# MEDIA MANUALS

**Motion Picture Film Processing**

# MEDIA MANUALS

# Motion Picture Film Processing

## Dominic Case

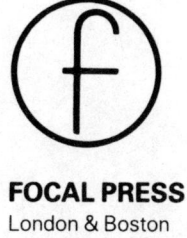

**FOCAL PRESS**
London & Boston

**Focal Press**
is an imprint of the Butterworth Group
which has principal offices in
London, Boston, Durban, Singapore, Sydney, Toronto, Wellington

First published 1985

**British Library Cataloguing in Publication Data**

Case, D.
    Motion picture film processing.—(Media manuals)
    1. Cinematography—Processing
    I. Title    II. Series
    778.5'32        TR886.2

ISBN 0-240-51243-X

**Library of Congress Cataloging in Publication Data**

Case, D. (Dominic)
    Motion picture film processing.

    (Media manuals)
    Bibliography: p.
    Includes index.
    1. Cinematography—Processing.    I. Title.    II. Series.
    TR88.2.C37    1985        778.5'32        85-4343
    ISBN 0-240-51243-X

Photoset by Butterworths Litho Preparation Department
Printed and bound in Great Britain by Biddles Ltd, Guildford and King's Lynn

# Contents

# Moving Pictures

Motion-picture photography relies on a number of quite separate techniques, all of which came together at the end of the nineteenth century. The magic lantern, in which a cut-out or painted image was projected onto a screen, dates from the seventeenth century. The illusion of motion was demonstrated in a number of Victorian toys such as the Zoëtrope and Praxinoscope, in which a continuous movement was represented by a rapid succession of gradually-changing still images. Photography, combining the technologies of optics and chemistry, was used to analyze motion in this way by Eadweard Muybridge in the 1870s, when he used 24 cameras to capture a couple of seconds of a horse's trotting movement.

George Eastman's flexible film, patented in 1889 for still photography, allowed a number of workers in several countries to develop motion-picture cameras capable of taking successive pictures on a single strip of film, together with projectors to show them. Although the original cellulose nitrate film base is no longer used, Edison's standard of 35-mm film with four perforations per frame has remained. At first, filming speeds varied from Edison's original 46 frames per second (fps), down to as slow as 12 per second. Although this caused jerky and flickery movement, the lower speeds allowed longer exposures in poor light, and conserved expensive film stock. The modern standard of 24 fps was established when sound on film called for standardization.

**The camera**
A roll of film is pulled down four perforations at a time, by a claw movement. As the claw disengages, the film is held steady by a spring-loaded back-plate, and in some cameras by an extremely precisely-fitting register pin which moves into the perforations and ensures that each frame is located in exactly the same way. Once the film is stationary the shutter opens and the frame is exposed. The shutter is a continuously-rotating disc with alternate segments cut away to allow the passage of light. By changing the angle of segment that is cut away, a longer or shorter exposure time is possible: usually the shutter is 180° open and 180° closed, allowing 1/48 th of a second between exposures for the claw to pull the film down. In a reflex camera the shutter is silvered, and when closed, reflects light into the viewfinder, giving the cameraman exactly the same view as the film in the gate. 16-mm cameras do not use register pins: the resultant image is nevertheless steady enough for all general work.

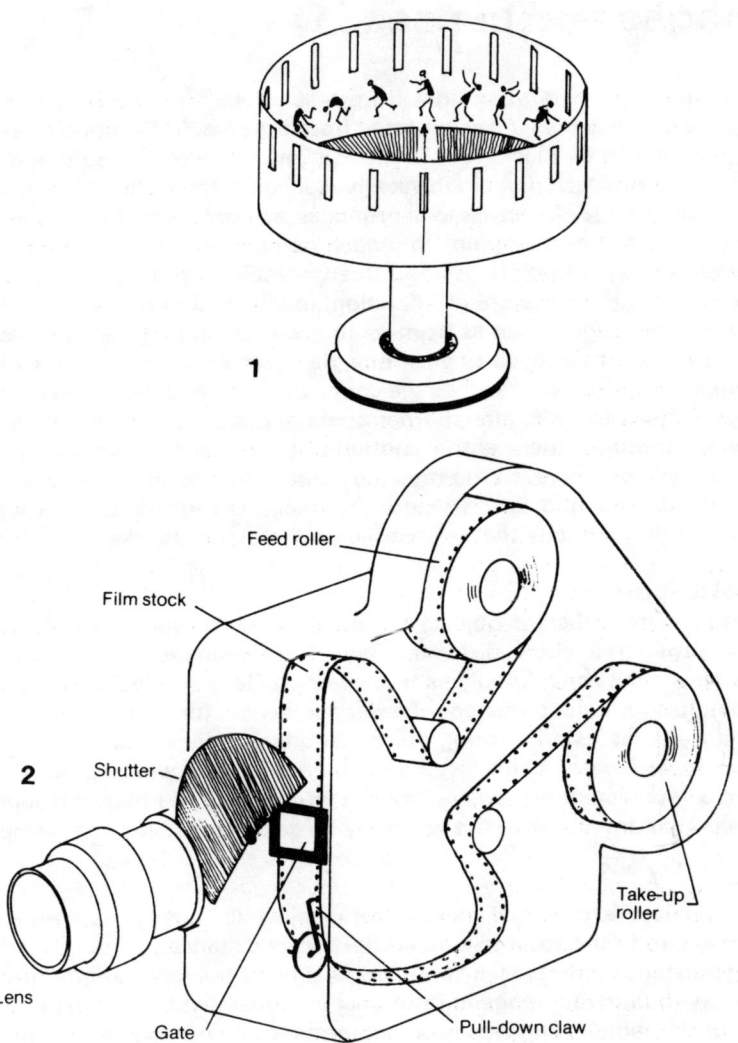

**1**

Feed roller

Film stock

Shutter

**2**

Lens

Gate

Pull-down claw

Take-up roller

**Moving pictures**

(1) The nineteenth-century Zoëtrope: as the cylinder is spun, each image is seen in turn through a slit, and an impression of motion is given.

(2) The twentieth-century cine camera: the claw pulls the film down one frame at a time while the revolving shutter is closed. When the shutter opens, light from the lens falls on the film and exposes it to an image.

# Images and Lenses (1)

An image is formed when light from a scene falls onto a screen in the same pattern in which it was reflected from the object. In a pinhole camera this is achieved by placing a pinhole in front of the screen so that only a single ray from each point in the scene reaches it. Naturally, this produces a very dim image. A convex lens produces a brighter image by collecting many rays of light diverging from each point and bending them so that they reconverge at points on the screen, forming a sharp image.

Lenses use the principle of refraction, in which light passing from one medium to another, such as from air to glass, is bent. The angle through which it is bent depends upon the angle at which it strikes the surface. When a bundle or rays reaches the convex surface of a lens, rays near the edge of the lens strike at a sharper angle and are bent more, while rays passing through the centre continue in the same direction. In a correctly-shaped lens, all the rays thus cross each other at a single point behind the lens, and this is where the image is formed. Convex lenses always form an image that is inverted and laterally reversed.

## Focal length

Light rays from distant objects are nearly parallel, and after refraction, reconverge in a short distance. Rays from much closer objects are diverging quite considerably as they reach the lens, and so reconverge at a point further behind the lens. The lens-to-screen (or film) distance must therefore be adjusted to bring objects at diferent distances into focus.

The *focal length* is the distance behind a lens at which parallel rays (from a very distant object) are brought into focus. The image distance for objects that are closer to the lens may be calculated using the formula

$$1/u + 1/v = 1/f$$

where u is the object distance (from object to lens), v is the image distance, and f the focal length. As the object distance is reduced, so the image distance increases. If the object is at twice the focal length from the lens, an equal-sized image is formed at an equal distance from the other side of the lens. A still-closer object forms a much more distant image. Another formula relates the object and image sizes:

$$\text{Magnification } M = \frac{\text{image size}}{\text{object size}} = \frac{v}{u}$$

Combinations of these formulae may be used to select the correct lens for a projector given the screen and theatre size; to set up a rostrum camera for a given reduction ratio; and so on.

**10**

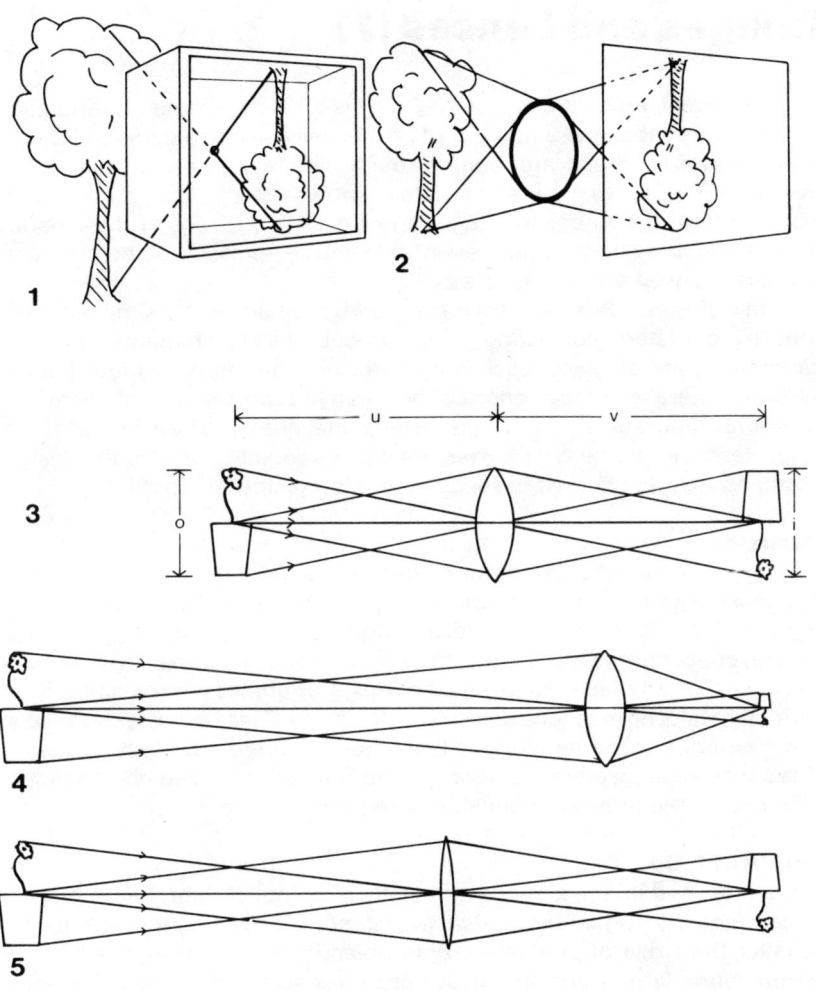

## Images and lenses

(1) In the pinhole camera, only a single ray from each point is used to form an image. The convex lens, (2), collects rays together to form a brighter image. (3) Object and image distances (u and v) are related to object and image sizes (o and i). A longer object distance, (4), results in an image smaller and closer to the lens, but a weaker lens forms a larger, more distant image, (5).

# Images and Lenses (2)

Unfortunately, no lens works perfectly. It is far from simple to grind glass to the ideal shape, and a number of problems arise: for example, different wavelengths of light are bent through different angles, resulting in coloured fringes to images, a defect known as *chromatic aberration*. Furthermore, the images of objects not directly in front of the lens are distorted, and light from even a centrally-placed object is only moderately-well refocused to a point.

Many of these defects can be reduced by replacing the simple convex lens by a system consisting of a number of lens elements, made of different types of glass, each one correcting the faults in the others. A typical camera lens may consist of between four and eight such elements. In some applications, of course, where the quality of an image is not important, simple convex lenses are quite adequate. This is the case in condenser systems used to focus light in projectors or spotlights.

## Aperture

In a lens of larger diameter, more light can be gathered, and the image is therefore brighter. However, image brightness is also affected by the focal length of the lens. A shorter focal length lens, by producing a smaller image, concentrates more light into the same area, thus making the image brighter. For any lens, however, the image brightness is the same if the ratio of focal length to lens diameter is the same. This ratio is expressed as the *f*/number of the lens and is known as the *aperture*. Most lenses are fitted with an adjustable iris which provides a variable-sized hole to reduce or increase the effective diameter as required.

## Depth of field

A well-focused image is made up ideally of points of light, but in practice each point is a minute disc, or *circle of confusion*. The better the lens, the smaller the circle of confusion. If an object is out of focus, the circle of confusion is larger, and the image becomes soft and blurred. The more the object is out of focus, the larger the circles of confusion, and the more blurred the image becomes. Circle-of-confusion size also depends upon the diameter of the aperture, so that by stopping down the iris, i.e. reducing the effective diameter of the lens, a blurred image can be made sharper. Depth of field is the range of object distances for any given focus setting that will result in an acceptably sharp image. An iris set at a smaller aperture will produce smaller circles of confusion, and so have a greater depth of field.

**12**

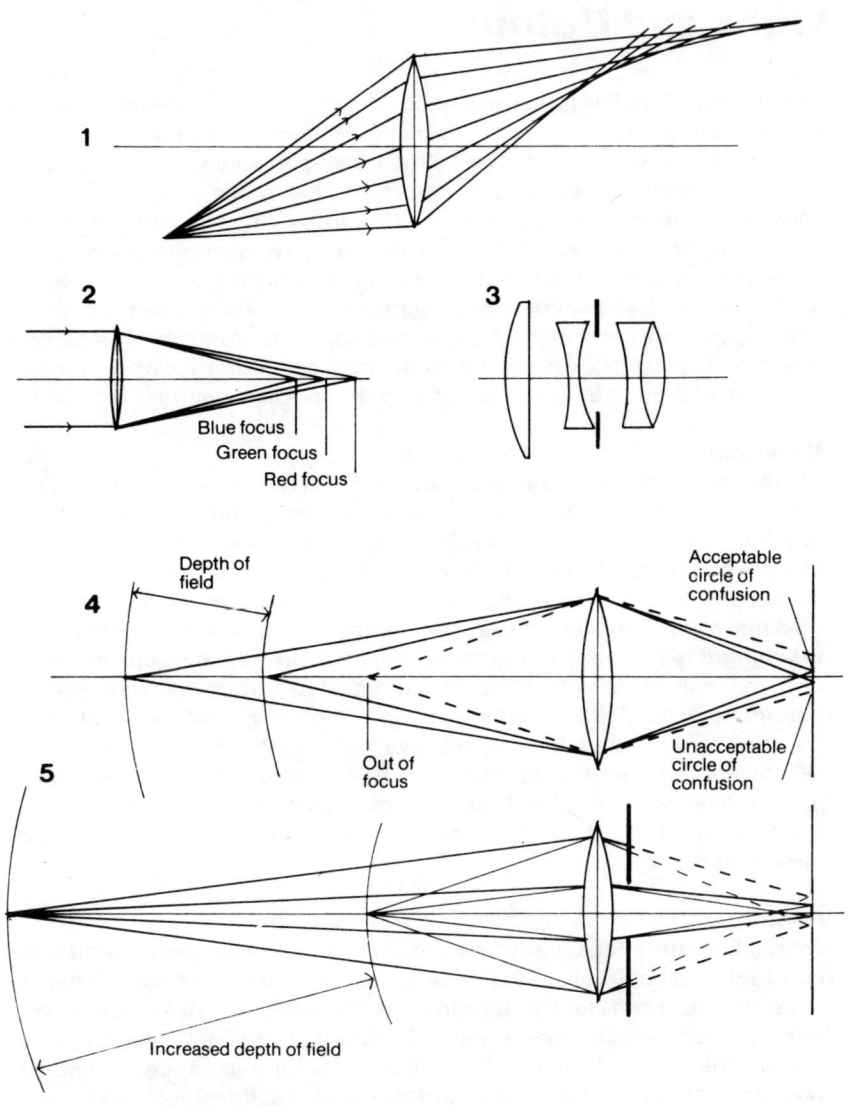

Blue focus
Green focus
Red focus

Depth of
field

Acceptable
circle of
confusion

4

Out of
focus

Unacceptable
circle of
confusion

5

Increased depth of field

## Focusing the image

(1) Coma is a lens aberration whereby rays from different sections of the lens meet at different points. Chromatic aberration (2) focuses different wavelengths at different points. Many aberrations can be corrected by using a compound lens (3), with different elements of different types of glass.

(4) Slightly out-of-focus objects can still given acceptably sharp results. (5) By reducing the lens aperture, out-of-focus images are made sharper.

**13**

# Light and Colour

Light is one of many forms of radiant energy – that is, energy which is transmitted by means of electromagnetic radiation. Other forms of radiant energy include X-rays, TV waves, ultra-violet, and so on. Several theories have attempted to explain the nature of this radiation: in particular, Newton regarded light as a stream of particles, and Huygens described light in terms of a wave theory. In this century, quantum physics has combined features of both theories, so that we may regard electromagnetic radiation as a stream of energy particles, or photons, which behave in some ways like a continuous wave of electromagnetic energy. The particle aspect of this model explains the photochemical properties of light, while the wave pattern is of use in describing its optical properties.

## Wavelength

All forms of electromagnetic radiation travel at the same speed (300 000 km per second in space, slightly slower in other materials), but they have widely differing wavelengths. Radio waves, for example, are measured in metres or even kilometres, while X-rays have wavelengths in the region of $10^{-10}$ metres (one ten thousand millionth of a metre).

Somewhere between these two extremes is visible light whose wavelength is normally measured in nanometres (equal to one millionth of a millimetre). Visible light has wavelengths ranging from 400 nm (nanometres) to 700 nm. Different wavelengths in this range produce different colour sensations in the eye, varying from violet or blue at 400 nm, through green and yellow, to deep red at 700 nm. Wavelengths outside these limits cannot be seen by the human eye, although the body responds to them by the feeling of heat (infra-red), or as sunburn (ultra-violet).

## Visibility

Although some things – such as the Sun, or car headlights – emit their own light, most objects are visible because they only reflect light. Different surfaces reflect different proportions of the light that strikes them, this making them appear either light or dark; often they reflect greater proportions of some colours than others, making them appear coloured. Mostly the light is scattered in all directions so that the object can be seen from anywhere: but shiny surfaces reflect more light in some directions than in others, producing highlights when the eye sees them from certain angles. Transparent objects allow most light to pass through them, and often reflect some as well. Light that is neither reflected nor transmitted is absorbed. Black surfaces that absorb light also absorb a lot of heat radiation, and get much hotter in sunlight than do white reflective surfaces.

**14**

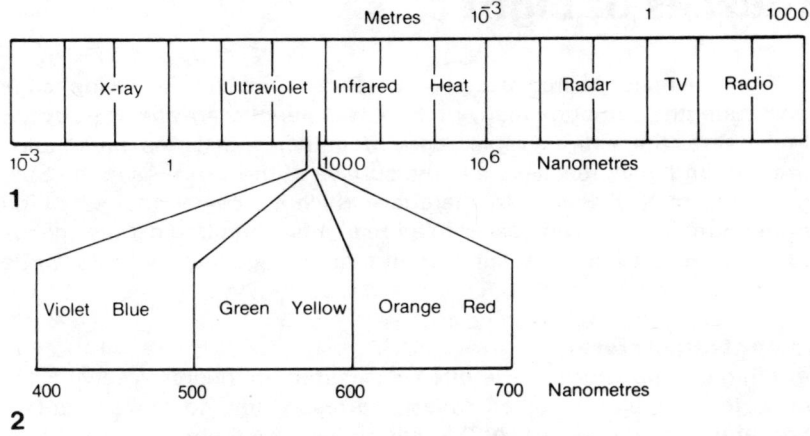

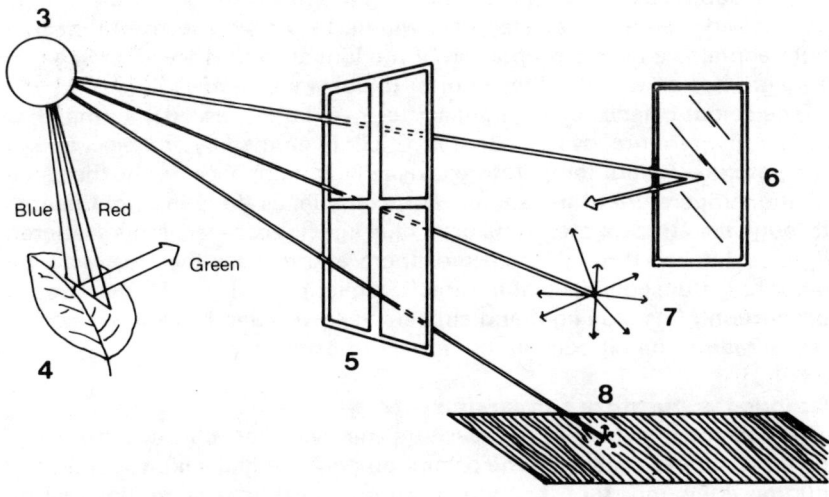

**The spectrum**
Visible light (2) forms a small section of the electromagnetic spectrum (1).

The Sun (3) emits rays of all colours: selective reflection by objects, (4), makes them appear coloured. Light may be transmitted, (5), reflected directionally, (6), or diffusely, (7), or absorbed, (8).

**15**

*Colour depends upon the light we see things by.*

# Sources of Light

The Sun, the major source of light on the Earth, emits rays of a wide range of wavelengths. Although many of these wavelengths are absorbed by the atmosphere, the entire visible range, together with some ultra-violet, infra-red, and heat, reaches us at the surface of the Earth. As in the Sun, light is normally produced by materials which are heated to a very high temperature. An iron rod heated in a fire to a few hundred degrees glows red; as it becomes hotter still it goes through orange and yellow to 'white hot'.

## Colour temperature

Very high temperatures are often measured in degrees Kelvin: the 'absolute' temperature of an object, corresponding to the amount of thermal energy it contains. At 0 Kelvin there is no thermal energy at all. The filament of an ordinary tungsten lamp burns at about 2800 K, while the Sun's surface is about 7000 K. (To convert degrees Kelvin to Celsius, simply subtract 273.) Although each light source emits radiant energy over a wide range of wavelengths, within the visible spectrum tungsten light contains a higher proportion of the longer (red) wavelengths, while sunlight has an excess of the shorter (blue) wavelengths.

The colour balance of any light source may be expressed in terms of its *colour temperature*, by comparison with light emitted by an object at that temperature. Colour temperature is usually, but not necessarily, the same as the temperature of the source. For example, as the Sun's light passes through the atmosphere, some of its blue light is scattered. (This scattered light is diffused through the atmosphere and reaches the Earth as blue skylight.) Consequently, the direct sunlight itself is deprived of a proportion of its blue light and appears yellower (and has a lower colour temperature) than it does in the upper atmosphere.

## Colour-temperature conversion filters

The balance of wavelengths reaching the eye after reflection from any given scene depends upon the colour temperature of the light source, and photography must take this into account. Conventionally, motion-picture film emulsions are balanced for tungsten light at 3200 K, while most amateur colour stills materials (which are more likely to be used in ordinary daylight) are balanced at around 5400 K. If a film is to be used under an unsuited source of light, colour-correction filters (e.g. Wratten 85 (orange) or Wratten 80 (blue)) are placed over the light source, or more conveniently over the camera lens, to absorb the excess blue or red component of the light, and match the balance of the light to the sensitivity of the film.

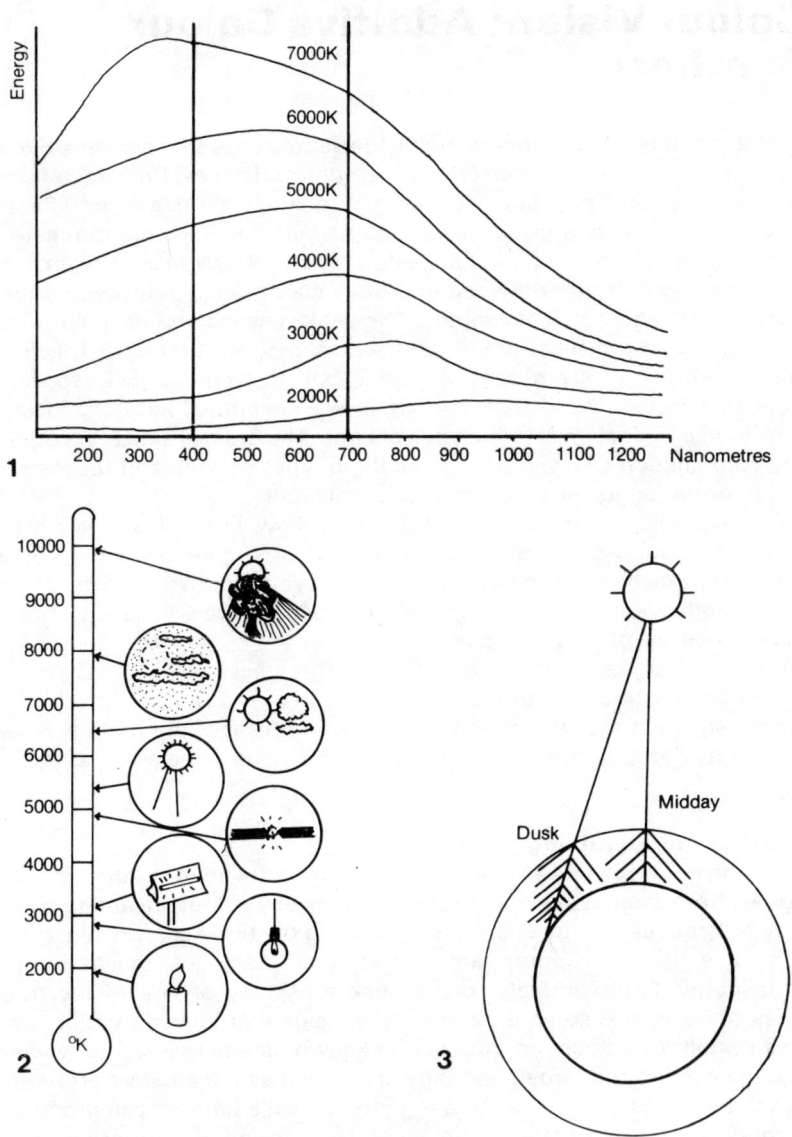

**Colour temperature**

(1) At higher temperatures, more shorter wavelengths are emitted, giving a bluer colour balance. (2) Light sources may be described in terms of colour temperature. (3) Although the Sun's surface is about 7000 K, some blue light is scattered by the atmosphere. At dusk, more blue light is scattered, giving a redder sun.

**17**

# Colour Vision: Additive Colour Synthesis

The retina of the eye is covered with specialized cells that are sensitive to light, and these cells fall into two types: rods and cones. Rods respond to lower levels of light, but they do not distinguish between different wavelengths: all colours produce the same reaction. Rods predominate in night vision, and thus colours are often hard to distinguish at night.

Cones may be further divided into three classes, distinguished by their response to different wavelengths. The peak sensitivity of each type falls respectively in the blue, green, and red ranges of the visible spectrum (about 440 nm, 550 nm and 610 nm), but the curves overlap to a considerable extent, so that any single wavelength of light produces a sensation or signal in all three types of cone. The brain is able to recognize any combination of signals from the three types of cone and reconstruct this information as evidence of a specific colour.

For example, a single wavelength of yellow light of about 580 nm produces roughly equal responses in the red- and green-sensitive cones, and a very much lower one in the blue-sensitive cones. Now, if light of two wavelengths, about 550 nm (green) and 640 nm (red) is used, then a similar pattern of responses is produced in the cones. The green light produces a signal in the predominantly green-sensitive cones, and a somewhat lesser one in the red-sensitive cones. The red light produces a further signal in the red-sensitive cones. In both cases the brain receives the same information, and so must interpret it in the same way – as yellow light.

### Additive colour mixing
Since the eye transmits all colour information to the brain in terms of three signals from three types of cone, the effect of any colour, including white, may be produced in the eye, simply by using the three colours red, green and blue in the appropriate proportions. Each of these colours corresponds approximately to the peak sensitivity of one of the three types of cone, and so controls mainly the signal produced by that cone. This system of colour reproduction is known as *additive colour mixing*, and the colours red, green and blue are known as the *additive primaries*. By mixing lights of these colours together two at a time we can produce a second set of three colours, the secondary, or complementary colours, yellow, magenta and cyan.

The three primaries when viewed together excite all three types of cone and so produce white light.

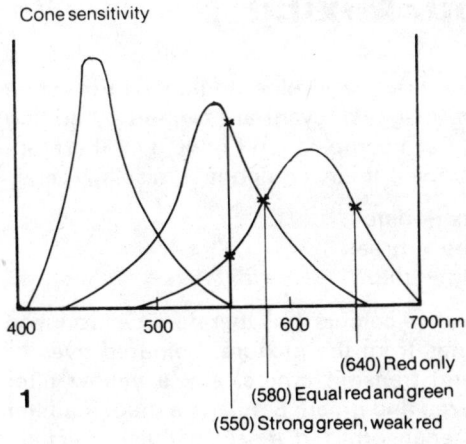

Cone sensitivity

400    500    600    700nm

(640) Red only
(580) Equal red and green
(550) Strong green, weak red

**1**

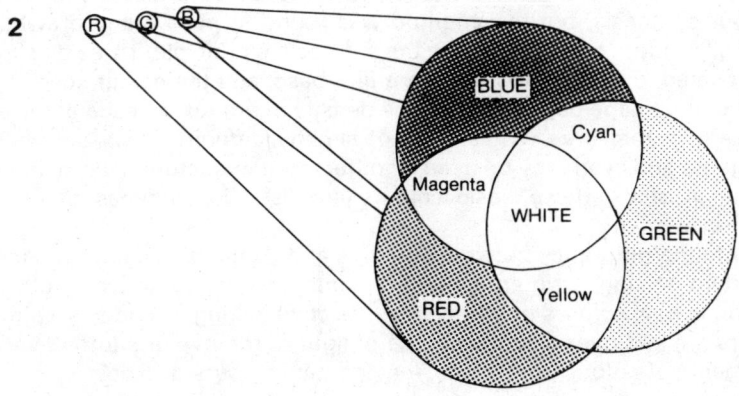

**2**

R  G  B

BLUE
Cyan
Magenta
WHITE
GREEN
RED    Yellow

**Additive colour**
(1) The sensitivities of the three types of cone overlap considerably so that any wavelength is detected by two or even all three cones. (2) Additive light mixing produces a full range of colours.

**19**

# Subtractive Colour Mixing

The three additive primaries, red, green and blue, together form white light. Secondary colours (yellow, magenta, cyan) are formed by adding together any two of these three. Each combination of two may therefore be thought of as white light with one primary component missing. Thus:

yellow (red + green)  =  white − blue
magenta (red + blue)  =  white − green
cyan (green + blue)  =  white − red

Starting from white light, secondary colours may therefore be produced by subtracting individual primaries from the mixture. Coloured dyes or filters absorb certain colours and transmit others, e.g. a yellow filter absorbs blue light and transmits red and green. Similarly a magenta filter absorbs green light and a cyan filter absorbs red. If pairs of these filters are overlapped, then two primaries will be removed from white light, leaving only a single primary.

All three filters overlaid together produce black, or no light at all, since each filter removes one of the three primaries. This series of combinations is known as *subtractive colour mixing*.

Early attempts at colour photography used the additive principle of colour synthesis, but this method was found to have many drawbacks, and all modern colour films use the subtractive principle. Three dye layers are coated, one over another, on a film base, and the colour seen in any part of the image depends upon the density or amount of each of the dyes present in that area. While dyes of slightly different shades of yellow, magenta and cyan may be used by different manufacturers, or in different types of stock, these basic colours are used in all types of modern subtractive film.

Note the difference between additive and subtractive colour mixing. In additive mixing, primary-coloured lights are added to each other to produce new colours or white. In subtractive mixing, secondary-coloured filters are laid over a single source of light to remove or subtract various elements of colour from white, leaving new colours or black.

Confusion sometimes arises from the apparent discrepancy between the above systems and the artist's rules of colour mixing that name the primaries red, yellow and blue. This is nothing more than a difference in naming colours: in fact, the painter's red, yellow and blue are quite similar to the photographer's magenta, yellow and cyan. Paints behave rather like filters, so that, for example, yellow and blue (cyan) paints mix to form green, just as superimposed yellow and cyan filters produce green.

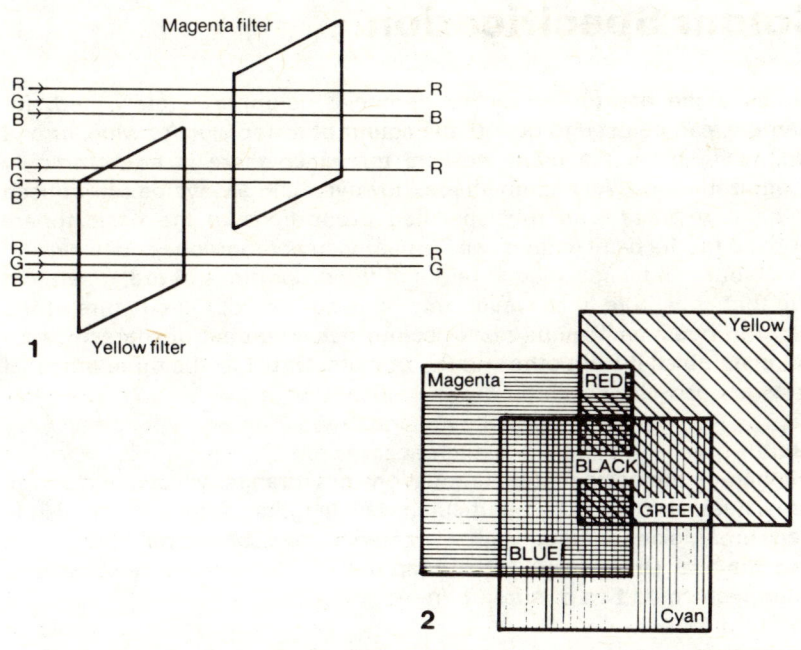

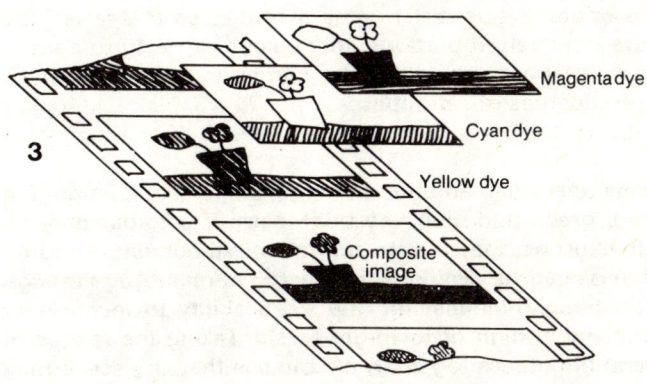

**Overlapping filters**
(1) Two filters together remove two primary colours, leaving a single primary, while various combinations of filters, (2), may be used to produce the full range of colours. (3) A colour film forms images in three superimposed dye layers. Here the components, when combined, show a yellow flower with a green leaf in a red pot on a black table.

**21**

# Colour Specification

Names alone are too vague to denote a colour accurately: red, for example, can be used to denote the colour of a stop sign, of wine, or of a dog, while there are many colours for which there is no commonly recognized name. Any given shade, however, can always be reproduced by paint retailers who mix specified proportions of the basic toners supplied for the paint in question. Similarly, in photography and television any colour can be specified in terms of the proportions of red, green and blue that constitute it. However, this does not describe the nature of the colour in question. Any particular colour has a number of characteristics that distinguish it from other similar colours. Of these, the three principal terms are as follows:

**Hue**
This names the basic colour in question: red, orange, yellow, and so on. Many hues correspond to particular wavelengths of light in the visible spectrum. Making a colour lighter or darker, or richer or paler, does not affect its hue. On average, the human eye has been found to be able to distinguish some two hundred different hues.

**Saturation**
This describes the richness or purity of the colour. Introducing a small proportion of the opposite hue desaturates a colour, so that when the opposing hues are in equal proportions, that colour varies from a pure, vivid colour to a neutral grey or white. The human eye can distinguish about one hundred degrees of saturation.

**Brightness**
Simply by varying the total amount of light, while maintaining the proportions of red, green and blue, the brightness of a colour may be changed without affecting the hue or saturation. About one hundred degrees of brightness can be distinguished by the human eye, although the range is considerably widened by the eye's ability to increase or decrease its sensitivity in high or low light levels. Taking the ranges of hue, saturation and brightness together, we can see that any scene may contain up to two million different shades of colour.

In colour television the term *chroma* is used to specify variations in hue, *purity* for saturation, and *level* for brightness. Video and broadcast equipment is set up in these terms; domestic receivers usually have 'colour' controls to vary the purity or saturation of the entire image (from black-and-white to glaring colour), and 'balance' to vary the overall hue of the image (over a fairly limited range).

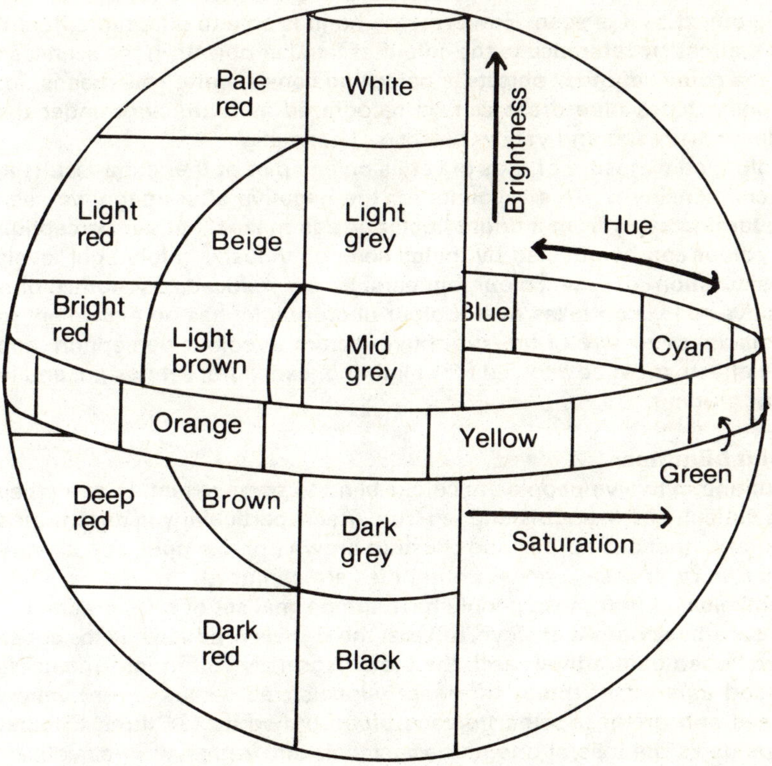
Pale red
White
Brightness
Light red
Beige
Light grey
Hue
Bright red
Light brown
Mid grey
Blue
Cyan
Orange
Yellow
Green
Deep red
Brown
Dark grey
Saturation
Dark red
Black

**The colour circle**
One way of arranging all colours to show the variation of hue, saturation and brightness.

*. . . . colours are not always what they seem.*

# Perception of Colours

Although colour may be described in purely objective terms (the proportion of various wavelengths of light reflected from an object), subjective colour – the apparent colour of an object as it is seen by the human eye – is affected by a number of factors. The colour temperature of the illuminating light source may vary: this determines the ratio of long to short wavelengths that fall on the object, and therefore influences the *hue* of the object as it is seen. However, the brain is able to adapt to different light sources by reference to the colour of familiar objects in the scene, so that the colour of other objects is perceived consistently. This means, for example, that a blue dress can be recognized as blue, even under the predominantly red and yellow balance of candlelight.

Prolonged exposure of rods or cones on any part of the retina results in reduced sensitivity. This accounts for the negative after-image we seen after turning away from a bright light, but also means that our perception of a colour can be affected by things seen previously. In low light levels the saturation of any colour appears to be reduced, as non-colour-sensitive rod vision takes over. Colour photography has no equivalent to rod vision, or to any of the subjective factors in colour perception, and these effects must be allowed for in lighting, exposure, set design, and in colour grading.

### Colour blindness

About one in twelve people are colour-blind to some extent. Usually they have difficulty in distinguishing red from green, particularly in desaturated colours, so that olive green and chestnut brown (for example) appear very similar. In rarer cases, yellows and blues are confused.

It is believed that these people have the normal set of red-, green- and blue-sensitive cones in the eye, but that the signals produced by the cones are confused before they reach the brain. Normally colour information is encoded as a set of three 'difference' signals: red versus green; yellow (i.e. red and green together) versus blue; and white (all three colours) versus dark. The loss of one of these signals still leaves all three colours 'visible', but the information required to distinguish some colours from each other is lost.

Colour blindness appears to be much commoner in males than in females, although some research has challenged this belief.

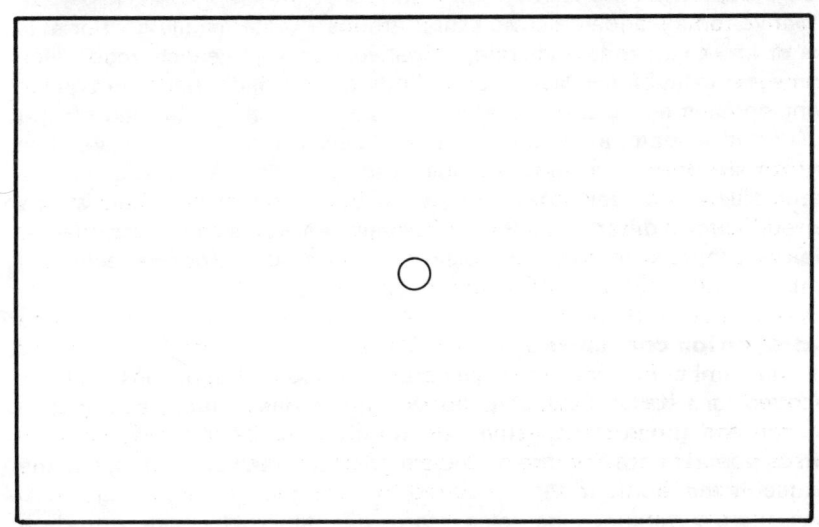

# WATCH THIS SPACE

**Brightness adaptation**
Stare steadily at the writing for at least a minute, in bright light. Then look at the white square. The white writing will have desensitized areas of the retina, thus causing a dull grey image of the writing to appear in the white square. Using a coloured filter in the first part would result in a complementary-coloured after-image.

**25**

*The building blocks of photographic materials.*

# Chemical Compounds and Ions

All substances can be classified into elements, mixtures, or compounds. An element is a substance consisting of just one type of atom, whereas mixtures and compounds are composed of two or more types of atom. Mixtures usually combine the properties of the various materials they comprise, but compounds, consisting of exactly fixed proportions of various elements, have properties quite unlike any of their components: thus common salt, sodium chloride, is quite unlike the reactive metal sodium or the poisonous gas chlorine.

The smallest unit of elements and compounds is a molecule: a specific grouping of two, three or more atoms. Water molecules, for example, contain two atoms of hydrogen and one of oxygen.

Atoms themselves may be thought of as positively-charged nuclei surrounded by negatively-charged electrons. Normally, the electrons' negative charge exactly cancels out the positive nuclear charge. When atoms combine as molecules, some of the electrons around each atom become 'common property'.

Many atoms – and some molecular groups – quite readily gain or lose one or more electrons, becoming negatively or positively charged. Such atoms are called *ions*. Many compounds are formed when one type of atom donates an electron to another type. The ions so formed do not usually stick together as individual molecules, but form crystal-lattice structures of many thousands of ions. In solution the individual ions move about freely and separately. Chemical reactions occur when atoms regroup to form different molecules. Usually, energy is either absorbed or released: thus, silver bromide releases silver atoms under the action of light.

### Hydrogen ion concentration
A small number of water molecules are ionized as hydrogen ions ($H^+$) and hydroxyl ions ($OH^-$). Curiously, the concentrations of these two ions in any solution, multiplied together, always gives the same result.

In pure water both concentrations are equal to 0.0000001 ($10^{-7}$), and the product is therefore $10^{-14}$.

Acids are compounds that release large quantities of hydrogen ions into solution: a few of these combine with hydroxyl ions (forming water), reducing the hydroxyl ion concentration and maintaining the constant value. Conversely, alkalis contain large quantities of hydroxyl ions, and the hydrogen ion concentration thus becomes lower than normal. The concentration of hydrogen ions in any solution is therefore a measure of the acidity or alkalinity of a solution. This concentration can vary between 1 (or $10^0$) and $10^{-14}$, and is usually expressed logarithmically as 'pH' (power of hydrogen), ranging between 0 and 14. A neutral solution has a pH of 7. Strong acids have pH of 0 and strong alkalis 14. Most solutions are only weakly acid or alkaline and have intermediate values of pH.

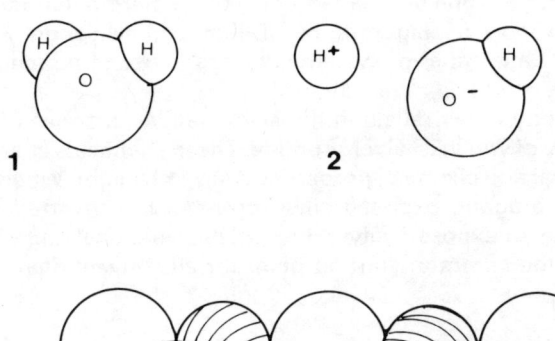

**1**          **2**

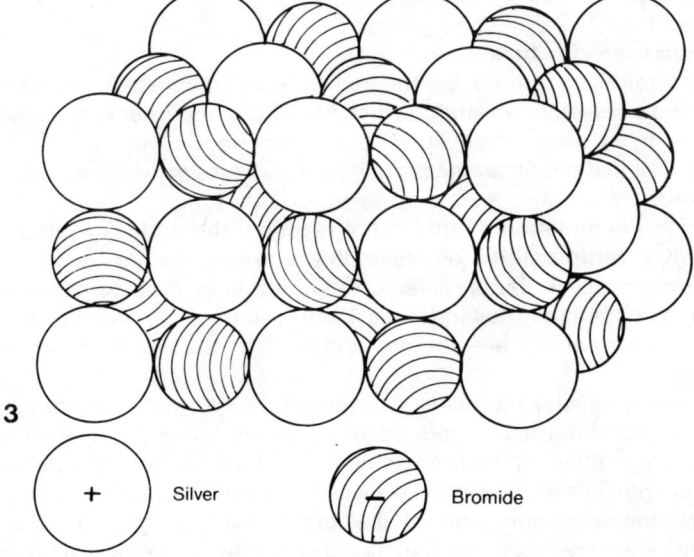

**3**

( + )  Silver          ( — )  Bromide

## Molecules and crystals

Water consists mainly of molecules, (1). A small number of these split up, (2), and form hydrogen ions, $H^+$, and hydroxyl ions, $OH^-$.

(3) Crystals of sodium bromide are large structures with equal numbers of silver, $Ag^+$, and bromide, $Br^-$, ions in a regular lattice.

*First, the emulsion must be mixed. . . .*

# Light-sensitive Emulsions

For hundreds of years scientists have been able to produce images of real scenes – for example, in the *camera obscura*, a large room that acted as a walk-in pinhole camera. It was not until the mid-nineteenth century, however, that anyone succeeded in making a permanent record of these images. The work of Daguerre, Fox Talbot, and Nicéphore Niépce, in the 1830s, led to a number of systems that made use of a range of chemical processes.

Photography today relies on the silver halides, a series of compounds the principal of which is silver bromide. These chemicals change certain of their physical and chemical properties if struck by light. When treated with a developing agent, exposed silver bromide is converted into metallic silver, while unexposed silver bromide is left unchanged. This basic reaction is the common starting point for all conventional photographic emulsions.

## Emulsion manufacture

Silver bromide is formed by the reaction between solutions of silver nitrate and potassium bromide, which are mixed, together with gelatin, in darkness, in an emulsion 'kettle'. Silver bromide is precipitated out of solution, but instead of coagulating, it forms a suspension (or emulsion) in the gelatin.

Following completion of this initial reaction, the emulsion undergoes 'ripening' at temperatures between 50°C and 80°C for up to two hours. During this process, large silver bromide crystals tend to grow, while small ones diminish, or even fall back into solution. The exact conditions and time of ripening are therefore crucial to the final nature of the emulsion.

After ripening, the emulsion is cooled to a gel, cut into shreds and washed to remove the by-products of earlier reactions. Next, is a second ripening stage followed by the addition of various 'doctoring' solutions to the emulsion. These may include dyes to extend or alter the sensitivity range of the emulsion, and in the case of colour emulsions, colour couplers which will take part in the development reaction to produce coloured dyes.

The gelatin itself plays an important – though not completely understood – part in the photographic process. Apart from acting as a physical binder for the emulsion, it forms a bond with silver bromide crystals, which prevents unexposed crystals from being developed. It absorbs the bromide produced during development, thus preventing it from recombining with the developed silver, and contains certain sulphur compounds that increase the sensitivity of the silver bromide.

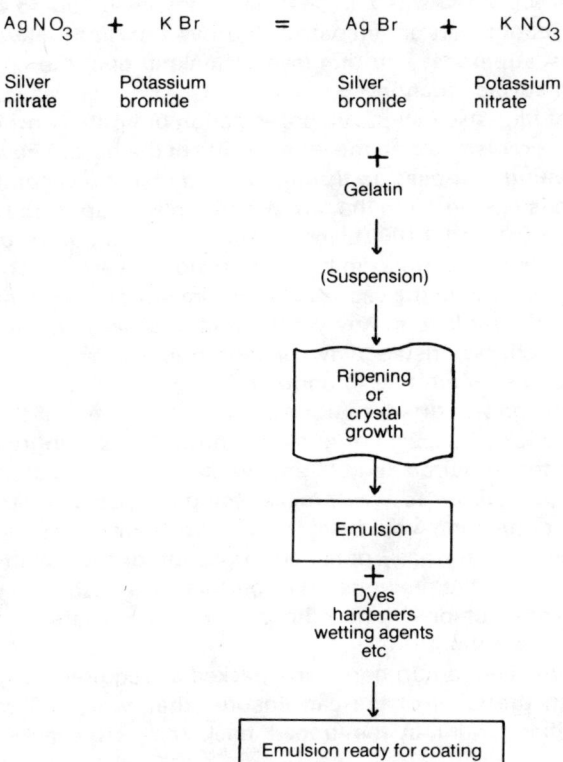

$$AgNO_3 \quad + \quad KBr \quad = \quad AgBr \quad + \quad KNO_3$$

Silver      Potassium         Silver         Potassium
nitrate       bromide           bromide      nitrate

+

Gelatin

↓

(Suspension)

↓

Ripening
or
crystal
growth

↓

Emulsion

+
Dyes
hardeners
wetting agents
etc

↓

Emulsion ready for coating

## Emulsion manufacture

Preparation of a photographic emulsion takes place in total darkness and under conditions of extreme cleanliness. Apart from the obvious hazards of dirt and dust particles, many everyday substances (handcreams, foodstuffs, etc.) can fog an emulsion and must therefore be prohibited from the emulsion-coating areas.

# Film Manufacture

The first flexible-film base was cellulose nitrate: however, not only is this material subject to considerable shrinkage over time, it is also highly flammable, and after some years decomposes to a highly-explosive powder. By 1951 all film was manufactured on a safety base of cellulose acetate. (More recently polyester bases have been used in some applications). The base is coated with a layer of silver bromide suspended in gelatin (the emulsion). As gelatin does not normally adhere to acetate, a 'subbing' layer acts as an undercoat to improve bonding between base and emulsion. A supercoat – or thin layer of gelatin over the emulsion – protects it from surface friction.

Many types of film also include an anti-halation or light-absorbing layer either below the emulsion or on the reverse side of the base. This prevents light from reflecting and passing through the emulsion a second time.

The emulsion is coated on to the film base in rolls of up to 150 cm wide and between 2000 ft and 10 000 ft in length, known as *parent* or *jumbo rolls*. The thickness and uniformity of emulsion layers are of critical importance, particularly in the case of colour-film stocks, which may have up to a dozen different layers. Any variation in thickness would result in changing image characteristics between one role and another, or even from one part of a single frame to another.

After the emulsion has dried, samples from various parts of the roll are taken and tested for all aspects of quality control. The parent roll is then slit to rolls of the required length and width, and perforated. These operations are carried out to very precise standards, as any variation in perforation size or position would result in picture unsteadiness. In 35-mm film, perforations are normally punched in groups of four, with a set of pilot pins moving into the previous set of perforations each time to locate the film. Tolerances of one hundredth of a millimetre are all that are allowed in this operation.

Finally, the film is edge-numbered and packed as required. A system of roll numbers on the label of the can ensures that every roll of film is uniquely identified and may be traced back through every stage of manufacture.

All stages of manufacture must be carried out in total darkness and in conditions of absolute cleanliness. Not only would dust particles produce a 'sparkly' image, they would also cause an uneven coating, and many contaminants would have a considerable effect on the photographic properties of the film.

After it is packaged, film is stored at a reduced temperature until it is ready for use.

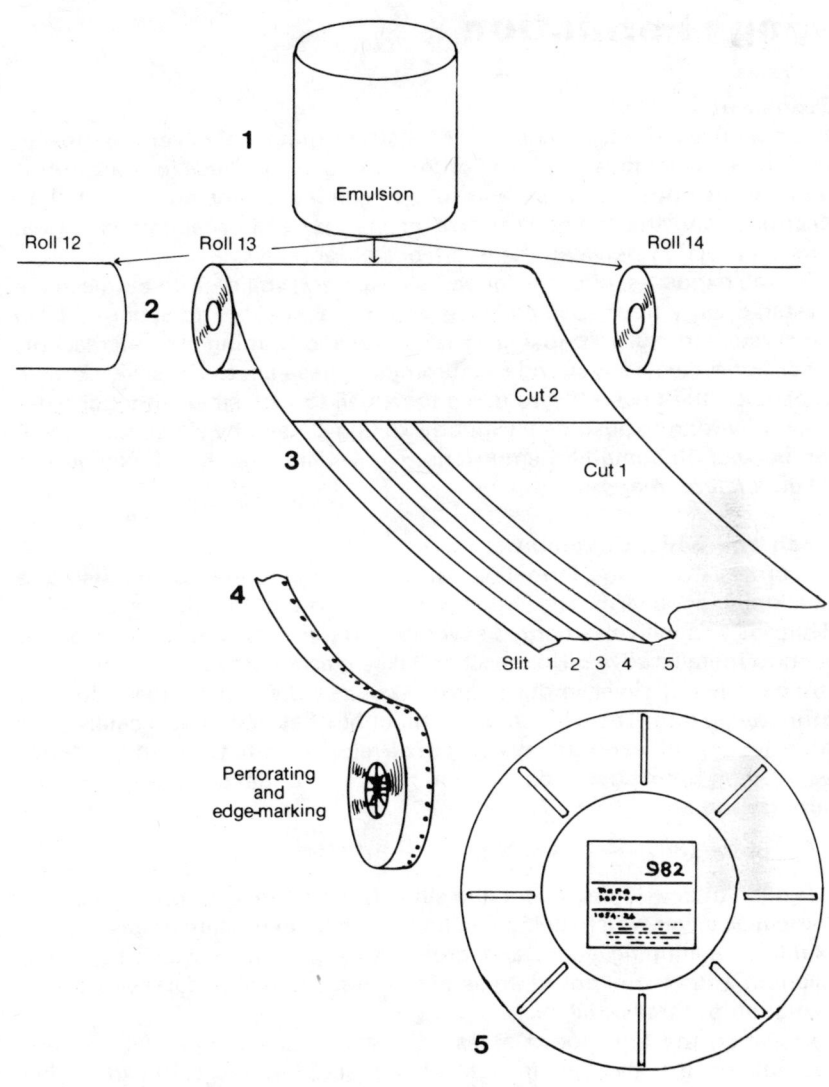

## Manufacturing history and identification

(1) One particular mix or batch of emulsion is used to coat a number of parent rolls, (2). Each roll is then cut to a number of lengths, (3), before it is slit and perforated, (4). After packaging, the can label carries numbers that identify each individual roll, (5).

# Image Formation

### Exposure

An unexposed emulsion contains crystals, or grains, of silver bromide, in the form of silver ions ($Ag^+$) and bromine ions ($Br^-$). These ions are atoms with an electric charge as a result of gaining or losing one of their electrons, and the lattice structure of the crystal is maintained by the strong attraction between the two types of ion.

During exposure, photons (or particles of light) collide with atoms in the crystal. Energy from each colliding photon causes ions to separate from the crystal structure, so losing their charge and forming sub-microscopic specks of metallic silver and free bromine. These specks of silver, known as *development centres*, are much too small to be visible, although after massively-long exposures a slight darkening caused by silver conversion can be seen in some film emulsions. The invisible record of exposure is called a *latent image*.

### Black-and-white development

The process of image formation can be much amplified by the use of a developing agent. This is a chemical reducing agent that acts by donating electrons to positively-charged silver ions in the emulsion and converting them to metallic silver. This reaction takes place most rapidly around the tiny particles of silver in development centres that have already formed during exposure. The silver may be thought of as acting as a catalyst for the reaction, and exposed crystals are developed up to two hundred times faster than unexposed ones. The reaction of development may be summarized as

$$Ag^+Br^- + (dev) --\!\!\gg Ag + (dev)^+ + Br^-$$

The initial developing agent and silver bromide react to produce grains of metallic silver which, being insoluble, remain in the film emulsion, and oxidized developing agent and bromine ions, both of which pass into solution. Thus the exposed areas of the film are visibly darkened by the formation of metallic silver.

However, the unexposed areas still contain silver bromide, and any attempt to view the film in light at this stage would result in further exposure and the steady reduction of these crystals also, to silver. The image can be made permanent by passing the film into a fixer solution, which dissolves away the unwanted silver bromide.

### Latent-image fade

If development is delayed after exposure, some of the silver atoms that form the latent image revert to the ionized form and fall back into the crystal structure. This latent-image fade occurs less at low temperatures.

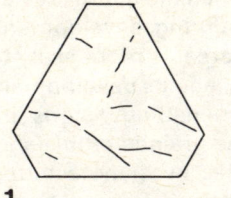
1

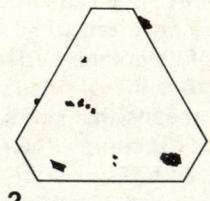
2

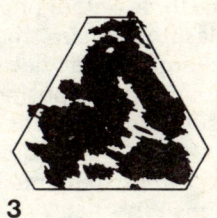
3

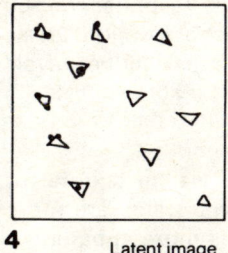
4    Latent image

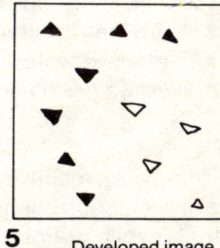
5    Developed image

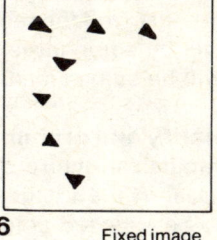
6    Fixed image

△  Unexposed silver bromide crystal

◭  Exposed silver bromide crystal

▲  Developed silver grain

## The silver image

Fault lines in the silver bromide crystals, (1), allow small 'development centres' of silver to form during exposure, (2). These centres spread during development until the entire crystal is developed, (3).

The invisible latent image, (4), becomes visible after development, (5), but is not stable until the fixer has removed the unexposed silver bromide crystals, (6).

**33**

# Speed and Grain

Silver bromide crystals become capable of development when photons strike the crystals and energy is absorbed. Not all collisions are effective; but once three or four photons have been absorbed then the entire crystal, regardless of its size, may be converted to silver during development. Now, a large crystal, because of its greater surface area, is more likely to receive sufficient exposing photons than a small one, and its development will result in more silver. This means that coarse-grained emulsions are faster – that is, they require less exposure – than fine-grained emulsions.

Further improvements in speed have been obtained by manufacturing emulsions with flat, or tablet-shaped crystals, all turned face-on to the surface, thus improving the photon-collecting chances of each crystal.

### Contrast

All grains of the same size have an equal chance of receiving sufficient exposure to be developed. If an emulsion contains such uniform grains, its response is limited: above a certain exposure all grains will be fully capable of development: below a certain limit none will receive sufficient light to be sensitized. This results in a very contrasty image.

If the size of grains is varied within an emulsion, its response will be more gradual, and the range of sensitivities is extended: at low light levels there will be some large grains that will develop: at much higher levels there will be some smaller-than-average grains still available.

### Granularity and graininess

The granular structure of the emulsion results in a visible texture, or graininess, in the image. Since larger, more sensitive, grains are more likely to be exposed at lower light levels, graininess is more apparent in the shadow areas, on negative films. Under-exposed images appear more grainy overall for this same reason. In reversal film, however, (see page 44) the larger, more readily exposed, grains are bleached away, leaving an image formed by the finer, slower grains.

The graininess visible in the projected image is not due to individual grains, which measure less than a hundredth of a millimetre across. Grains are distributed at random in the emulsion, and tend to form larger clumps, with sparsely-filled gaps in between, rather than a regularly-arranged distribution. These larger clumps are clearly visible at only small amounts of magnification.

The term *graininess* is used to describe the subjective impression of the granular structure of the image, while *granularity* is a scientific measurement (using a microdensitometer) of the mean variation in an area of overall uniform density. This, of course, is dependent not only on grain size but also on the contrast of the image.

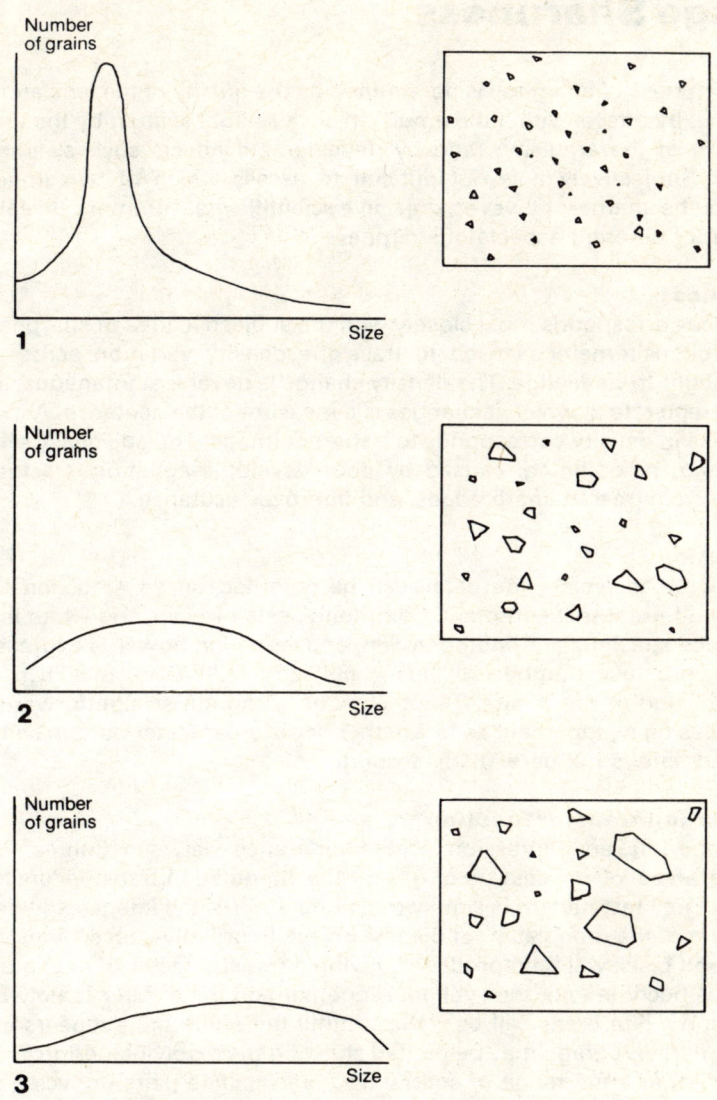

**Distribution of grain size**
(1) A uniformly fine-grained emulsion gives a film of slow speed and high contrast.
(2) A wider range of grain sizes results in a medium-speed, lower-contrast film. (3)
The inclusion of larger grains results in a more sensitive emulsion, but with a
grainier image.

# Image Sharpness

The sharpness of an image is determined by the quality of the lens and its focusing, by effects within the emulsion such as light scatter, by the grain structure of the emulsion, and by development effects such as image spread. Subjectively it is not difficult to assess which of two images appears the sharper; however, objective scientific measurement reveals a number of different aspects of sharpness.

**Acutance**
Acutance corresponds most closely with the subjective idea of sharpness. A microdensitometer is used to trace the density variation across an abrupt light-to-dark edge. The density change is never instantaneous, and the average rate at which it changes is a measure of the acutance. A more rapid rise in density corresponds to a sharper image. The adjacency effect – fringing, or outlining, caused by poor developer-agitation – actually steepens contrast at sharp edges, and improves acutance.

**Resolution**
The degree to which fine detail can be recorded on an emulsion is a slightly different measurement. Commonly, sets of black and white lines of various spacings are photographed, and resolving power is expressed as the greatest number of line pairs per millimetre that can be distinguished in the image. This technique, although straightforward in use, relies on a judgement as to whether or not a particular pattern can be resolved, and is not particularly accurate.

**Modulation-transfer function**
*Modulation* is an expression of the difference between lightest and darkest areas of the test pattern, and the modulation-transfer function (MTF) of any test pattern is simply the modulation of the image expressed as a ratio of the modulation of the test object. In broadly-spaced lines, full white and black will be reproduced, giving a transfer factor of one, but as the lines become finer they will blur together and the difference between black and white areas will be reduced until the entire area appears as a uniform grey. A graph may be plotted showing the resolving performance of the film at a full range of spacial frequencies (line pairs or cycles per millimetre). The MTF can be measured for each element in a system (lens, negative stock, print stock and so on), and the factors at each stage multiplied together to find the MTF of the system as a whole.

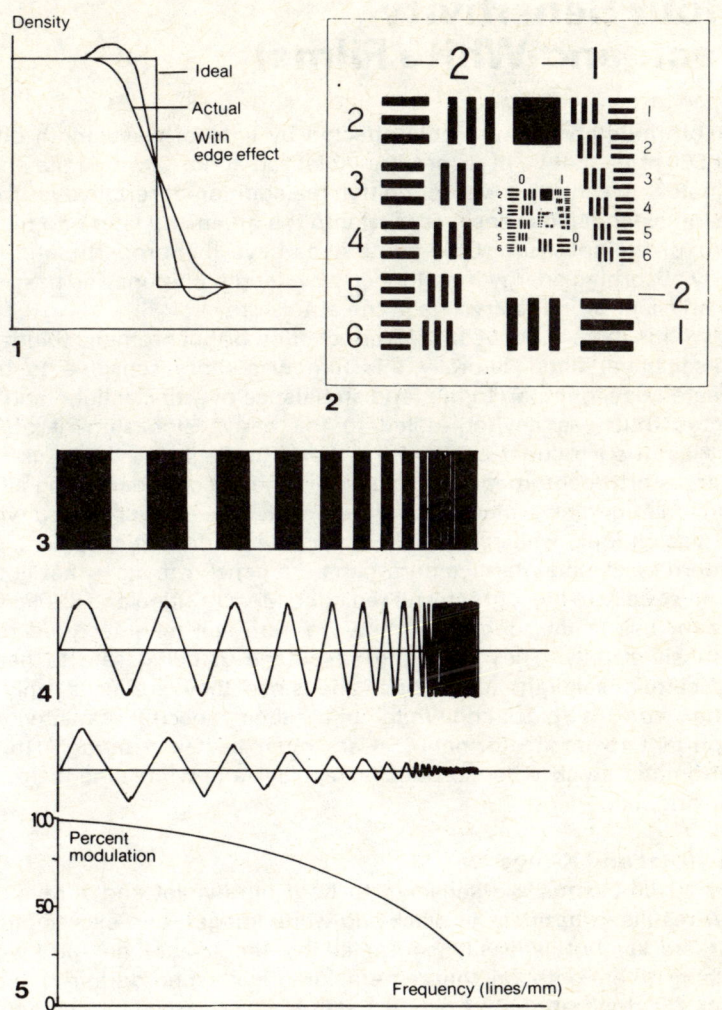

## The image in detail

(1) An ideally sharp edge is reproduced as a blurred gradient from black to white. Some development effects can make this appear sharper by forming an outline. (2) Resolution charts give a visual check on the film's (or lens's) ability to reproduce a repeating pattern. (3) A modulation transfer test chart shows stripes at a steadily-increasing frequency. Ideally it is reproduced with constant amplitude, (4), but in practice there is a progressive loss of contrast at higher line frequencies. A graph of this, (5), shows the performance of the system at any scale of detail or definition.

# Colour Sensitivity
# (Black-and-White Films)

Silver bromide crystals are only affected by light of wavelength below about 500 nm – that is, blue, or ultra-violet radiation. Towards the end of the nineteenth century it was found that the addition of certain dyes to the emulsion extended its sensitivity first into the green and later into the red regions of the spectrum. Only some dyes have this property, and they work by absorbing energy from longer-wavelength photons and passing it on to adjacent bromide crystals in the emulsion.

Early films (before about 1926) were shot on orthochromatic (blue- and green-sensitive) film. Naturally this film was more sensitive to blue-dominated daylight than to the reddish balance of artificial light, and this factor as much as any other led to the early establishment of film industries in such sunlit parts of the world as California and Australia. Further, as orthochromatic emulsions had the effect of darkening all red colours and lightening blues, performers with blue eyes appeared with a rather vacant look, while even pale lips appeared dramatically dark.

Modern black-and-white camera films are panchromatic – that is they respond equally to blue, green and red light. Most printing and duplicating stocks for use in the laboratory, however, are still manufactured to be blue-sensitive only. They have the advantage of being safe to handle under certain safelight conditions, and since they are used only for printing from a black-and-white film, their spectral sensitivity is unimportant to image formation. Care must be taken though, to use panchromatic stock when producing a black-and-white image from a colour original.

### Ultra-violet and X-rays

Nearly all emulsions are sensitive to both ultra-violet and X-rays. The former results in haziness in black-and-white images, and excess blue in colour stocks, but is easily controlled by the use of an ultra-violet-absorbing filter, both on the camera for original photography, and in printers for duplication and printing stages. X-ray sensitivity presents a problem mainly at airport security checks: like any exposure, the effect is cumulative, and repeated exposure to X-rays, even when exposure is minimized by metal cans, will cause fogging.

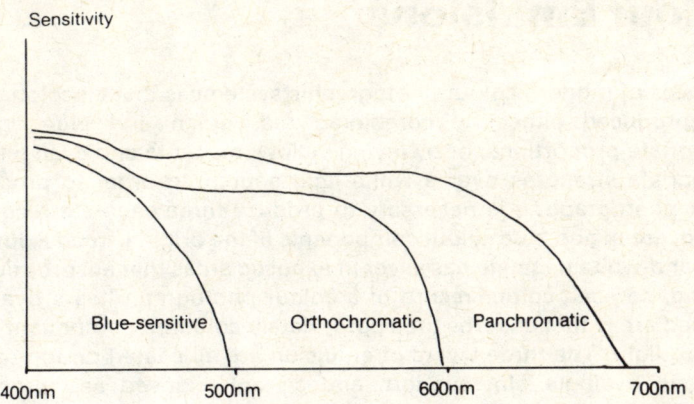

Sensitivity

400nm       500nm       600nm       700nm

Blue-sensitive     Orthochromatic     Panchromatic

| Blue-sensitive | Orthochromatic | Panchromatic |
|---|---|---|
| 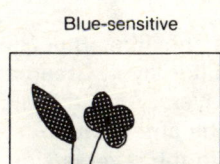 | 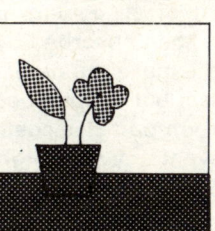 | 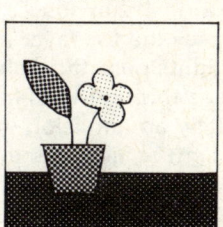 |

## Colour in black-and-white
Non-panchromatic films see many colours as darker than they should be. A red
flowerpot, for example, appears too dark on blue-sensitive and orthochromatic
film, while a green leaf is rendered correctly on orthochromatic and panchromatic
emulsions. A yellow flower is too dark on blue-sensitive film, but slightly lighter on
orthochromatic film, due to the green component of yellow light.

**39**

# Colour Emulsions

The basis of modern colour photographic systems is that all colours may be reproduced either by combining red, green and blue light in appropriate proportions, or by laying yellow, magenta and cyan filters of appropriate strengths over a white light source. In order to produce a colour photograph, it is necessary to produce three separate records of the red, green and blue colour components of the original image. Just as a black-and-white negative has silver in exposed areas that absorbs light on viewing, so each colour record of a colour photograph has a dye in its exposed areas that absorbs the appropriately-coloured component of the viewing light. The three layers of emulsion are all coated on top of each other on a single film support, and all are exposed and processed simultaneously. Such film is known as *integral tripack film*.

In a colour negative, the top emulsion layer is sensitive only to blue light. Immediately under this is a blue-absorbing filter, and below this there are green-sensitive and finally red-sensitive layers. Although these last two are also sensitive to blue light, this has been removed by the filter layer before the light reaches them.

In addition to silver bromide crystals and sensitizing dyes, each emulsion layer contains another chemical known as a *colour coupler*, which, after development, will form the coloured-dye image. There is a different coupler for each layer.

During its exposure, light of all colours strikes the film. Blue light exposes the top layer and is then absorbed by the filter layer. Green and red lights pass through and expose the other two layers. After this, light passes through the film base, but is absorbed by the anti-halation layer (usually an emulsion of carbon particles coated onto the reverse side of the film), which acts to prevent any stray light from reflecting internally and re-exposing the film.

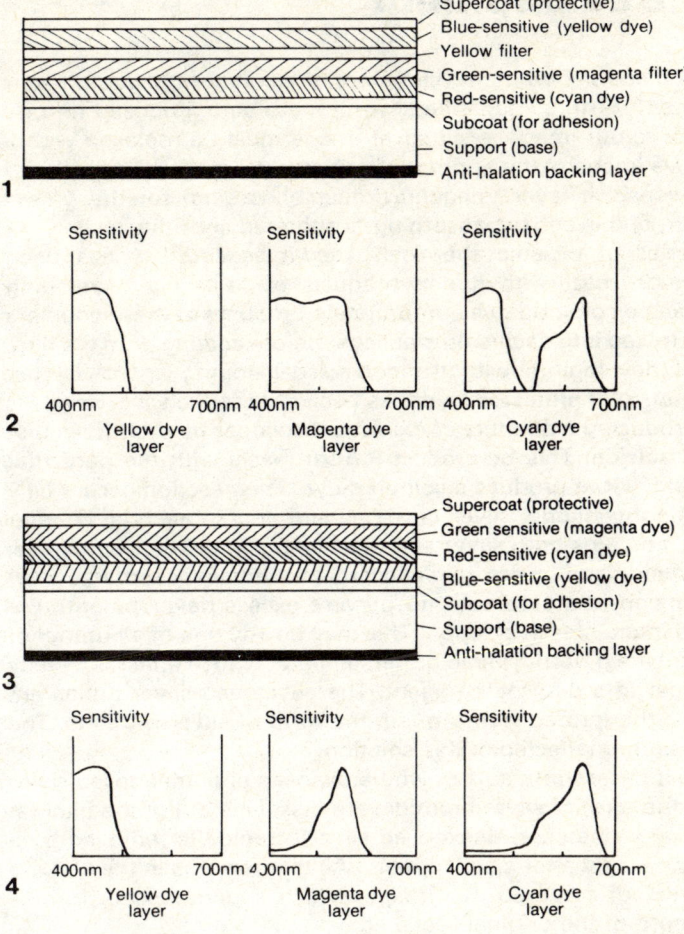

**1**

Supercoat (protective)
Blue-sensitive (yellow dye)
Yellow filter
Green-sensitive (magenta filter)
Red-sensitive (cyan dye)
Subcoat (for adhesion)
Support (base)
Anti-halation backing layer

**2**

| Sensitivity | Sensitivity | Sensitivity |
| --- | --- | --- |
| 400nm    700nm | 400nm    700nm | 400nm    700nm |
| Yellow dye layer | Magenta dye layer | Cyan dye layer |

**3**

Supercoat (protective)
Green sensitive (magenta dye)
Red-sensitive (cyan dye)
Blue-sensitive (yellow dye)
Subcoat (for adhesion)
Support (base)
Anti-halation backing layer

**4**

| Sensitivity | Sensitivity | Sensitivity |
| --- | --- | --- |
| 400nm    700nm | 400nm    700nm | 400nm    700nm |
| Yellow dye layer | Magenta dye layer | Cyan dye layer |

**Layers in a colour film**
(1) Colour negative is coated with the blue-sensitive emulsion on top with a yellow filter layer under it. This is necessary because the other two layers are also sensitive to blue light, (2). In colour-positive emulsions the magenta-forming, green-sensitive layer is on top for maximum sharpness, (3). Blue sensitivity of the red and green layers is minimal, (4). Film base is of approximately 0.005-in thickness, and each emulsion layer is about 0.0001-in thickness.

**41**

*The silver is developed then removed, leaving a dye image.*

# Colour Development

Conventional black-and-white development of a colour film would result in the production of three separate silver images superimposed on one another. For a colour image, each silver image must be replaced with a transparent dye image of the appropriate colour: yellow (blue-absorbing) for the blue-sensitive layer, magenta (green-absorbing) for the green-sensitive layer, and cyan (red-absorbing) for the red-sensitive layer.

Now, a series of organic chemicals known as *couplers* has been produced, which react with the by-products of particular developing agents to produce coloured dyes. Appropriate amounts of these couplers are therefore mixed into each emulsion layer before coating onto the film. The effect of developing (with the correct developing agent) is that wherever a particular emulsion layer has been exposed, a silver image is developed, producing a quantity of oxidized developer by-product in that part of the emulsion. This by-product in turn reacts with the particular coupler in that layer to produce a coloured dye. This reaction occurs only as a result of conventional silver development, and so each layer, after development, contains both silver and dye images in the exposed areas, and silver bromide and unchanged couplers in the unexposed areas.

After immersion in a stop bath (to prevent excess development), the film is passed into a bleach solution. This may be any one of a number of oxidizing agents (e.g. ferricyanide or persulphate) whose effect is exactly opposite to that of a developing agent. The developed silver grains are reconverted to the ionized form $Ag^+$, in the form of silver bromide. The coloured dyes are unaffected in this solution.

The film next passes into a fixer, where exposed and unexposed silver (both now in the form of silver bromide) are dissolved out of the film. (In the colour positive process, unexposed silver bromide is removed by a first fixer immediately after development.) All that remains in the film are the three layers of coloured dye image, which superimposed, form a full-colour record of the original scene.

Just as a black-and-white negative is darkest where the exposure was greatest, so a colour negative has greater density at brighter parts of the scene. In addition, however, since each colour component of the original scene is recorded by its complementary dye, red parts of the scene appear in the negative as cyan, yellow as blue, and so on.

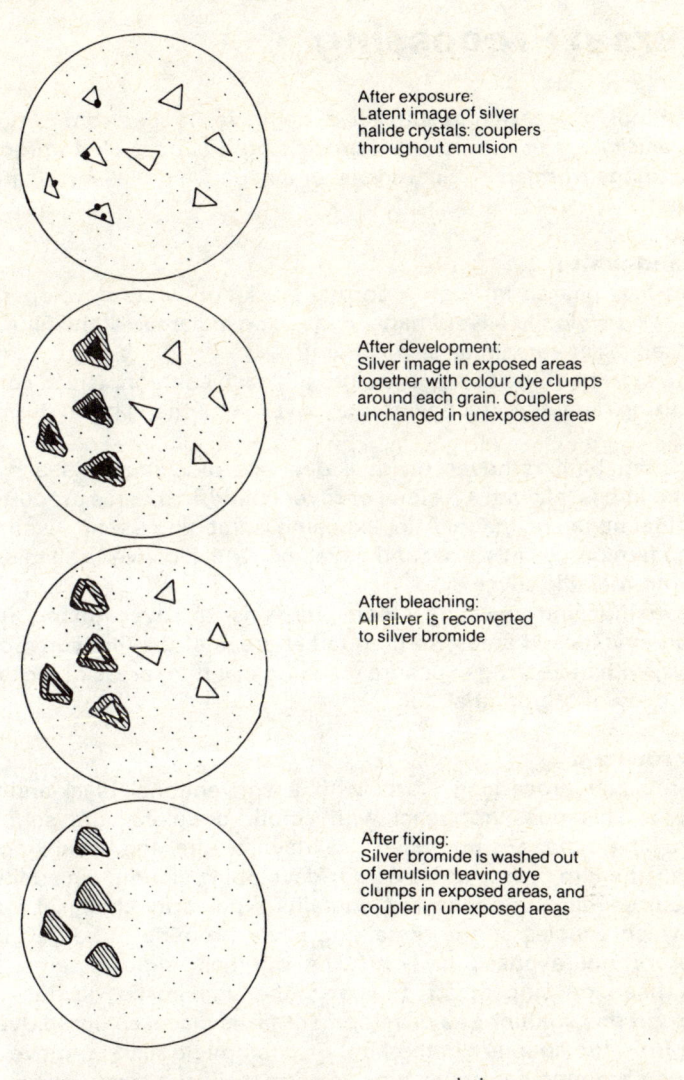

After exposure:
Latent image of silver
halide crystals: couplers
throughout emulsion

After development:
Silver image in exposed areas
together with colour dye clumps
around each grain. Couplers
unchanged in unexposed areas

After bleaching:
All silver is reconverted
to silver bromide

After fixing:
Silver bromide is washed out
of emulsion leaving dye
clumps in exposed areas, and
coupler in unexposed areas

△  Unexposed silver bromide crystal

◬  Exposed silver bromide crystal

◣  Developed silver grain

⋰  Undeveloped coupler

◭  Developed colour dye

**The stages of colour development**
Silver development is necessary for the formation of a dye image, but all silver is
subsequently washed out of the emulsion.

**43**

# Reversal Processing

Conventional processing results in a negative image from a positive subject and *vice versa*. In reversal processing it is possible to produce a positive image from an original scene, or a negative directly from another negative.

### Black-and-white

The film first passes through a normal black-and-white developer. This results in a developed silver image in the exposed areas of the film, while unexposed areas remain as silver bromide.

After a stop bath the film passes into a bleach solution, which contains an oxidizing agent to reconvert the silver into the ionized form and dissolve it.

A clearing bath removes residual deposits of oxidized bleach, after which the film is left with a residue of silver halide, in inverse proportion to the original negative image. After exposing or fogging the film with white light, the film passes into a second developer which converts all this silver halide into metallic silver.

After fixing and washing, there remains a silver image in the originally-unexposed areas, so that darker areas of the film corresond to shadows, with increasing exposure resulting in lighter areas of the image: a direct copy of the original.

### Colour reversal

Colour-reversal processing starts with a conventional black-and-white developer. This does not react with colour douplers, and so only a negative silver image is produced in all layers. After the usual stop bath and rinse, the film passes into a colour-developing solution. In addition to the colour-developing agent, this contains a powerful chemical fogging agent which enables all the remaining silver bromide to be developed, whether or not exposed to light. The originally-exposed areas have already been developed, so it is only the unexposed residue which develops in this solution. As development takes place, coloured dyes are formed from the couplers in the film. Bleaching and fixing remove silver and silver bromide from the film, leaving only the dyes. These were formed in the unexposed areas of the film, and so the resultant image is clear in areas of maximum exposure, and has colour and density in the darker areas of the original scene, thus forming a positive copy.

BLACK-AND-WHITE
REVERSAL

COLOUR
REVERSAL

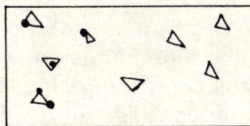

Exposure: exposed crystals have
microscopic spots of silver,
forming a latent image

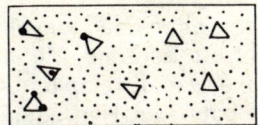

Exposure: neither silver nor colour
dye images are visible at this stage

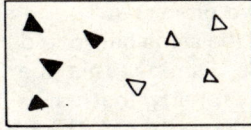

First developer: exposed crystals
are converted to silver grains

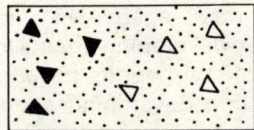

First developer: exposed crystals
are converted to silver but the
couplers are left unaffected

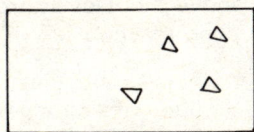

Bleach: developed silver grains
are converted to soluble silver
dichromate and removed

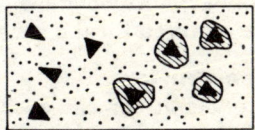

Colour developer: the remaining
crystals are fogged and developed:
the colour developer by-products
form dye clumps

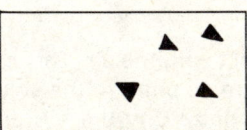

Second developer: the remaining
silver halide is fogged and
developed to silver, producing a
positive silver image

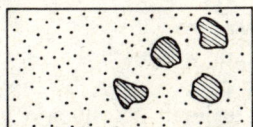

Bleach and fix: all the developed
silver is dissolved leaving a
positive dye image

△  Unexposed silver bromide crystal

◭  Exposed silver bromide crystal

◢  Developed silver grain

⋮  Undeveloped coupler

  Developed colour dye

**The stages of reversal processing**
The positive image is formed in those areas unaffected by exposure or first
development.

**45**

# Constituents of a Developer

### Developing agent

The most often-used developing agents are a group of compounds derived from benzene. Metol and phenidone give high emulsion speed, but also tend to develop unexposed areas, this resulting in high fog levels and low contrasts. Hydroquinone produces higher contrast but is a fairly slow-acting agent. However, a mixture of hydroquinone and metol not only combines the best features of each, but is considerably more active than the sum of the two components: a phenomenon known as *super-additivity*. Varying proportions of these agents are used in low-contrast negative and high-contrast positive processes.

Colour-developing agents are all members of the same benzene-derived group of compounds based on paraphenylene diamine. This is a fairly slow-acting developing agent, but it has the property that its oxidized by-product will react with couplers to form coloured dyes. The pH of a solution – its degree of acidity or alkalinity – has a considerable effect on the speed of development. Metol is quite effective in neutral solution (pH about 7), while hydroquinone requires higher levels of pH. Colour-developing agents will develop silver at any pH above 7, but levels around 10.3 are required for the secondary, colour-coupling reaction.

### Alkali and buffer

The pH of a solution can easily be raised by the addition of a strong alkali such as sodium hydroxide. To maintain it at a steady value, however, it is preferable to add larger quantities of a weak acid salt such as sodium carbonate, or borax. These form a stable, buffered solution whose pH is not changed by the by-products of development.

### Preservative

Developing agents are easily oxidized by contact with the air. This can be reduced considerably by the addition of sodium sulphite to the solution. As this is itself a reducing agent, it is also oxidized by the air, and so enough must be added to ensure that it is not exhausted. As sulphite also has an accelerating action on the developer, its concentration must be carefully controlled.

### Restrainer

Developers have a tendency to develop unexposed silver halide grains as well as exposed ones. The presence of bromide in the solution slows all development, but has a greater effect on this fogging development. Since development yields bromide as a by-product, only a small amount is needed in the original formulation.

### Penetrating agent

Some developers (e.g. colour-reversal first developers) include a small amount of thiocyanate. This has the effect of swelling the emulsion, allowing more rapid penetration of the developer and removal of by-products.

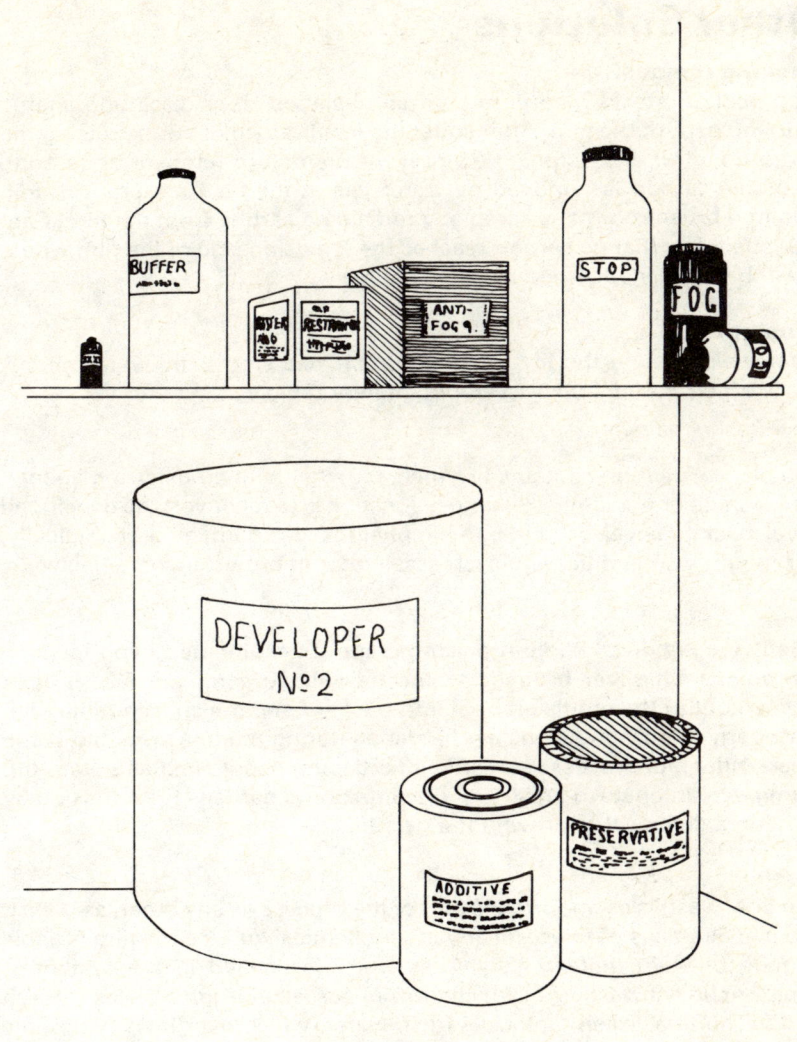

**A mixture of ingredients**
Developer solution forms a complex system of reactions, each component held in balance by the others.

**47**

*Every solution has its own function.*

# Other Solutions

### Backing removal
Many colour stocks incorporate an anti-halation layer of carbon coated onto the back of the film. After softening in a prebath of borax (raising the pH to about 9) and sulphate (to prevent premature removal of carbon), insoluble carbon is removed by water jets in the backing-removal unit. Rotating brushes or pads scrub any remaining carbon from the film. Care must be taken that no carbon reaches the emulsion side of the film where it will be rapidly absorbed by the gelatin.

### Stop bath
After development the film passes into an acid stop bath, which simply lowers the pH and stops development very rapidly.

### Bleach
The bleach solution contains bromide, together with an oxidizing agent – ferricyanide or persulphate – whose function is to reconvert the developed silver back to silver bromide. Persulphate is less damaging ecologically, but requires an additional bleach accelerator in order to work effectively.

### Fixer
This is a solution of sodium or ammonium thiosulphate ('hypo'), which combines with silver bromide to form a soluble complex. This is then washed out of the emulsion both into the fixer and the subsequent rinse.

Modern colour emulsions are hardened during manufacture, but some black-and-white processes include a hardening agent such as potassium aluminium sulphate in the fixer. This shrinks and hardens the emulsion by forming a chemical bond with the gelatin.

### Wash
The final wash is as important a part of the process as any other, as it must remove all traces of fixer and any other chemical, or else the film is liable to fade or stain quite rapidly. Less water is needed in the system of counter-current washes, in which the film passes through a series of wash tanks. The final wash tank uses fresh water, which overflows (with only the very last traces of contamination) into the previous tank and so on. Although the first wash therefore carries most of the washed-out chemicals, it still removes considerable chemical from the heavily fixer-laden emulsion. A three-stage counter-current wash requires about one tenth of the water used in a single-tank system.

### Stabilizer
In the final stabilizer solution, formaldehyde reacts with unused colour coupler molecules (which would otherwise slowly attack the magenta dye) thus stabilizing the colour of the image. It also hardens the emulsion. A wetting agent breaks down surface tension in the water and prevents the forming of water spots on the film, thus promoting even drying.

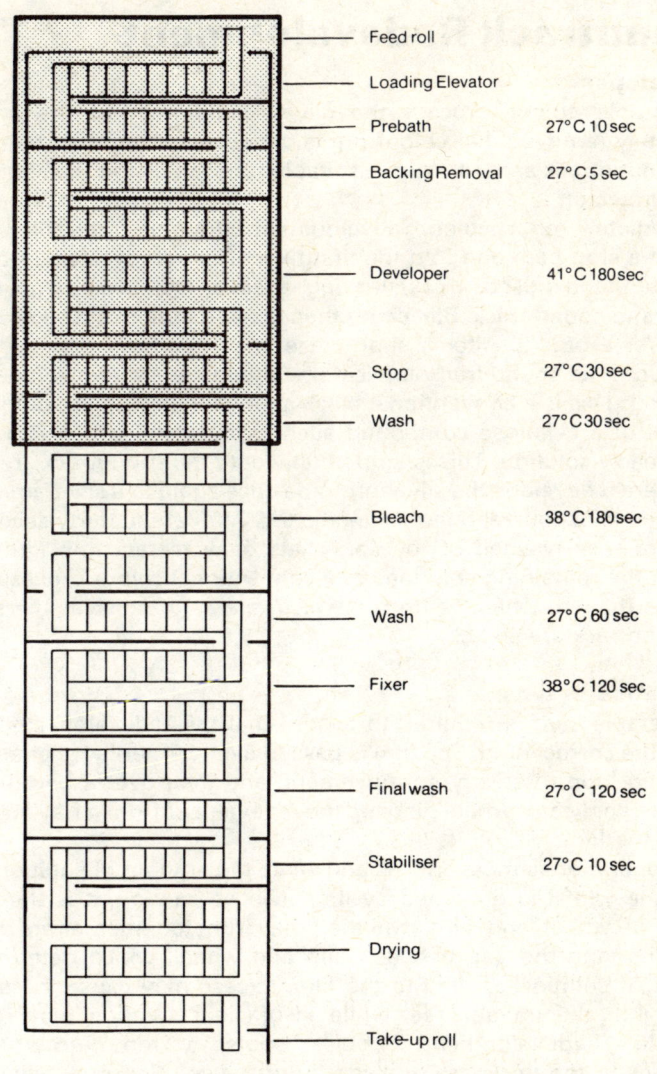

| | |
|---|---|
| Feed roll | |
| Loading Elevator | |
| Prebath | 27°C 10 sec |
| Backing Removal | 27°C 5 sec |
| Developer | 41°C 180 sec |
| Stop | 27°C 30 sec |
| Wash | 27°C 30 sec |
| Bleach | 38°C 180 sec |
| Wash | 27°C 60 sec |
| Fixer | 38°C 120 sec |
| Final wash | 27°C 120 sec |
| Stabiliser | 27°C 10 sec |
| Drying | |
| Take-up roll | |

**The ECN-2 colour-negative process**
Developer time and temperature are critical: other solution times are minimum
requirements but may be exceeded slightly with no effect on the image. Total
processing time, including drying, is about 20 minutes.

# Soundtrack Redevelopment

### Redeveloper

In a simple colour process the silver component of the image is completely removed. For colour prints, however, silver must be retained in the soundtrack area to make it suitable for scanning in the sound head of the projector.

Immediately after colour development, therefore, the film passes through a stop bath and into the first fixer. This removes silver bromide only from unexposed areas, leaving a silver-plus-dye image in both picture and sound track. Bleaching then converts the exposed silver back into silver bromide. After a short rinse and superficial drying, the film passes into the sound track applicator station where a redeveloper stripe is applied. This is a conventional black-and-white developer, but with the addition of a cellulose compound such as Natrasol, which results in a thick, treacly solution. This is striped only onto the soundtrack area of the film where it develops the silver bromide once again to a silver image. The picture area, of course, remains unaffected. After about thirty seconds the redeveloper is washed off by spray jets of water and the film passes through the remaining solutions of a conventional colour process. Fixing removes the silver halides from the picture area, but leaves the silver in the soundtrack area.

### The applicator wheel

Considerable care is required to ensure that the redeveloper is applied only in the correct area. The film is passed over an inertia roller assembly or sprung loop to steady its movement, and then over a back-up roller where an applicator wheel picks up the redeveloper from a tray and paints it on to the film.

This operation is most critical, and while the amount of solution picked up by the wheel is governed by its speed of rotation, it is the relative speeds of wheel and film, whether they run together or in opposite directions, and the gap between film and wheel, which determine the amount of solution applied to the film. Excess may cause the stripe to spread into the image area, while insufficient solution may result in incomplete redevelopment, bubbles, spots, or too narrow a track. Variations in the thickness or viscosity of the solution may have similar results.

Bubbles or applicator miss will result in a series of pops or a rumbling hiss on the soundtrack as the projector scans non-silver areas. If redeveloper spreads, leaving silver in picture areas, this may be removed quite effectively by reprocessing the film, remembering of course to reapplicate the soundtrack. Silver cannot, however, be restored to a track which has already been bleached and fixed.

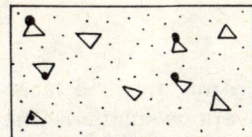

Exposure: latent image in image and track areas

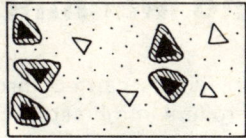

Colour developer: silver and dye formed in both image and track areas

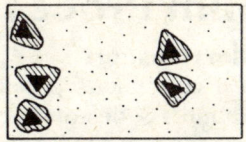

First fixer: unexposed silver bromide removed

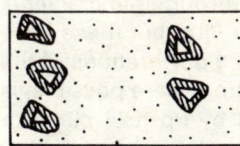

Bleach: silver reconverted to silver bromide in image and track areas

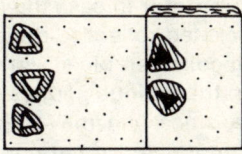

Redeveloper: applied to track area only: converts silver halide to silver

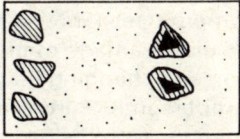

Second fixer: silver halide removed from image area leaving dye image; silver retained in track area

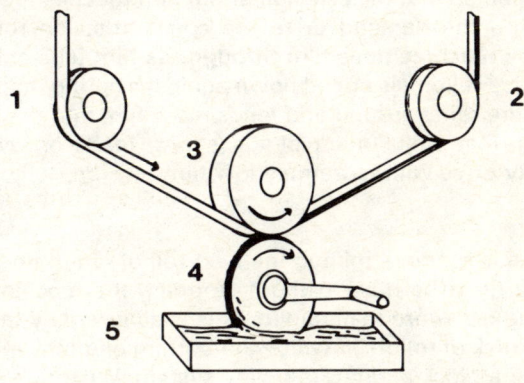

### Sound redeveloper application
Partially-dried film is guided between rollers, (1) and (2), around a flat back-up roller, (3). Viscous redeveloper is picked up by the applicator wheel, (4), from a constantly-filled trough, (5), and painted onto the film in a narrow stripe.

*Wet film must be driven very gently.*

# Film Processing Machines

## Film transport

In a continuous processor, film is carried through the machine laced around a series of racks of rollers immersed in the various solutions; the time the film spends in each solution being proportional to its path length through the corresponding set of racks. A machine running at 300 feet per minute may have a total path length of 6000 ft, with a total process time of 20 minutes. This machine would have several hundred rollers, a number of which must be driven by a motor to ease the film through the machine. Some processors use sprocketed rollers to drive the film, but these have the disadvantage of placing considerable strain on the perforations of the film, and changing between the various gauges of film, where possible, is cumbersome. Furthermore, since film may expand by up to 4 per cent when wet, provision must be made for varying amounts of slack in any section of the machine.

Sprocketless machines use various systems of friction drive in which the film is carried over, and driven by, rollers with a soft dimpled tyre that supports the film over its entire surface. To avoid emulsion damage, these are always arranged so that the cell side of the film touches the rollers. In one such system – the demand drive – a constant-speed roller at the take-up end of the machine pulls film through: as film tension increases over any other drive roller it is pulled down against a spring onto a driving shaft that drives the roller around and feeds more film into the loop, thus reducing tension. Fine adjustment of the spring loads on every roller results in a steady drive with extremely low film tension.

## Joins

Once the machine is running, joining the next roll of film onto the end of the previous one must be done without stopping the machine, so that correct processing times are maintained. This is achieved by the use of a *feed elevator* – a rack of rollers in which the bottom end may move freely up and down, like a block-and-tackle pulley system. When the end of the film is reached it is stopped by means of a brake, but the film continues to feed from the elevator onto the machine as the bottom set of rollers rises. Provided that the next roll of film is joined on – usually with staples or waterproof tape – before the bottom set of rollers reaches the upper limit of its travel, processing can continue uninterrupted. When there is no more film to be processed, a roll of machine leader – dummy film with no emulsion, often made of polyester for strength – is loaded onto the machine so that it always remains completely threaded with film.

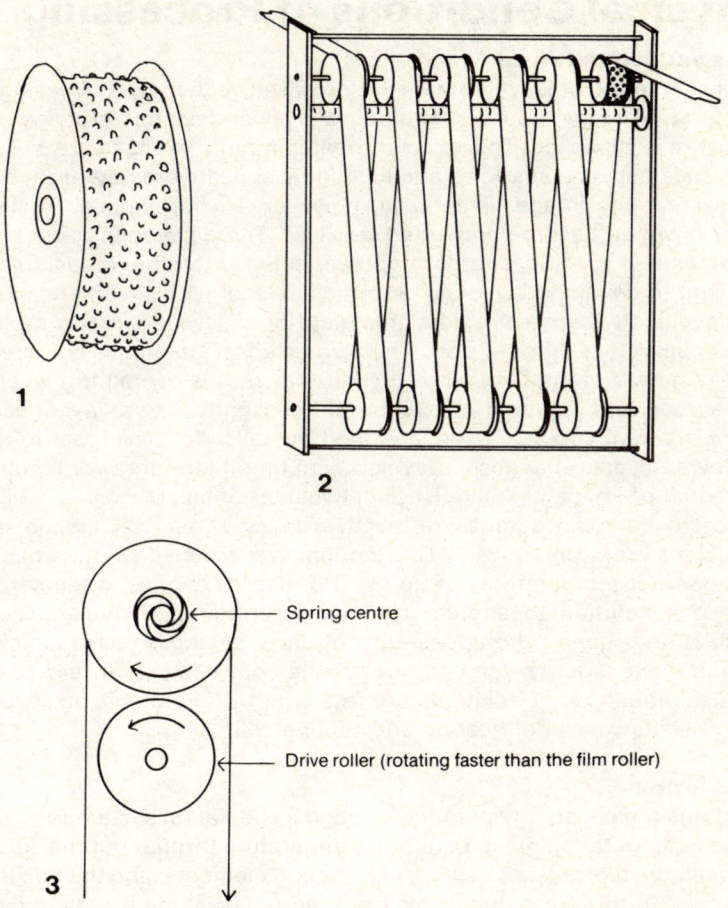

1

2

Spring centre

Drive roller (rotating faster than the film roller)

3

## Film rollers

(1) Tyres support the base side of the film. (2) Film follows a helical path across each rack. (3) In the demand-drive system film is pulled through the machine: if tension increases, the roller is pulled down on its sprung centre until it touches the drive roller which causes it to speed up so that tension is reduced.

Processing machines can use PVC, rubber, glass, or stainless steel for their construction. Stainless steel is attacked in bleach tanks and titanium must therefore be used. Most other materials are either attacked by the chemicals, or have a fogging action on the film.

# Physical Conditions of Processing

### Time and temperature

As the amount of development is increased, either by increasing the temperature or the time, so the amount of silver developed for any given exposure is increased. This effect is greater in more exposed areas, so the difference between shadows and highlights appears greater, producing a more contrasty image. Eventually, however, all the exposed grains of silver bromide become converted to silver. The developer's action now becomes less specific, and development extends to other areas. Crystals adjacent to developed crystals become 'infected' with silver, and start to be developed themselves, and the developer also attacks completely unexposed areas of emulsion. The former effect dramatically increases the graininess of the film, while the latter increases overall fog level.

In a multilayer colour film, reactions differ slightly in each layer because of the different couplers used, and the time taken for developer to reach the lower layers. Changes in development time therefore may result in a mismatch of image characteristics between each layer.

Most developing agents are inactive below about 13°C, while many emulsions break up above 27°C, although forehardened colour stocks are processed at temperatures of up to 43°C. Rapid changes in temperature from one solution to another may cause cracking of the emulsion – reticulation – giving the appearance of crazy paving. Precise control of development requires temperatures to be controlled to an accuracy of 0.1°C (although other solutions are less critical), and this is achieved by thermostatic control of heating and cooling coils.

### Circulation

Solutions are constantly pumped through a circulation system for several reasons: first, to maintain a uniform temperature throughout the solution between the thermostat, heating and cooling elements, and the film itself; secondly, to mix fresh chemicals from the replenishment system evenly throughout the solution; and thirdly, to pass solution through a filter system.

### Turbulation

The process of development results in a layer of used developer around the film surface, and this slows down further development. This can produce a streaky effect on the film, and light fringes around heavily-exposed areas where development has been the greatest. The passage of film through the developer is not sufficient to overcome this, and submerged jets are directed at the emulsion every few seconds during development. Since this affects the supply of fresh developer to the emulsion, a change in turbulation has an overall effect on the degree of development.

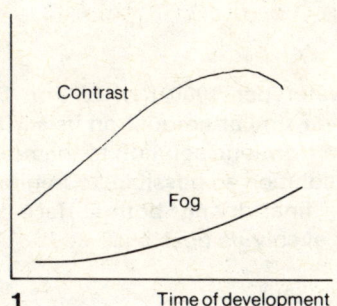

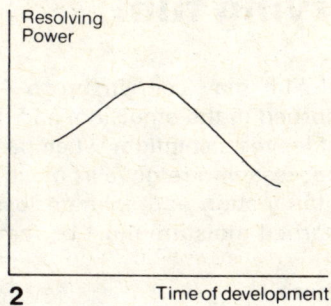

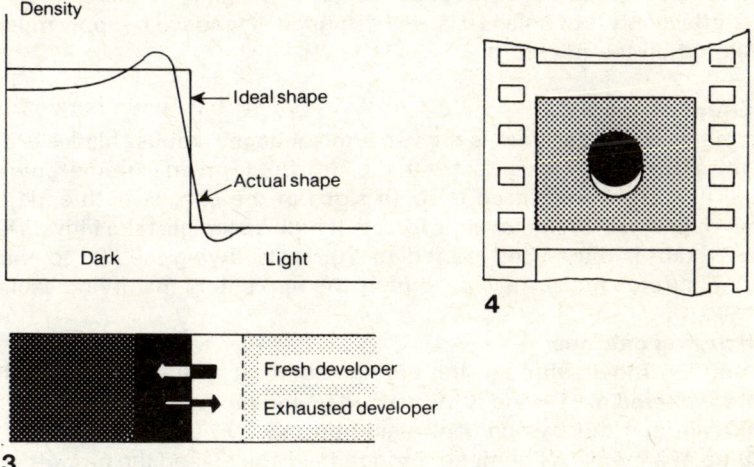

## Development and agitation

(1) Increased development time or temperature increases contrast, up to a point: beyond that, increased fog level becomes more significant. (2) More contrast results in better resolution, until image-spread and granularity become too great, and resolution falls off. (3) Insufficient turbulation reduces the supply of fresh developer to exposed areas except at image edges. The black outline thus formed can improve apparent sharpness. (4) In extreme cases, the film's travel through the machine is the only form of turbulation, and a directional 'ghost', formed by the stream of exhausted developer, appears.

**55**

*The film must finish up dry and clean.*

# Drying film

Wet film may contain up to 4 kg of water per 1000 ft of 35-mm film absorbed in the emulsion, and may carry a similar amount on its surface as it leaves a solution. When passing film from one solution to the next it is necessary to remove as much surface solution as possible, to minimize contamination and solution loss. During final drying, both surface and absorbed moisture must be removed as evenly as possible.

### Wipers
The simplest way of removing surface moisture is by use of wiper blades or squeegees made of rubber or nylon. Although quite efficient, these introduce a grave risk of scratching the film if they become worn or collect any dirt or grit. An alternative is to use air knives which blow off surface moisture. These are scratch-free, but can cause splashing of solution if they are set inaccurately. A rubber roller, or wringer, removes moisture quite effectively, but unless it is well designed, it tends to re-apply much of the liquid on the next turn.

### Vacuum squeegees
The most efficient system is the vacuum squeegee: rubber blades are set so as not to come into contact with the film, but form an extremely narrow gap. These sets are placed on both sides of the film, at both ends of a vacuum enclosure, so that air is forced at high speed past the film surface. This system is often used immediately prior to drying the film to ensure that no surplus moisture is present as the film enters the drying cabinet.

### The drying cabinet
As the film moves through the drying cabinet it is dried by a stream of heated, filtered air. Drying is influenced by the temperature and humidity of the air, and this can be controlled not only by heaters by also by the volume of air which is pumped through the cabinet, and the proportion of moist exhaust air which is recirculated.

In wet film, the swollen emulsion causes the film to curl, emulsion out. As the emulsion dries and shrinks, the film flattens, and eventually curls the other way, with the emulsion in. The film should normally be flat about a third to a half way through the cabinet, allowing plenty of time for the emulsion to dry right through.

Drying in excess humidity can result in *shorelining,* or contour marks around the perforation edges where the emulsion has dried unevenly. Overheated drying results in a film whose surface is dry and hard, but which is still moist and soft underneath. Such film is extremely liable to damage upon projection, and even correctly-dried film is soft for a day or two after processing, until it has reached a stable and uniform condition throughout.

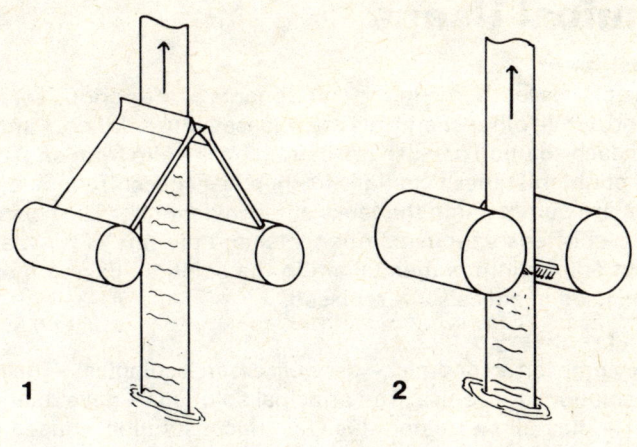

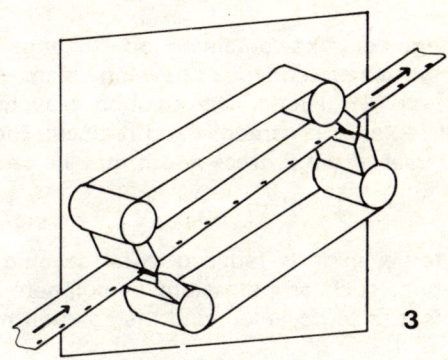

**Removing surplus moisture**
(1) Wiper blades. (2) Air knives. (3) Vacuum squeegees suck air at high speed past the film as it passes into and out of the enclosure.

# Chemical Usage

### Replenishment
As film is processed, some of the components of the various solutions are consumed, while other chemicals are released into solution. Furthermore, traces of each solution or wash are carried by the film from one tank to the next. To counteract these changes in chemical concentration, replenisher solutions are pumped into the tanks at a constant rate. The concentration of the replenisher's various components, and the rate of flow, are set so that exact equilibrium is maintained in the solution. Excess by-products overflow, used chemicals are replaced.

### Chemical recovery
It has become an economic – as well as an ecological – necessity to reclaim solutions for re-use. The principal solutions – developers, bleach, and fixer – may all be treated this way. Reconstitution of used chemical components is achieved simply by addition of fresh chemical up to the normal concentration; the removal of excess by-products is more complex, but several methods are available.

### Ion exchange
The solution is passed through columns containing ion exchange resins, which absorb unwanted ions such as bromide in developers and replace them with harmless hydroxyl ($OH^-$) ions. The solution may then be reconstituted up to normal replenisher strength and re-used. The resin may be reclaimed by a reversal of the process and it may be re-used a number of times.

### Regeneration
In the bleaching process, ferricyanide is reduced to ferrocyanide. The addition of an oxidizing agent such as potassium persulphate to the overflow solution reconverts it to ferricyanide, and the solution may be re-used.

### Silver recovery
Silver from the emulsion is dissolved into the fixer, and it may be recovered from this solution by electrolysis. It is common to fit electrolytic cells to fixer tanks and to circulate solution continuously through the cell and back into the machine. This maintains the silver at a sufficiently low level for fixing to continue, but more silver may be extracted from the overflow fixer to make the solution suitable for reconstitution as a fixer replenisher. The reclaimed silver is, of course, a valuable product, and efficient recovery should have a considerable effect on a laboratory's overall operating costs, as well as helping to maintain world supplies.

Invariably, due to carryover, there are traces of silver in the final wash, and some laboratories have found it economical to remove these fractions of a gram per litre either by electrolysis or by reverse osmosis (a form of molecular filtering). This has the added benefit of producing well-purified water which may itself be recycled with considerable saving in heating as well as water expenses.

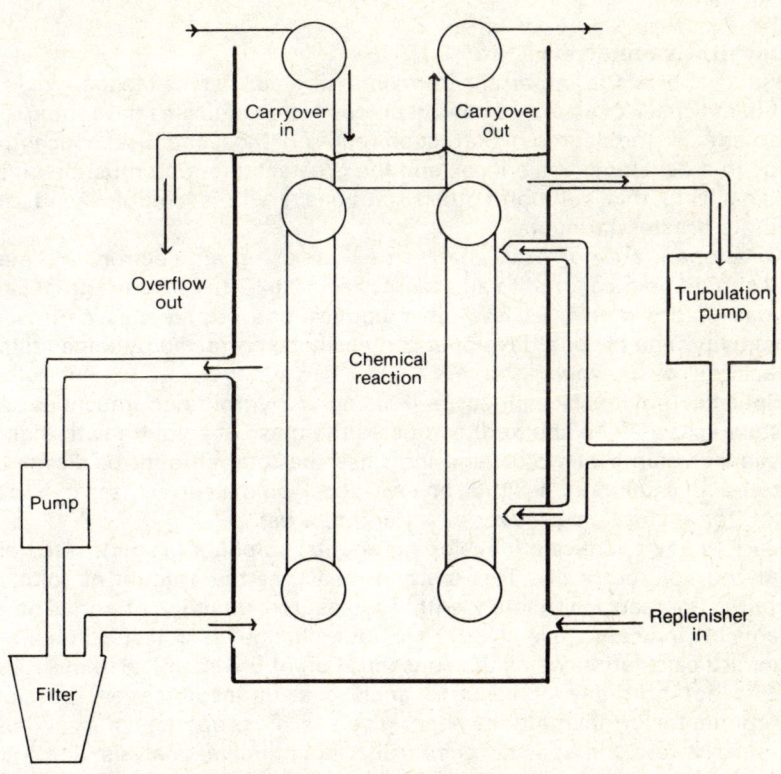

**Solution circulation and exchange**
In addition to chemicals used or released in chemical reactions, solution is lost
through carryover. Replenisher is fed in at a measured rate to balance these
changes. The solution that overflows may be saved for regeneration. There is also a
continuous-circulation system for filtering (and silver recovery in the case of a
fixer), and a separate turbulation system.

**59**

*... . and regularly checked.*

# Chemical Analysis

While times, temperatures, replenishers, etc. are all controlled to maintain the correct conditions for processing, it is still necessary to test the system to ensure that correct results are being obtained. Visual assessment of picture quality can be supported by sensitometric tests, but some degree of chemical analysis provides a direct check on the condition of various solutions.

## Quantitative analysis

Regular analysis is important in maintaining consistent results, while a complete check of an out-of-control process often indicates the source of a problem and the degree of correction required. Most chemical concentrations in a developer are critical, and the greatest attention must be given to analyzing this solution: other solutions are less complex and can tolerate greater variations.

Developers are normally analysed for pH using an electrolytic meter, and should be measured to an accuracy of ±0.02. This calls for great care in use of the meter, as few other applications require this degree of sensitivity. The pH of a developer can easily be corrected by the addition of acid or caustic soda.

Specific gravity, SG, (measured using a hygrometer, much as car battery acid may be checked) compares the mass of solution with that of an equal volume of water, and indicates the total amount of dissolved material in a solution. It is thus an easy check on the correctness of a mix, or of (for example) carryover of water into a bath.

Certain key chemicals (developing agents, sulphite, bromide, etc.) are analyzed volumetrically. This method measures the amount of solution required to react completely with a measured quantity of some other chemical, indicated usually by a colour change in a test solution. A standard calculation yields the concentration of the chemical in question.

It is not normally practical to analyze solutions for every possible component. Normal methods either give specific properties of a solution, or simply test for specific chemicals. Quantitative analysis does not provide a complete assay of every substance present in a solution, and some types of contamination might have a sensitometric effect on the film but be difficult to trace by chemical methods.

Chemical analysis is not a complete control system in itself and apparent variations should be checked, and confirmed by sensitometric trends in the film itself before any attempt is made to correct the solution. Chemical changes rarely occur in isolation, and correcting one factor alone will often result in a less, rather than more, stable process.

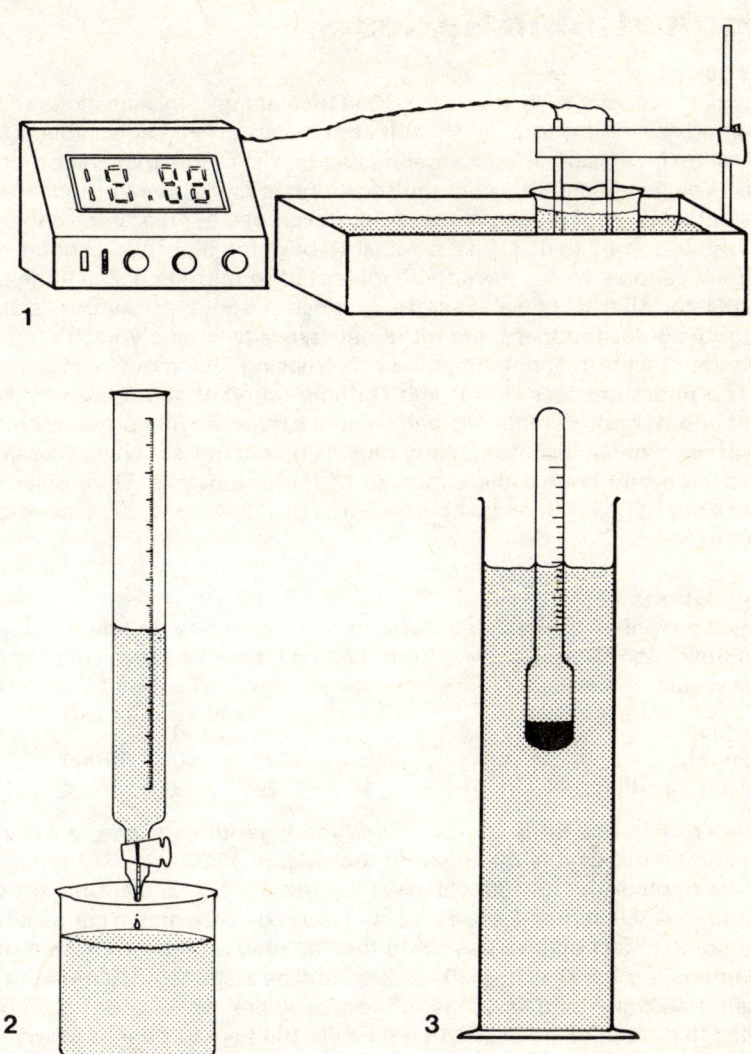

**Chemical analysis**
(1) pH is measured at a constant temperature using a pH meter. (2) A burette is used for volumetric analysis. (3) specific gravity, also measured at a standard temperature, is determined with a hygrometer or float.

**61**

# Logarithmic Series

### Weber's law

The psychologist Weber found in 1890 that changes in sensations such as heat, pain, brightness and loudness, became less noticeable as the stimulus increased. The change in level of a stimulus that will produce a 'just noticeable difference' in the sensation is found to be proportional to the actual level of that stimulus: so, for example, if three candles together produce a light that is just detectably brighter than two candles, then twenty candles would have to be increased to thirty to achieve the same just detectable increase. Thus to produce a series of uniform steps of brightness (or loudness, etc.) it is necessary to multiply each step by a constant factor, resulting in steadily increasing increments.

The photographers Hurter and Driffield found at about the same time that photographic emulsions behave in a similar way. In order to produce a series of negatives of regularly increasing darkness it was necessary to give each one double the exposure of the one before. Thus a series of steps might be produced with exposures of 1, 2, 4, 8, 16, 32, seconds, and so on.

### Logarithms

It is convenient to express each term in a series as the number of multiplication steps it is away from the first term. In a series with factor 10 this would appear as

| Step: | 1 | 2 | 3 | 4 | 5 | 6 |
|---|---|---|---|---|---|---|
| Number: | 1 | 10 | 100 | 1000 | 10000 | 100000 |
| Multiplications: | 0 | 1 | 2 | 3 | 4 | 5 |

The terms in this third line are called the logarithms of the terms in the second line: thus 4 is the logarithm, or log, of 10000.

The numbers 1, 10, 100, etc. have logarithms 0, 1, 2, etc. On a graph of numbers against their logs, a smooth curve could be drawn connecting all the points. Fractional values could then be read off this graph so that, for example, log 2 = 0.30, log 30 = 1.48, etc. The statement '10 multiplied by itself 1.48 times equals 30' is, of course, quite meaningless (compared with '10 multiplied by itself three times is 100') but this series of numbers behaves in just the same way as the basic series of whole number logarithms. For any series of numbers with a common multiplication factor, there is a corresponding series of logs of those numbers with a common addition factor.

The quantities measured by Weber, and by Hurter and Driffield, fit this type of arithmetic quite well, and log scales are used to measure such things as density, exposure, and sound level or loudness. The key feature of all these units is that an increase of 0.3 in the log scale corresponds to a doubling of the original quantity, while an increase of 1.0 denotes a ten times increase in the quantity itself.

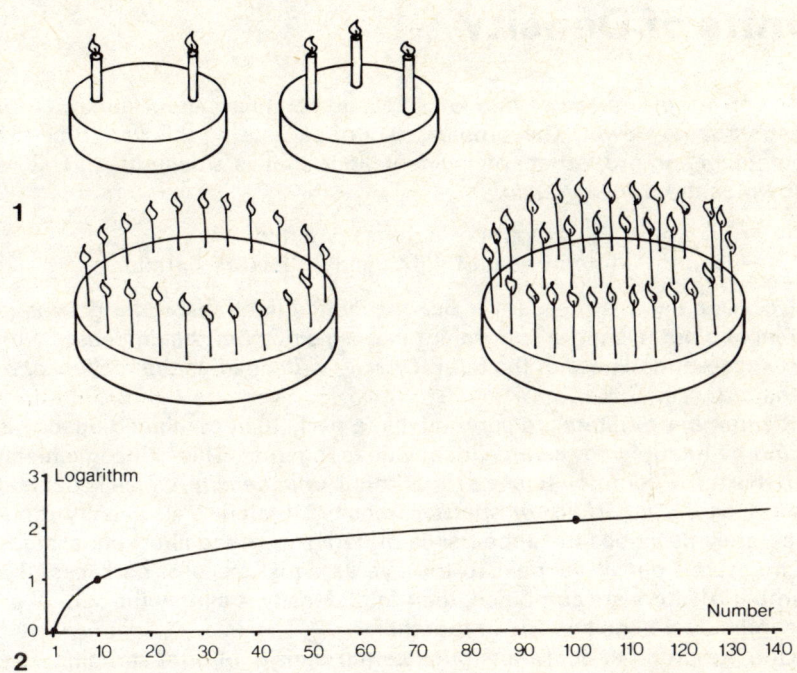

**1**

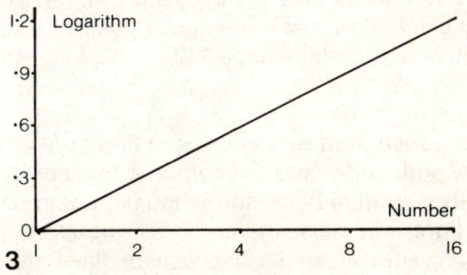

**2**

| NUMBER | LOG |
|--------|-----|
| I | 0·0 |
| 2 | 0·3 |
| 4 | 0·6 |
| 8 | 0·9 |
| 10 | 1·0 |
| 16 | 1·2 |
| 32 | 1·5 |
| 64 | 1·8 |
| 100 | 2·0 |

**3**

## Constant factors

(1) For a given change in brightness, the increase in lighting must be proportional to the original lighting power.

(2) Numbers and their logarithms are linked by the rules $\log(y) = x$ where $y = 10^x$.

(3) Every time a number is doubled, its log is increased by 0.30.

# Units of Density

The density of a piece of film is a measure of its apparent darkness, or light-stopping power. The simplest way of expressing this would be the percentage or proportion of incident light that is transmitted. This is known as the *transmittance:*

Tr = T/I where T = amount of light transmitted
and      I = amount of light incident (before filtration)

Occasionally this measure is used to define light-absorbing gauzes in projectors but it is more convenient to have a number that increases with the apparent darkness of the filter. *Opacity* is defined as the *reciprocal of transmittance:* O = I/T.

If a number of filters are combined in a pack, their combined opacity is found by multiplying the individual values together. This is inconvenient, and it is more common to use a logarithmic unit, *density*, which is defined simply as the *logarithm of opacity*. Density D = log (I/T). Density more accurately describes the appearance of darkness of the filter: equal steps of measured density appear to the eye as equal steps of darkness. If a number of filters are combined, their total density is simply the sum of all the individual densities added together.

One hundred per cent transmittance (no density or light stopping) is a density of 0. Clear film base usually has a density of about 0.03: (about 94 per cent transmittance). A filter of 0.30 density transmits 50 per cent of light, while film of density 3.00 transmits only 0.1 per cent of light, and may be regarded as effectively black. This material may be used as black spacing in chequerboard negative cutting (*see* page 112).

## Diffuse and specular density

A certain proportion of the light transmitted by any piece of film or filter is scattered away from its original path. In the case of coloured films or dye filters this is a very small proportion, but in black-and-white films as much as ten per cent of transmitted light may be scattered. In a more extreme example, a ground glass may scatter 80 or 90 per cent of the light it transmits. Most densitometers collect all transmitted and scattered light; the reading so obtained is called the *diffuse density* of the film. If only the directly-transmitted light is collected, the result is termed *specular density*. In contact printing, all light transmitted by the negative falls on the raw stock. However, in an optical printer or a projector, only the directly transmitted light is gathered by the lens system, and all scattered light is lost. Dark areas therefore behave as though they were somewhat darker, with the result that the contrast appears to be increased.

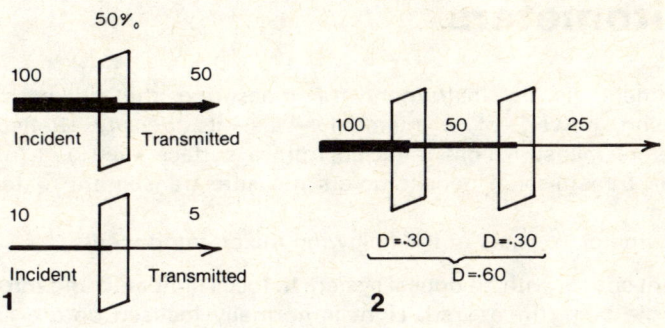

50%

100 Incident — 50 Transmitted

10 Incident — 5 Transmitted

**1**

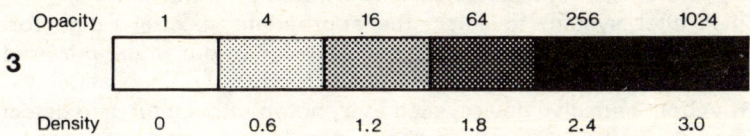

100 — 50 — 25

D = ·30   D = ·30

D = ·60

**2**

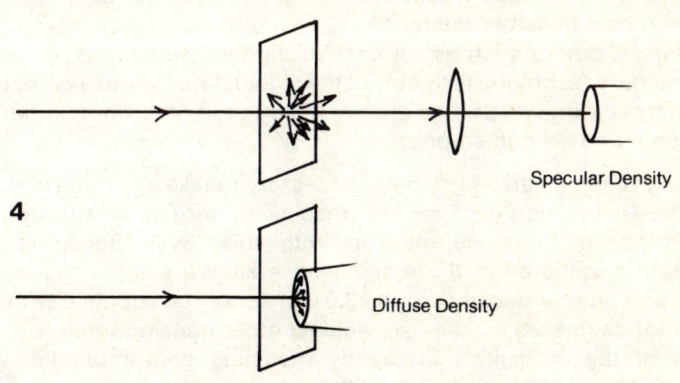

| Opacity | 1 | 4 | 16 | 64 | 256 | 1024 |
|---|---|---|---|---|---|---|

**3**

| Density | 0 | 0.6 | 1.2 | 1.8 | 2.4 | 3.0 |
|---|---|---|---|---|---|---|

Specular Density

**4**

Diffuse Density

**Transmittance and density**
(1) A filter transmits the same proportion of light however bright the source. (2) Combining two filters requires the densities to be added. (3) Density units are conveniently small. (4) Scattered light is measured only in a diffuse-density system.

# Densitometers

A densitometer is an instrument for measuring the darkness, or light-stopping power, of a material – i.e. its *density*. Reflection densitometers measure light reflected from a surface such as a paper print, while transmission densitometers measure transparent materials such as film.

A densitometer consists of the following major components:

(1) A light source with an optical system to focus light onto and through the sample being measured. Light is normally focused onto a small aperture on the base stage of the instrument. A 2 mm or 3 mm circular aperture is usual for most work, but optical soundtracks are read using a slit of 0.3 or 0.4 mm width. The film sample is placed directly over this aperture and an optical collector is lowered onto the sample.

(2) A filter system to select the appropriate spectral range for the reading being taken (red, green or blue for colour films, infra-red for optical soundtracks, etc.).

(3) A light-sensitive device, such as a photomultiplier tube, to detect the amount of light passing through the sample, and an amplifier to convert this into a readable signal. The output of this stage must be converted electronically into a logarithmic form, in order that the result may be interpreted as a density reading.

(4) A display device such as a meter or digital display unit. A useful supplementary technique is to output the signal directly into a computer or microprocessor, which may plot the result on a graph or compare it to a given standard and so on.

Before any reading can be taken it is necessary to take a reading with no film sample in position and set the display to zero; any subsequent reading is based on a comparison with this level. Readings are standardized by calibrating the meter with a known sample: usually a neutral carbon filter of density around 3.0 which may be supplied with the instrument or calibrated by the user against other densitometers.

Because of the difficulties in exactly matching photomultiplier and amplifier response curves, it is unlikely that two densitometers will produce exactly the same readings throughout the entire range, even if both are calibrated against the same standard. For this reason, comparisons of process results, etc., should always be carried out on the same instrument.

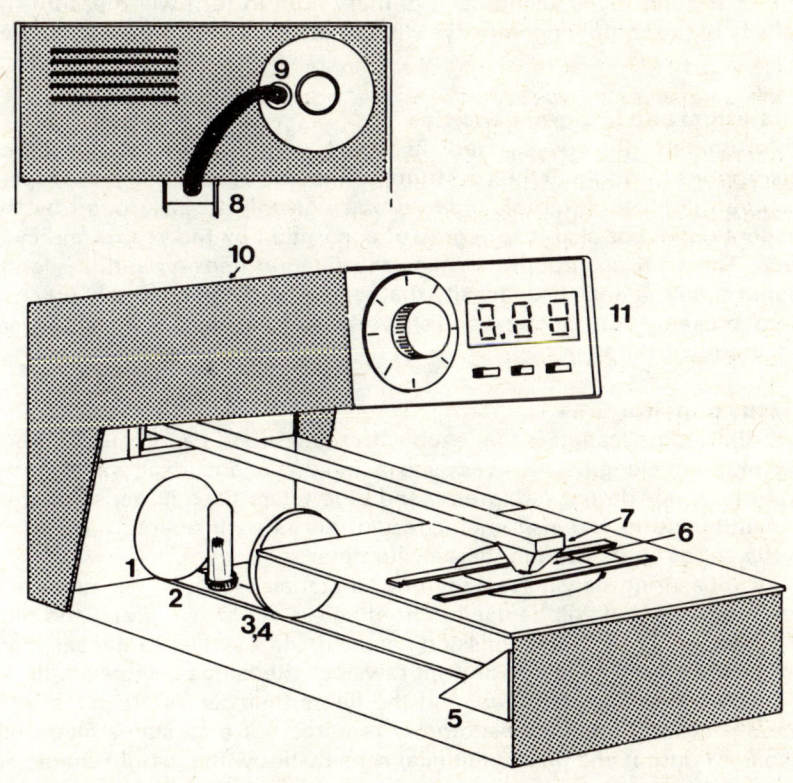

## Densitometers

A rear mirror, (1), collects light from a lamp, (2), through focusing condensers, (3 and 4), and a 45-degree mirror, (5), so that the filament is focused upon the aperture (6) where the film sample is placed. Transmitted light is collected by a diffuser, (7), and passed by way of a fibre optic, (8), through the required colour filter, (9), into a photocell, (10). The signal is amplified and measured and displayed as a density reading, (11).

*Three readings for three dyes in one piece of film.*

# Colour Densitometry

In colour film, three dye layers are used to control light in the three broad bands of the spectrum: red, green and blue. The density of each dye layer must be read separately to gain full information about any part of a film image. Since each of the three primary colours of light is absorbed by only one of the film dyes, using each primary light in turn will measure the density of the complementary dye without interference from the other two dyes.

### Analytical and integral densities

Unfortunately the dyes used in colour films all have unwanted absorptions throughout the spectrum, so that the density of a piece of film to green light, for example, will be due not only to absorption by the magenta dye, but also to a degree of absorption by the yellow and cyan dyes. The total absorption is called the *integral density*, and is slightly higher than the analytical density that would be obtained if only one dye were present. For routine control work, integral density readings are sufficiently accurate.

### Status densitometry

A further complication is that even within the broad bands of red, green and blue wavelengths, the dyes used in film do not absorb all wavelengths uniformly, nor do the red, green, and blue filters used in densitometers transmit uniformly. Densitometric results will vary considerably according to the set of filters used in the densitometer.

For measuring densities of pre-print materials – that is, negatives and intermediates that will be used in printing – a set of red, green and blue filters is chosen with transmission characteristics similar to the sensitivities of the emulsion layers of print rawstock. Readings using such filters are called *status M densities*, and the filters themselves are *status MM filters*. Accurate status densitometry requires not only status filters but also light-output and photomultiplier sensitivities with the right characteristics.

Materials intended for projection are measured using a slightly different set of filters having transmission characteristics closer to the sensitivity distribution of the eye. These are known as *status AA filters*, and result in *status A densitometry*.

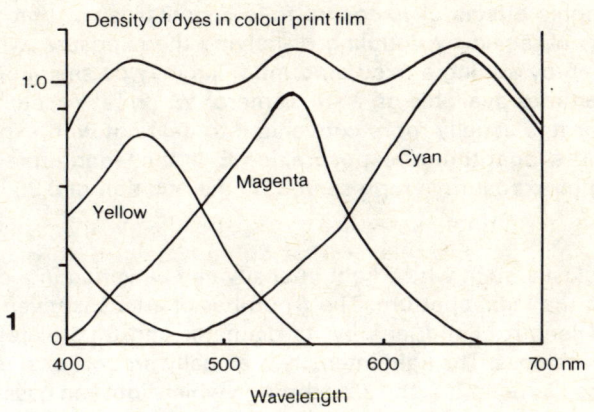

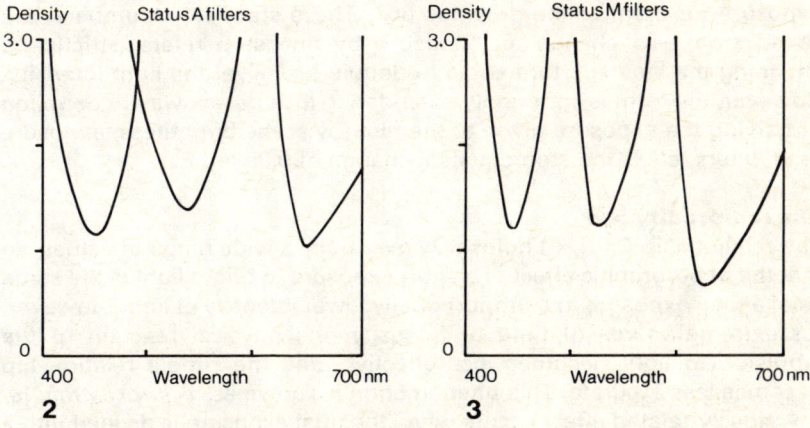

**Spectral response**
(1) Dye densities overlap into each others' region of the spectrum, so that each dye makes a slight contribution to density readings of each other dye. (2) Status A filtration is chosen to correspond to peak visual sensitivities while, (3), Status M filtration, corresponds more exactly to print-stock sensitivites.

*Low light for a long time, or a short, bright exposure.*

# Units of Exposure

The amount of light that falls on a photographic emulsion is the product of two factors: intensity of light, and time or duration of exposure.

Weber's law describes human responses to various sensations: the photographic effects of exposure follow similar laws: that is, a certain change is obtained by doubling or halving the exposure, whatever it is, rather than by adding a fixed amount. (This may be seen in the range of exposure times available on a still camera: ½, ¼, ⅛, 1/16, etc). Because of this factor it is usually more convenient to deal not with exposure itself, but with the logarithm of exposure, log E. In the logarithmic scale, every doubling of exposure is represented by the addition of 0.30 log E.

### Stops

The simplest way in which light intensity can be varied in a camera is by changing the lens' aperture. The *f*/number of a lens is given by dividing the focal length of the lens by its diameter and this relates directly to image brightness. The light intensity is actually proportional to the square of the lens diameter (i.e. the area through which light can pass to reach the film). The iris control, or aperture, is usually calibrated in steps of doubling this area, so that each division on the scale represents twice (or half) the exposure (or area) of the previous one. These steps (or *f*/numbers) are called *stops*. To change an exposure by one stop refers, strictly, to changing the lens aperture so as to double (or halve) the light intensity. However, the term is commonly extended to include any way of doubling or halving the exposure given to the film (by scene brightness, exposure time, filters, etc.) One stop equals a change of 0.30 log E.

### The reciprocity law

The relationship $E = I \times t$ holds true over quite a wide range of values, so that the photographic effect of a short exposure to bright light is the same as of a long exposure to a proportionally lower intensity of light. However, for extreme values of time or intensity, the physical reaction of the emulsion to light becomes less effective, and the simple relationship becomes less accurate. This phenomenon is known as *reciprocity failure.*

A closely-related effect occurs when the total exposure is divided into a number of short exposures. This is known as the *intermittency effect*. In general, a number of short exposures with intervals between them have less total effect than a single exposure of the same total duration.

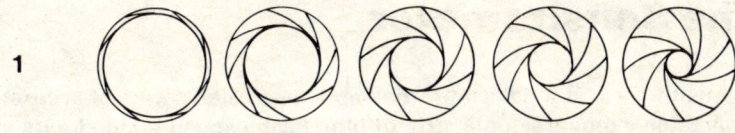

| Focal length | 40mm | 40mm | 40mm | 40mm | 40mm |
|---|---|---|---|---|---|
| Diameter | 20mm | 14mm | 10mm | 7mm | 5mm |
| Aperture | f/2 | f/2.8 | f/4 | f/5.6 | f/8 |
| Lens area | 400mm$^2$ | 200mm$^2$ | 100mm$^2$ | 50mm$^2$ | 25mm$^2$ |
| Relative exposure | 1 | 1/2 | 1/4 | 1/8 | 1/16 |

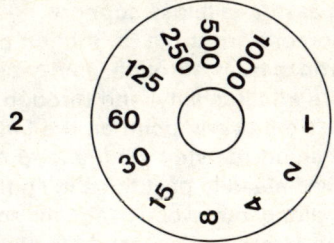

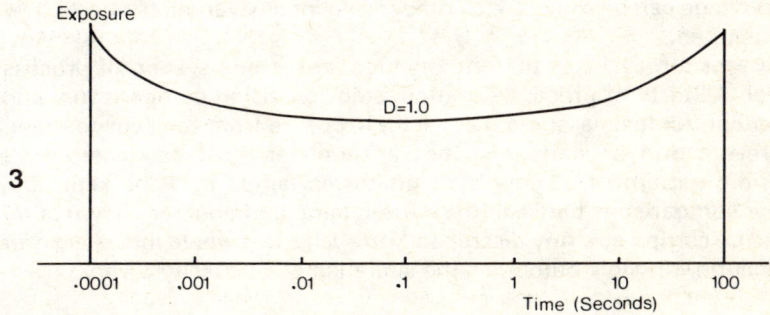

## Exposure

(1) Each aperture setting gives half the exposure of the previous one. (2) Still-camera shutter speeds: each is half the previous one. (3) Reciprocity failure: if the exposure time is very long or very short, a greater exposure (l × t) is required for the same effect on the film.

# The Sensitometer

A sensitometer is a device for making a graduated series of accurate and repeatable exposures on a strip of film. Each exposure step bears a fixed relationship to the next, so that after processing, the effects of steadily increasing steps of exposure can be measured.

A time-scale sensitometer is one in which the different steps of exposure are obtained by allowing each one a longer exposure time, with constant intensity of light. In an intensity-scale sensitometer on the other hand, every step receives the same exposure time, but the intensity of light is varied by placing a 'step-wedge' in the light path. This is a strip of neutral-density filter with steps of increasing density, and is usually made of a carbon emulsion coated onto a glass or cellulose support.

In a typical intensity-scale sensitometer used in a motion-picture laboratory, light from a tungsten lamp passes through any necessary filters to correct the colour temperature and intensity, and through a slit, whose width determines the exposure time at any point on the film. The film itself is supported immediately behind the step wedge, and during exposure the film and wedge are moved steadily past the slit, so that, in effect, a narrow slit of light passes along the wedge, and is steadily decreased in intensity as it reaches the film. The distance between lamp and film determines the overall intensity of the light, and both this and the lamp voltage can be changed to compensate for any variation when a new lamp is fitted.

The sensitometer sets the primary standard in any system of process control. All tests of process variation, stock emulsion comparisons, and printer control tests assume a constant exposure from the sensitometer. To prevent drift of standards, the sensitometer must be treated as a precision instrument. A supply of pre-tested lamps must be kept, and regular comparisons between the current lamp and another known lamp should be carried out. Any discrepancy in such a test would indicate a drift in the current lamp's output, as the spare lamp is unlikely to vary.

### The step wedge

The step wedge usually has 21 steps, in density increments of 0.15 log E, thus providing an exposure range of 3.00 log E (10 stops) in half-stop intervals. For some high-contrast emulsions, exposure steps of 0.15 log E are inconveniently far apart, and an alternative wedge with 21 0.10 log E steps is sometimes used. Another type of wedge, used by one stock manufacturer for pre-exposed strips, has 11 steps of 0.30 log E intervals.

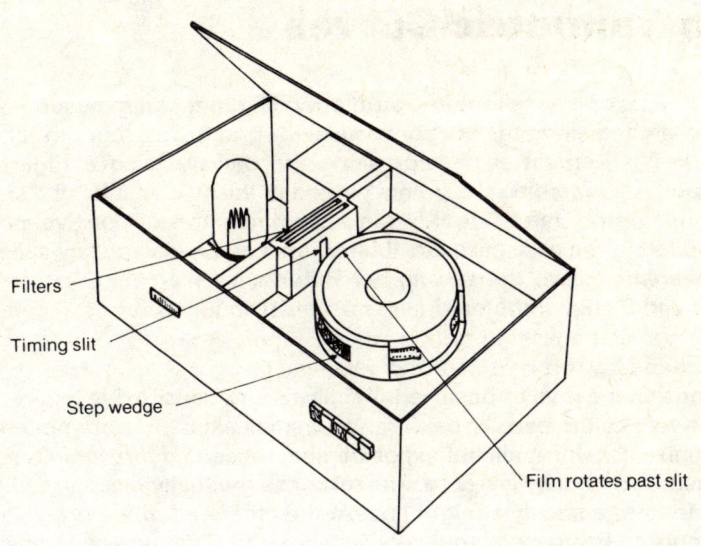

Filters

Timing slit

Step wedge

Film rotates past slit

Lamp moves past film

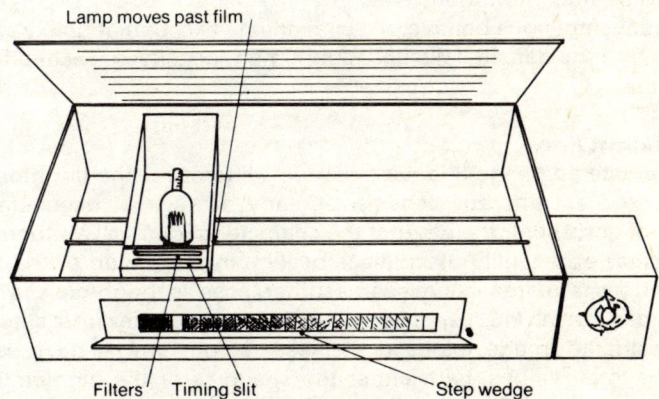

Filters    Timing slit    Step wedge

**The sensitometer**
Two designs: in each machine a short length of film is clamped behind the step
wedge which is then swept by a slit of light.

# Sensitometric Curves

The 21 steps of a sensitometric strip provide a range of exposures which may be plotted along the horizontal axis of a graph, on a logarithmic scale (log E). The vertical scale represents the density (also a logarithmic function). A line joining the points plotted in this way results in a smooth curve rising from left to right in the case of negative or positive, or from right to left in the case of reversal films. This graph is variously called the *characteristic curve*, the *sensitometric curve*, or the *H & D curve* (after Hurter and Driffield, the originators of this technique).

### The curve shape

Unexposed negative or positive film has a slight density due to developer fog, as well as the base of the film. Very small exposures are not enough to increase density at all, but exposure above a certain *threshold* results in a measurable density increase. The response gradually increases until the curve follows a steady straight line. At the other end of the graph, where the emulsion has been completely converted to silver or dye, increases in exposure can have no further effect on the film, and the curve levels off again at the maximum density.

Reversal emulsions behave in a similar way except that unexposed film is black, and the density falls until a minimum density is reached for large exposures.

### The straight line

To reproduce an image it is necessary for different scene brightnesses to be recorded as different densities. Clearly a range of exposures lying entirely at one end or the other of the characteristic curve would result in a totally clear or a totally black piece of film. In the region of the toe and shoulder parts of the curve, some differences in brightness would be reproduced, but as the response of the film varies as the curve steepens or flattens off, an image exposed in these regions would have severely-distorted tonal values, with either the shadows or the highlights being very indistinct.

The straight line portion of the curve — where the line is not only at its steepest, but more importantly where it slopes consistently — is the region where tonal values may be recorded most faithfully. Exposures within this range will result in a distinct image where densities vary in exact proportion to the brightnesses in the original scene.

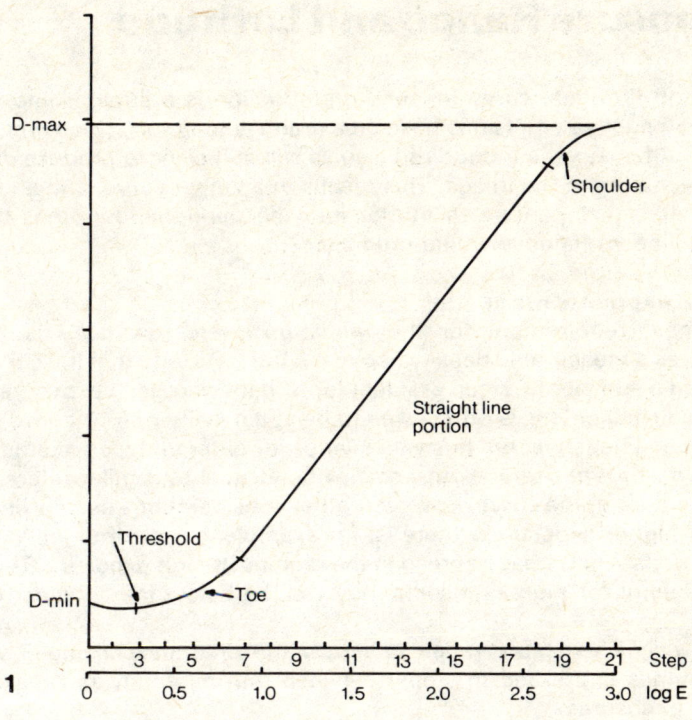

1

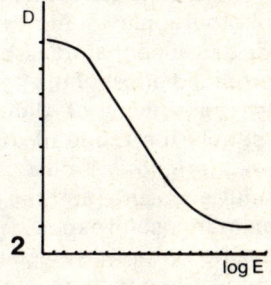

2

## The characteristic curve

(1) Negative or positive process. (2) Reversal process. Over the straight-line portion of the curve, density is directly proportional to exposure (log E).

# Exposure Range and Latitude

Although the ideal curve for tone reproduction is a straight line, many camera negative emulsions have an extremely long toe region where the slope of the curve, although reduced, is still sufficient to produce distinct tonal variation in the image. This results in a longer curve, and an image with detail that penetrates further into the dark shadow areas than a strictly linear response would produce.

### Useful exposure range
The main requirement for the *minimum useful exposure* is that it produces a measurable density above the fog level, and that the curve has reached a sufficiently steep gradient for a slight change in exposure to be distinguishable. This is often taken to be at a density of 0.10 above d-min for original negative, but this value varies for different types of emulsion.

The *maximum useful exposure* may be located by similar reference to the shoulder of the curve. However, other considerations usually limit the use of higher exposures: there is, for example, a loss of definition as a result of flare and image spread in the regions of high exposure. Thus the cut-off point for high exposures may well be below the shoulder of the curve.

The *useful exposure range* is simply the difference of log E values (sometimes expressed in stops) between the minimum and maximum useful exposures.

### Brightness range and exposure latitude
Any scene to be photographed, or film image to be duplicated, has a range of brightnesses or densities that must be recorded. In original photography, this is the combined effect of the lighting contrast (between light and shadow), and the reflectivity of different surfaces in the scene. In duplication it is simply the range of densities in the film to be copied. Naturally, the lowest brightness must produce an exposure greater than the minimum useful exposure, and the brightest part of the scene must fall below the maximum useful exposure. The amount by which an overall exposure may be varied without exceeding upper or lower limits is termed the *exposure latitude*. Clearly, there is more latitude for a low-key scene, and less for a very contrasty subject. In extreme cases it may be impossible to fit both ends of the range on to the curve at once, and unless steps are taken to reduce contrast (e.g. by extra lights to fill the shadows), either shadow or highlight detail will be lost.

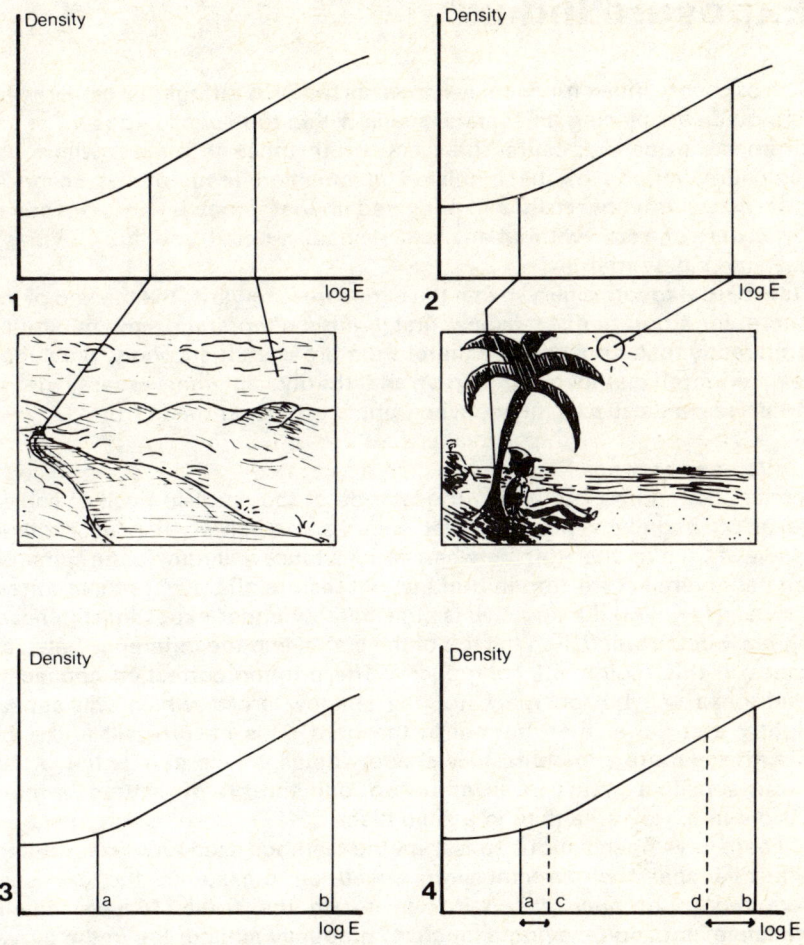

**Exposure range**

(1) Exposures from scenes with soft or flat lighting fall on a relatively short section of the characteristic curve. (2) Strong lighting uses the full length of the curve.

(3) The useful exposure range for an emulsion extends between a point on the toe of the curve (a) and the top of the straight line (b). (4) Most scenes have a brightness range (c to d) that fits well within the useful exposure range of the emulsion, allowing a certain latitude of acceptable exposures.

# Exposure Index

The exposure index (previously known as the ASA rating) of a camera film is a guide for placing an average scene within the useful exposure range of an emulsion. Exposures may vary from those indicated, within the exposure latitude of the emulsion in question (and for the scene in question). Conventionally a film is rated so that it may be under-exposed by ⅓ to ⅔ of a stop without any loss of shadow detail, and this provides a working safety margin.

It is usual to rate a film so that the exposure is towards the toe end of the curve, for a number of reasons: first, light is often at a premium, and an apparently faster emulsion is therefore more useful; secondly, resolution is maximized by low exposures; and thirdly, an unnecessarily dense negative may cause difficulty when prints are being made from it.

**Under-exposure**

Variations in exposure within the latitude of the emulsion will of course result in negatives that are overall darker or lighter than each other. However, the relationship between various tones will remain the same, so that an overall correction in printing will restore all tones to their correct values. However, if a negative is considerably under-exposed, significant shadow detail will fall on the toe of the curve, and the difference between tones in this region will be reduced. The printing correction applied to mid-tones will be too much for the shadow areas, which will appear lighter and flatter than normal in the print. This in turn will make the graininess more apparent, since shadow detail is recorded by the larger, more sensitive grains in an emulsion, and the grainy pattern is more visible in a grey area than in a solid black.

There have been various sensitometric methods used for measuring the effective speed of an emulsion, based on measuring the exposure required to produce a certain density on the curve. Modern colour negative emulsion, having a long and gradually sloping toe in the curve, cannot be accurately rated by these methods, and recent practice has been simply to rate the film at the speed that gives the best screen results. Higher speed ratings will result in more noticeable grain, and so it is often possible to rate an emulsion faster in 35 mm than in 16 mm, where the smaller image size makes grain a more significant feature of screen quality.

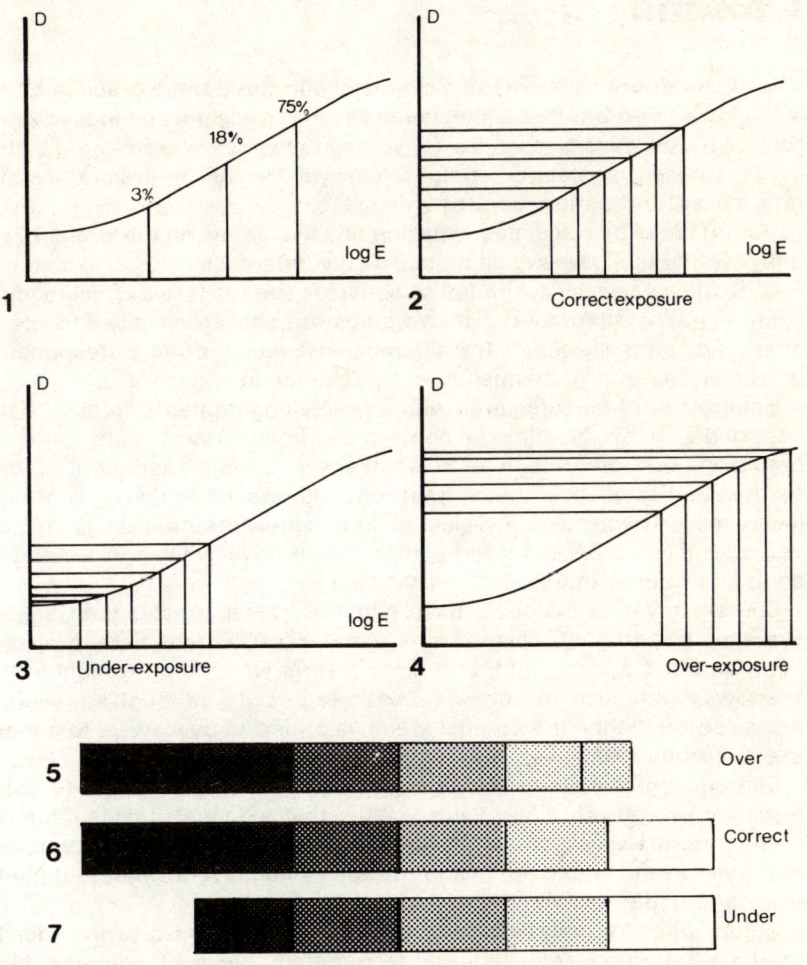

**Correct exposure**
(1) Exposure tests are often based on an 18 per cent reflectance grey card: this represents the average reflectance in a scene which typically ranges between 3 per cent and 75 per cent. (2) Correct negative exposure results in a print, (6), with a uniform tonal scale. (3) An under-exposed negative compresses shadows so that a corrected print, (7), will have thin blacks. (4) An over-exposed negative compresses highlights, (5); a corrected print will lack clean whites.

*The slope of the curve measures the contrast of the emulsion.*

# Gamma

The most important feature of a characteristic curve is the gradient of the straight line portion. This is the *gamma* of the emulsion, and indicates the rate at which density changes for a given change in exposure. For the same subject, a steeper straight line will result in greater density differences, and a more contrasty image.

Gamma may be calculated by taking any two points on the straight line, and dividing their density difference by the difference in log E exposures. Frequently a specially calibrated setsquare is used to take a direct reading from a graph; alternatively, if two steps are chosen exactly 1.00 log E apart, the gamma is simply the difference between the two corresponding densities. Gamma = change in density/change in exposure.

Emulsions are manufactured with a variety of gammas according to the intended use of the film. In copying an image from reality onto an emulsion, or from one film to another (in printing and duplication), gamma indicates how much the contrastiness of the image will be increased or decreased. A value of 1.00 represents no change; higher values will result in increased contrast; and lower values in a reduced contrast or flatter image.

Camera reversal materials have gammas rather greater than 1 – on average, 1.30 to 1.60. This value is partly offset by lens flare, projector flare, ambient theatre light, and other factors which tend to lighten the shadows and reduce the contrast. The screen image, although still slightly more contrasty than the original scene, is preferred by viewers to a more exact reproduction.

Camera negative emulsions have gammas in the region of 0.50 (0.65 for black-and-white). This low value means that a much greater range of scene brightnesses can be accommodated within the density range available on the negative. This in turn gives negative a wider latitude to over- and under-exposure than reversal film.

Colour positive materials need a wide range of densities in order to produce saturated colours. This requirement fits well with the high gamma (around 3.0) required to compensate for a very low gamma in the colour-negative stage. Taken together, colour negative printed onto colour positive produces an overall image contrast (gamma product) which is found by multiplying each individual gamma together: in this case $0.5 \times 3.0 = 1.5$, which is very similar to the single-stage reversal system, and produces a screen image that is most preferred by viewers.

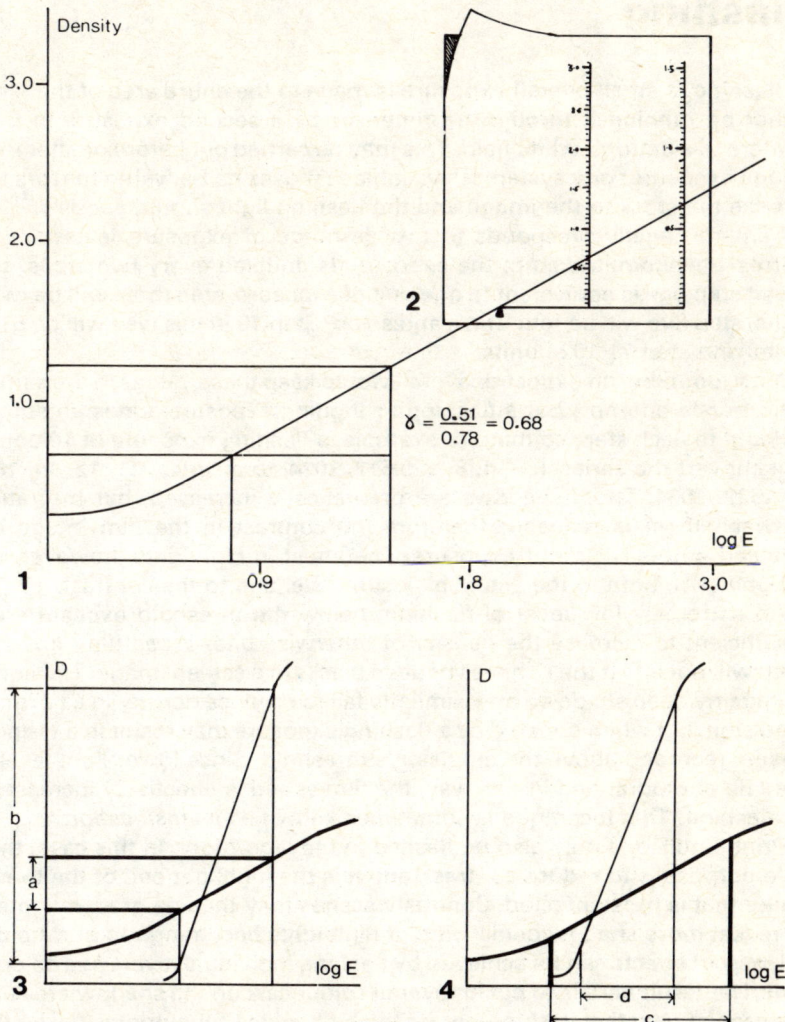

Density

3.0

2.0

1.0

$\gamma = \dfrac{0.51}{0.78} = 0.68$

0.9   1.8   3.0   log E

**1**

**2**

**3**   D   b   a   log E

**4**   D   d   c   log E

## Gamma

(1) Density change is divided by exposure change to obtain the gamma. (2) A 'gammeter' may be used to measure the slope of the line. (3) A low-contrast negative emulsion gives a smaller change in density (a) for a given exposure change, than a high-contrast print emulsion (b) does. (4) However, a low-contrast emulsion can reproduce a wider range of exposures (c) on its straight line portion than a high-contrast emulsion (d).

# Flashing

In flashing, a small overall exposure is made to the entire area of the film either by running it through a printer, or by a second exposure in the camera to a uniform white field. This may be carried out before or after the image exposure: or a system is available that uses half-silvered mirrors to expose the stock to the image and the flashing light simultaneously.

Camera negative responds to a wide range of exposure levels: in a normal sensitometric strip, the exposure is doubled every two steps, so that if step one is equivalent to one unit of exposure, step three will be two units, step five will be four units, and so on. Step 19 in this way will be 512 units, and step 21 1024 units.

Now, doubling an exposure overall would keep these values in the same ratio to one another; but a flashing or fogging exposure addes an equal amount to each step, so that, for example, a flashing exposure of 10 units will convert the series 1, 2, 4, 8, . . . .512, 1024, to a series, 11, 12, 14, 16, . . . .522, 1034. Thus, shadows are dramatically increased, but the ratio between them is reduced; therefore the contrast in the film image is reduced in this region of exposure. The effect in highlights, however, is insignificant, both to the actual exposure level and to the contrast.

An extremely low level of flashing, below the threshold exposure, is insufficient to increase the density of otherwise unexposed film, and as such will not affect the richness of deep blacks in a screen image. The light from fairly deep shadows may similarly fail to produce density in a normal emulsion, but when boosted by a flashing exposure may result in a visible image, recorded above the emulsion's threshold. Since lower light levels may be photographed in this way, the film speed is effectively increased by flashing. This technique is sometimes known as *latensification.*

Print emulsions may also be flashed in the laboratory. In this case, the sole purpose is to reduce contrast, and it is the highlight end of the tonal range that is most affected. Contrasty scenes may thus be graded lighter to reveal more shadow detail without highlights becoming too burnt out.

Unusual effects can be achieved by flashing individual layers of a colour film. The result here is to put an overall colour cast on the shadow area (in the case of negative flashing), or on the highlights (if the print is flashed).

| Step | 1 | 3 | 5 | 7 | 9 | 11 | 13 | 15 | 17 | 19 | 21 |
|---|---|---|---|---|---|---|---|---|---|---|---|
| Exposure | 1 | 2 | 4 | 8 | 16 | 32 | 64 | 128 | 256 | 512 | 1024 |
| log E | 0 | 0.30 | 0.60 | 0.90 | 1.20 | 1.50 | 1.80 | 2.10 | 2.40 | 2.70 | 3.00 |
| Exposure +10 units | 11 | 12 | 14 | 18 | 26 | 42 | 74 | 138 | 266 | 522 | 1034 |
| log E | 1.05 | 1.07 | 1.15 | 1.26 | 1.42 | 1.61 | 1.87 | 2.14 | 2.43 | 2.71 | 3.00 |

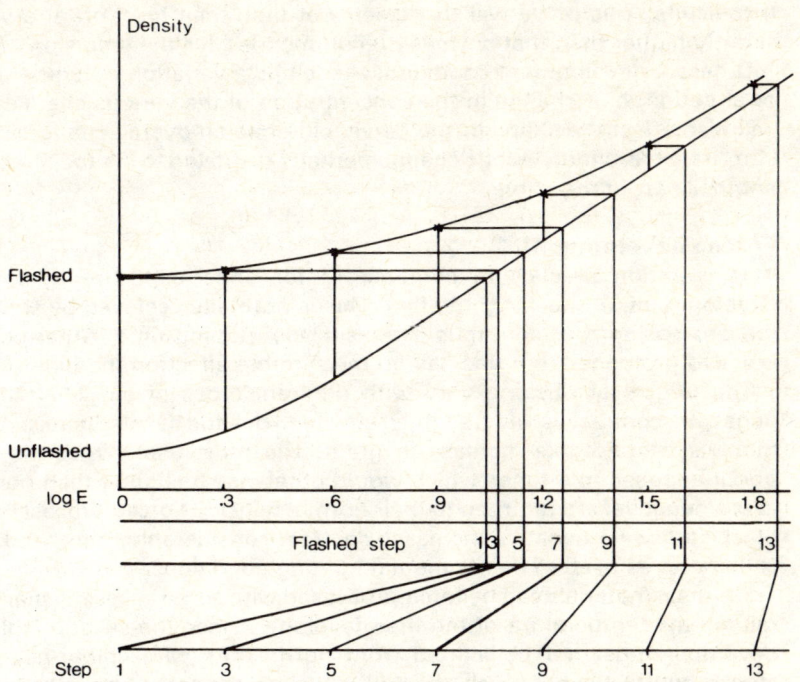

## Flashing

An overall fogging exposure has the greatest effect on the shadows of the image
exposure: contrast is reduced progressively, resulting in a long shallow curve
instead of a straight line.

# Gamma and Process Variation

The characteristic curve is affected not only by the type of emulsion, but also by the processing, since more or less development produces more or less light-stopping silver or dye image.

If a series of sensitometric strips is processed for progressively longer times and curves are plotted for each result, the gammas for each process time may be measured. A *time-gamma curve* may then be drawn to relate the results. This curve will rise steeply at first, then level off at a value slightly higher than that normally recommended for the emulsion.

Different development conditions – such as a variation in temperature or agitation, or a change in the concentration of the various chemicals – will also affect the shape of the curve, either as an overall change in the gamma, or as a more subtle change perhaps restricted to the toe region or another part of the curve.

**Forced development**
It is common practice to compensate for under-exposure by forced development, or 'pushing' the film. This is normally achieved by slowing the processing machine, thus increasing developing time. Other stages are also prolonged, but this has no measurable effect on the film.

The effects of pushing vary with different types of stock. In colour negative, contrast is only slightly affected, but fog levels increase and there is a noticeable increase in grain. The most useful result is that under-exposed mid-tones which would otherwise be lighter than normal in the negative, are returned to their normal density. Forced processing of black-and-white negative increases contrast considerably more, and this is sometimes used to overcome flat lighting conditions.

Reversal materials can be force-processed with some sucess: usually by raising the temperature of the first developer, since the second (colour) developer must not be altered from normal. As with colour-negative stocks, contrast is not much affected, but since the entire image becomes lighter there is a tendency for shadows to appear grey and 'washy'. However, since the enlarged grains produced by extended first development are all removed in the bleach stage, there is only a slight increase in graininess in forced reversal film.

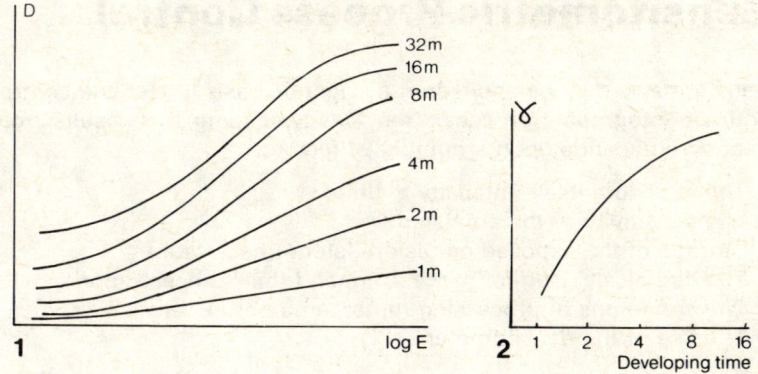

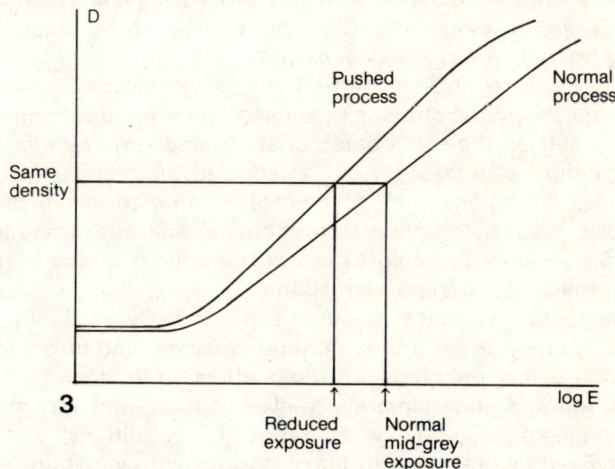

## Gamma control

(1) Gamma increases with developing time up to a point and then levels off. Further development merely increases the overall fog level. (2) A time-gamma curve summarizes the curves in (1). (3) Pushed (or forced) processing compensates for under-exposure by returning negatives to their ideal density.

*Consistent processing aids consistent results.*

# Sensitometric Process Control

Sensitometry may be applied on a scientific basis to test and control the entire photographic process. The density reading that results from an exposure depends upon a number of factors:

The exposure itself (intensity × time)
The sensitivity of the emulsion
Storage of the exposed emulsion (latent-image fade)
The chemicals used for processing, and their concentration
The conditions of processing (time, temperature, etc.)
The use of the densitometer

It is possible to observe the effect of variation of any one of these by holding all the others constant. Thus the effect of exposure variation on a given emulsion is determined by making a series of exposures (a sensitometric strip) on that emulsion, and processing it in a standard way. Similarly, different emulsions may be compared by exposing and processing them all in an identical manner.

Routine process control is carried out by processing – at regular intervals – sensitometric strips, all exposed under identical conditions in the sensitometer on the same batch of stock, and stored under identical conditions before processing. Any variation in the results – barring an error in these conditions – must indicate a variation in the process. If sensitometric results, together with chemical analysis, are interpreted logically, it is usually possible to locate the source of any variation in results and make appropriate corrections.

Fortunately most chemical variations occur fairly gradually, and by processing frequent tests, trends may be detected, and errors identified and corrected before they have a serious effect on the film.

The laboratory is sent camera negative of many different types and batches, exposed under a wide range of conditions, not always favourable. Even laboratory print films are subject to variations in printer exposure. Whilst occasions may arise when processing is varied to compensate for some other factor such as under-exposure, it is important that the laboratory process is maintained as accurately and consistently as possible. In this way a cameraman, working on the same scientific basis as the laboratory, can confidently predict the outcome of his exposures.

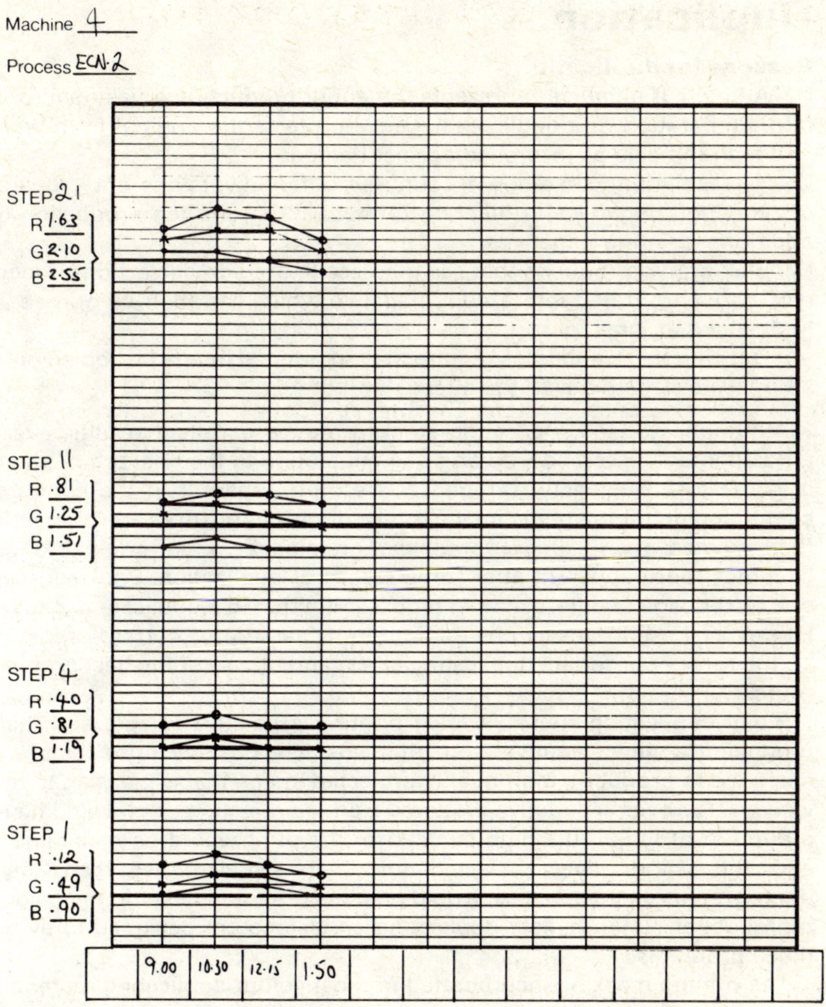

Machine __4__

Process __ECN·2__

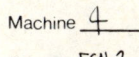

STEP 2 |
R |·63 ⎤
G 2·10 ⎬
B 2·55 ⎦

STEP || |
R ·81 ⎤
G 1·25 ⎬
B 1·51 ⎦

STEP 4 |
R ·40 ⎤
G ·81 ⎬
B 1·19 ⎦

STEP | |
R ·12 ⎤
G ·49 ⎬
B ·90 ⎦

9.00  10·30  12·15  1·50

## Trend chart

Aims for a process are established by processing test strips in a correctly-mixed and analyzed bath at the specified time and temperature. Once standards are established, the process may be monitored by regular processing of test strips (sensos), and comparison of selected steps with the standard result.

**87**

*The original image must be reproduced for many reasons.*

# Duplication

### Reasons for duplication

(1) A final cut negative represents the entire production investment of a film. Preparation of a duplicate negative protects the original from wear and tear and acts as insurance against damage.

(2) Release printing in different countries, different versions, and blow-up or reduction negatives in different formats all require the production of additional printing negatives.

(3) Bulk printing requires that scene-to-scene grading corrections, fades, etc., be incorporated into a dupe negative which can then be printed at high speed at 'one light'.

(4) Optical effects and titles require that an original image be copied onto a duplicate negative with the effect incorporated.

Although modern duplicating stocks produce excellent results, every time an image is copied – adding one generation to the final print – there is some loss of quality. Differences become apparent in the contrast, colour and definition of the image. While duplicating stocks are inherently finer-grained than camera originals, graininess in an original often becomes more apparent after some stages of duplication. Printer losses due to slippage and flare tend to reduce definition in a duplicate negative. However, these losses can be minimized by setting the correct exposure on the most appropriate duplicating stock, and by use of the best printing route.

Many duplicating routes involve printing a positive image, and then producing a new negative from that positive. Positive print films are designed to produce a high-quality projected image that is pleasing to the viewer. However, a negative prepared from a projection print would have a number of faults: the high contrast of the print would be maintained, and the colour dyes, selected for their visual rather than their photographic characteristics, would result in poor and desaturated colour reproduction. Intermediate duplicating emulsions are designed to avoid these problems.

The orange masking incorporated in most colour duplicating materials helps maintain colour purity, while the long straight line portions of their characteristic curves allow a wide range of tones to be copied accurately.

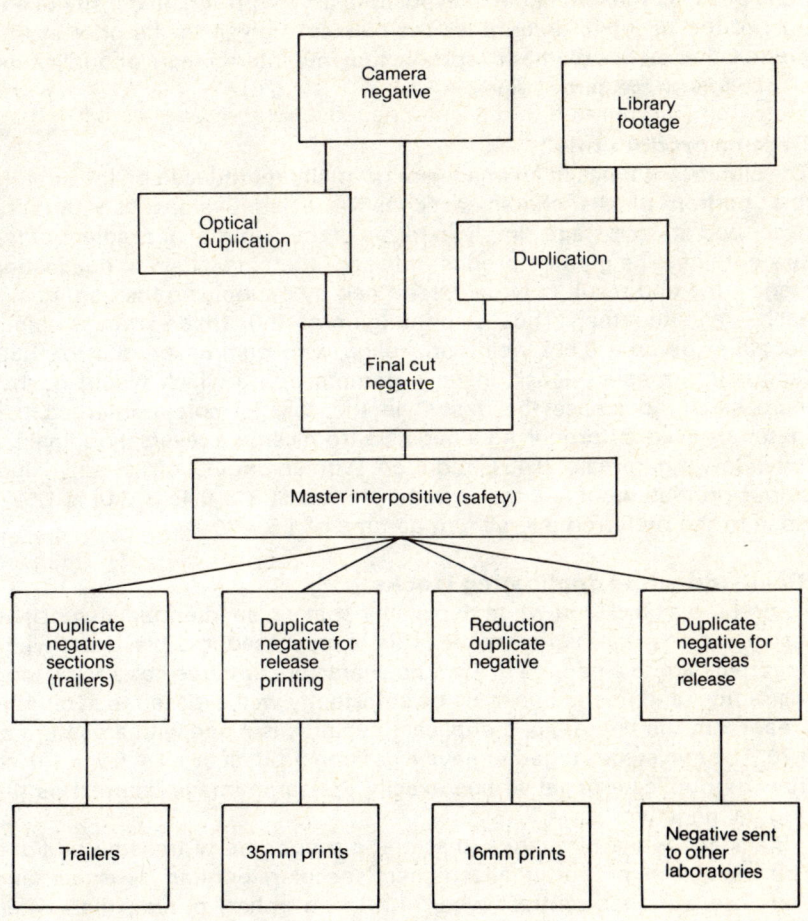

```
              ┌─────────────┐              ┌─────────────┐
              │   Camera    │              │   Library   │
              │  negative   │              │   footage   │
              └─────────────┘              └─────────────┘

      ┌─────────────┐                ┌─────────────┐
      │   Optical   │                │             │
      │ duplication │                │ Duplication │
      └─────────────┘                └─────────────┘

              ┌─────────────┐
              │  Final cut  │
              │  negative   │
              └─────────────┘

      ┌───────────────────────────────────────────────┐
      │          Master interpositive (safety)          │
      └───────────────────────────────────────────────┘
```

| Duplicate negative sections (trailers) | Duplicate negative for release printing | Reduction duplicate negative | Duplicate negative for overseas release |
| --- | --- | --- | --- |
| Trailers | 35mm prints | 16mm prints | Negative sent to other laboratories |

**Reasons for duplication**
Both individual shots and complete negatives may be duplicated in the laboratory.

# Film Duplication Characteristics

The way in which a scene is reproduced on a negative is described by the characteristic curve of the negative emulsion, relating exposures to densities. When a positive print is made from that negative, its scale of densities becomes the scale of exposures for the print. The density of any part of the negative determines the exposure given to the print at that point. Other stages of image reproduction into intermediate or duplicating stocks follow the same principle.

### Gamma product rule
The significant tones in an image are normally reproduced on the straight line portion of the characteristic curve. Image values can thus be described at each stage simply in terms of the gamma, or gradient of the straight line. The gamma product rule says that, in a chain of duplicating stages, the end result may be determined by multiplying the gammas of each stage together. Thus, a print (gamma 3.0) made from a colour negative (gamma 0.50) yields an image with gamma product of 1.50. Colour intermediate stocks have a gamma of 1.0 which would neither increase nor decrease this result. In the case of colour internegative materials used for producing a negative from camera reversal originals, a much lower gamma of 0.45 is required. With an original of 1.2, and a final colour print stage of 3.0, the gamma product ($1.2 \times 0.45 \times 3.0$) is 1.62 – close to the preferred overall film gamma of 1.5.

### Black-and-white duplicating stocks
To prepare a black-and-white duplicate negative, an intermediate positive (called a *fine grain*) is first made. This is processed in a black-and-white negative bath to a gamma of 1.4. The characteristic curve has a fairly long toe region, and fine grains must be sufficiently well exposed to avoid this area. From the fine grain, a duplicate negative is made with a gamma of 0.70. The two stages together have a gamma product of $1.4 \times 0.7 = 1.0$, so that the duplicate negative has exactly the same image contrast as the original negative.

Black-and-white film tends to scatter a proportion of transmitted light. This results in proportionally higher (specular) printing densities, and therefore a higher contrast when run in an optical printer, than when contact printing is employed. Optical duplicate negatives are therefore developed to a lower gamma – often around 0.55 – to counteract this.

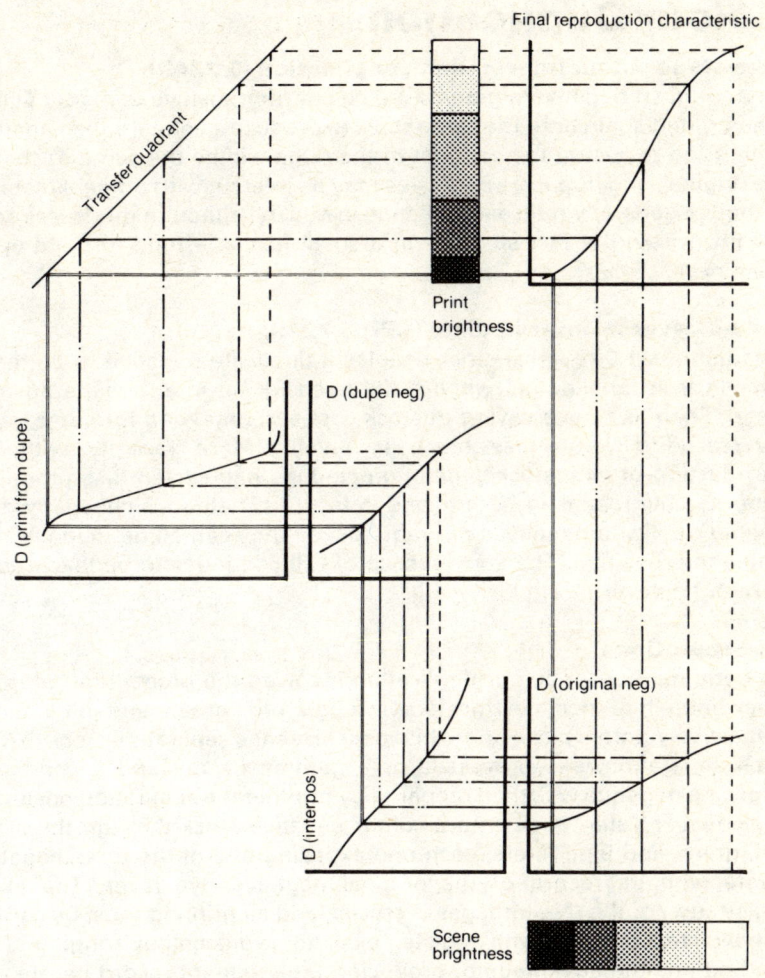

Final reproduction characteristic

Transfer quadrant

Print brightness

D (dupe neg)

D (print from dupe)

D (original neg)

D (interpos)

Scene brightness

## Tone reproduction
The tonal range of a scene may be traced through various stages of duplication, as the densities produced in each film stage become the exposure range for the next stage. A geometrical 'transfer quadrant' is drawn to match the final print tones with the original subject tones and obtain the overall reproduction characteristic.

*.... from a range of alternative systems.*

# Colour Duplication

### Two-stage colour intermediate duplication (5/7243)

From original negative a gamma 1.0 colour interpositive is made. This is then printed again onto the same stock to produce a colour dupe negative. With good exposure the contrast of the dupe will be the same as that of the original, and duplicate negatives may be intercut with original material without a generally noticeable change in quality, although this is less so in 16 mm, where the two stages – in a small format – tend to build up in graininess.

### Colour-reversal intermediate (CRI; 5/7249)

This gamma 1.0 reversal stock enables a duplicate negative to be made directly from an original without the need for an intermediate positive stage. There is thus a saving in stock cost and time, and for some years reversal duplication was much in favour. More recently with the introduction of new stocks, the interpos-dupe neg system has produced better quality results in 35 mm, and in fact this method is cheaper where several duplicate negatives are required, as they can all be made from a single interpositive. The convenience of CRI continues to be favoured in 16 mm, however.

### Tri-separations

An early method of colour duplication involved the preparation of three black-and-white positive masters through red, green and blue filters respectively onto a black-and-white panchromatic separation stock (5235). Each separation was processed to a gamma of 1.0, and a combined duplicate negative was then prepared by printing the separation positives, in perfect register, back onto a colour negative stock through the same red, green and blue filters, each one exposing one of the three negative layers with its record of the original negative dye layer. The exact registration of the three images is crucial, and all printing must be carried out on step printers with register pins, to avoid colour fringing. This method has the advantage of producing a permanent record because of the excellent keeping properties of silver images. Separations, however, are rarely used today except for some special optical effects.

92

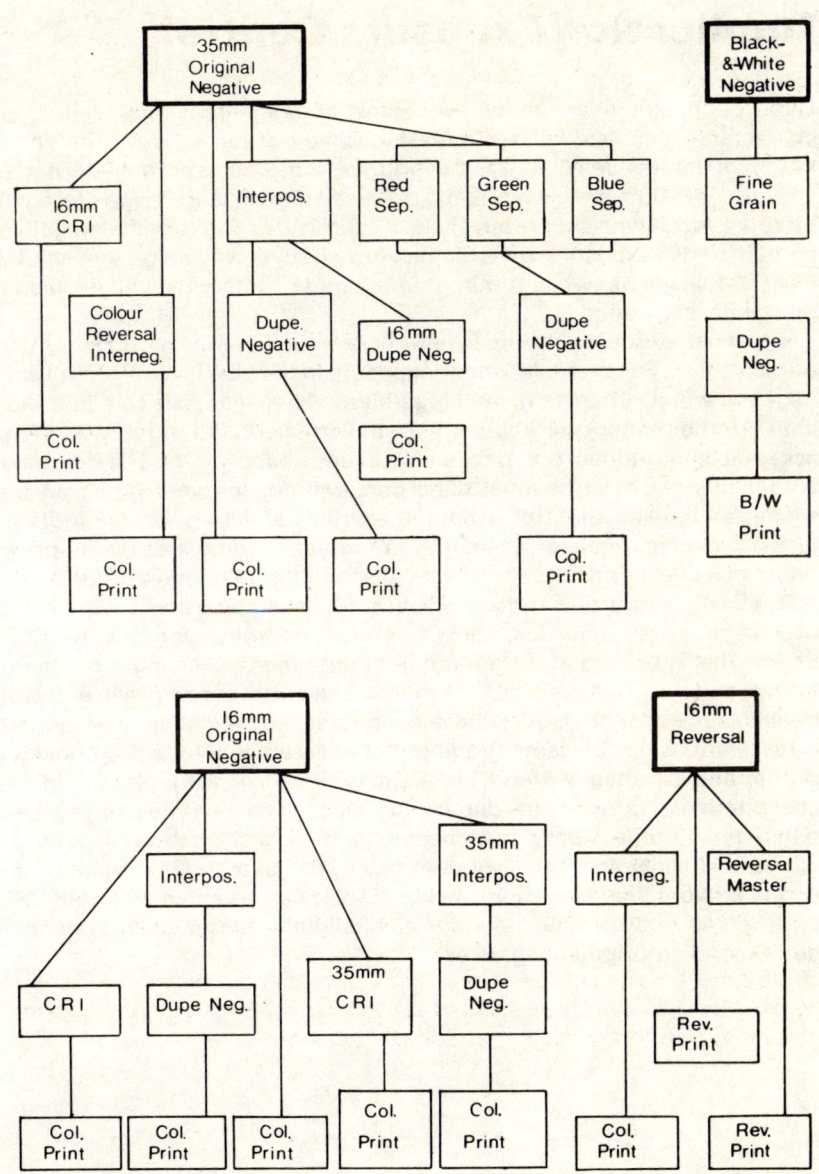

**Duplication routes**
A number of options are available depending upon the original material and the end product.

# Duplication Exposure Control

Duplication stocks are made with long straight line portions in their characteristic curves. For accurate duplication of tonal values the entire range of image densities in the original must be reproduced on this straight line. Outside this range the curves flatten off, and image detail will be reproduced with progressively less contrast. As with original negative, overall under-exposure of a duplicate negative will result in 'smoky' flattened shadows, while a thin, under-exposed interpositive will yield a print with flat, veiled highlights.

Incorrect exposure in just one colour layer will produce colour mismatching. For example, under-exposure in the blue layer of a duplicate negative will result in an overall blue-biassed negative, but with less blue shift in the flatter toe region. When corrected, the print will show acceptable mid-tones, but excess blue in any shadow area. The degree of colour mismatch, or of tonal distortion, will depend very much on the scene; a high-key shot, for example, with few shadows, will be more or less acceptable, while a scene with important shadow areas will appear badly distorted. Certain colours may also shift in relation to others.

Duplication control is most easily accomplished by using a negative of precise mid-grey densities, known as the *laboratory aim density (LAD) patch.* This is printed at a standard light onto the duplicating stock being tested, and the printer is adjusted so that a given set of red, green and blue densities is obtained. Under these conditions, any negative may then be duplicated, using the same grading that is acceptable for colour positive prints, and all shadows and highlights will be correctly placed on the characteristic curve of the duplicating stock. The densities of the LAD patch for various stocks are chosen to be exactly half way between extreme shadow and highlight densities – that is, at the mid-point of the useful straight line – for each stock. LAD aim figures show that both CRIs and 5/7243 intermediates are normally slightly denser or heavier than corresponding original negatives.

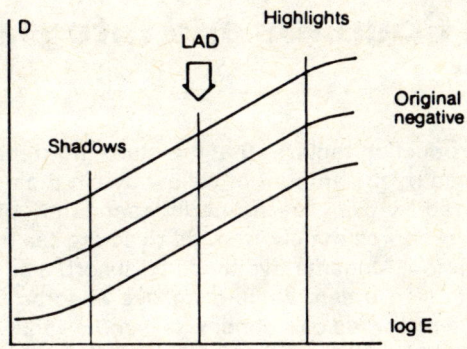

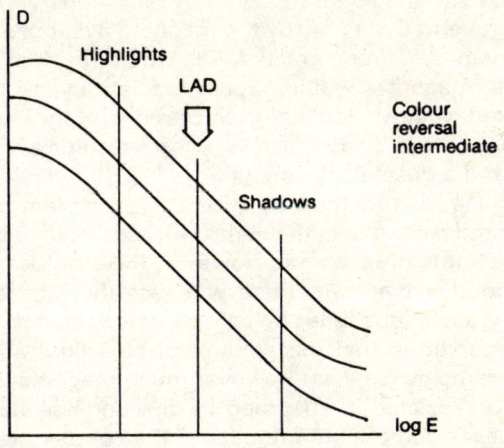

| LAD STANDARDS | STOCK TYPE | R | G | B |
|---|---|---|---|---|
| Original negative | 5247/7291 | 0.80 | 1.20 | 1.60 |
| Interpositive | 5243/7243 | 1.10 | 1.50 | 1.90 |
| Dupe negative | 5243/7243 | 0.90 | 1.30 | 1.70 |
| C R I | 5249/7249 | 0.90 | 1.30 | 1.70 |
| Colour positive | 5384/7384 | 1.09 | 1.06 | 1.03 |

**Duplication exposure control**
Correct placing of the mid-grey laboratory aim density (LAD) will ensure that the full
range of tones in the original is reproduced on the linear part of the duplication
curve.

# Coloured Couplers and Integral Masking

Perfect colour reproduction requires that the blue light transmitted by the negative is governed by the amount of yellow dye in the negative, green by magenta, and red by cyan: each one independently of the other. In practice this is only approximately true, as dyes are far from perfect in their colour absorption. Magenta dye tends to absorb a small amount of blue light in addition to green, while cyan dye absorbs both blue and green as well as the major red component. This means that the amount of blue light transmitted by the negative is affected not only by the yellow dye, but also by the magenta and cyan dyes. Similarly, the green light transmitted is governed not only by the magenta dye, but also, to a lesser extent by the cyan dye. If uncorrected, this would result in a print having impure colours: magentas would appear reddish; cyans and blues dark and muddy, and yellows too light. Successive stages of duplication, moreover, would have a cumulative effect, resulting in poor colour reproduction, and a desaturated image.

Integral masking is a method by which this problem can be largely overcome. The magenta dye in the negative absorbs, in addition to green light, a small quantity of blue light. However, the emulsion also contains undeveloped coupler wherever there was less than full exposure. The integral masking technique relies on using a pale yellow (blue-absorbing) undeveloped coupler so that the amount of blue light absorbed in the magenta layer remains constant however much magenta dye is present. In unexposed areas, blue is absorbed by the undeveloped coupler: as exposure increases, increasing amounts of the coupler are converted to the slightly blue-absorbing magenta dye. Thus a constant amount of blue light is absorbed, regardless of the amount of magenta dye, giving the negative an overall ye'low cast.

A similar compensation for the unwanted green and blue absorptions of cyan dye is provided by using a pale-orange-coloured coupler in the red-sensitive layer. As this coupler is developed, its orange colour is replaced by the unwanted orange bias of the cyan dye. The combined effect of these two couplers is to give the negative its characteristic orange cast. This can be compensated for in printing quite simply by increasing blue and green exposures. In projection materials (original and print reversal film, and positive print film), no further stage is available for correction, and so masking cannot be employed.

Note that the orange colour of a negative is an integral part of the image in the emulsion layers (whether as an undeveloped coupler or as dye). It is not an orange-tinted base, nor is it a separate filter layer.

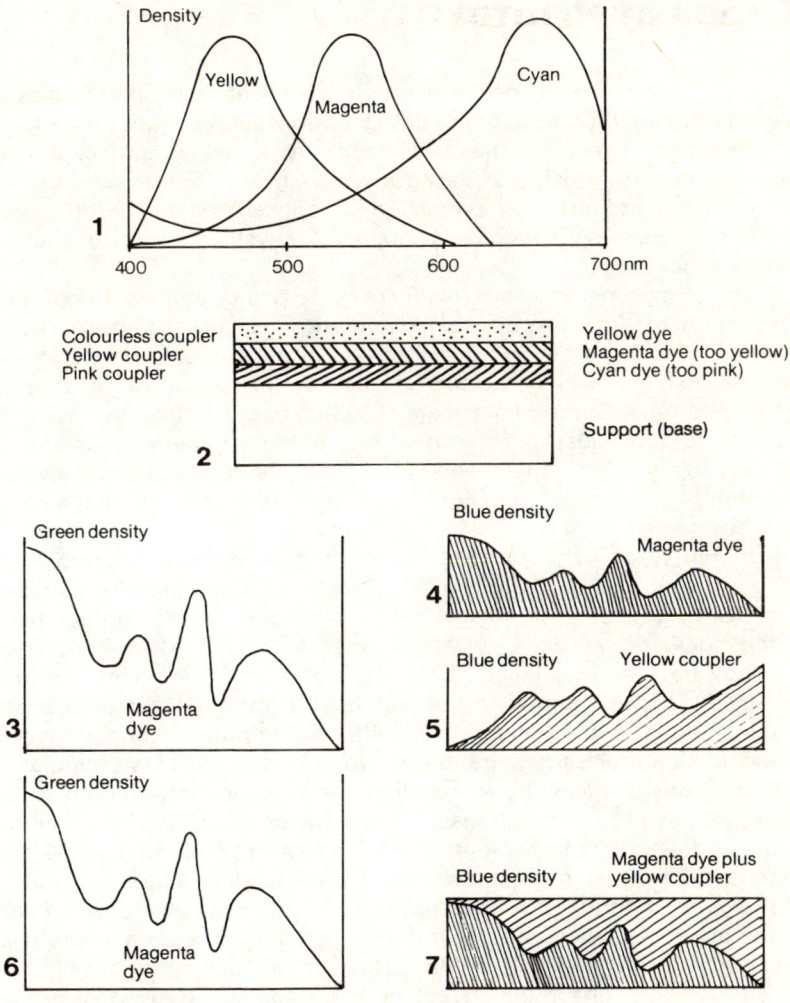

## Unwanted absorption

(1) Dye absorption overlap, resulting in false colours (2). (3) Magenta dye correction: as the green density varies with more or less magenta dye, so does the unwanted blue absorption in this layer (4). However, the formation of magenta dye reduces the amount of yellow-coloured coupler in the layer (5). The effects of unwanted blue absorption, and the blue density of the yellow-coloured coupler cancel each other out so that for any density of magenta dye (6) the blue density of the layer is constant (7).

**97**

# Types of Printer

During printing, the image on a processed negative or intermediate is copied onto another piece of film (rawstock) by passing light through one onto the other. The image may be formed in two ways: in contact printers, negative and rawstock are placed in contact, emulsion-to-emulsion, in front of a light beam: in projection or optical printers, light shining through the negative is focused through a lens system to form an image in the rawstock.

Printing machines may also be divided into two categories according to the method of film transport. In step printers, film is passed through a gate frame by frame, in the same manner as in a camera or projector. The image is exposed while the negative and rawstock are at rest, a complete frame at a time. Some printer gates have a pilot pin which moves into a film perforation just before exosure, to ensure perfect steadiness. Continuous printers, on the other hand, move negative and rawstock together past a narrow slit of light, exposing the entire length of the film in a steady sweep.

Different types of printer are appropriate for different requirements. *Step printers*, because the film is always stationary during exposure, produce the steadiest image, and a *contact step printer*, being independent of any lens system, produces the best definition. These printers are therefore ideal where steadiness and sharpness are most important: in the manufacture of high-quality intermediates or duplicate negatives, or for producing optical effects components and projection plates (where precise registration of two or more images is essential).

*Continuous printers*, by eliminating the need for intermittent movement, are able to run much faster (at speeds of up to 1000 ft per minute, compared with a typical step printer at 16 frames per second, or 60 ft per minute (35 mm) or much slower, and are therefore more suitable for high-volume printing of release prints, or for the fast turnaround of work prints or rushes. Image and sound are printed together in a single pass, and scene-to-scene exposure changes are made fully automatically.

*Optical printers* have the advantage that original and rawstock are run separately. In normal production this allows reduction or blow-up from one gauge to another, and more sophisticated machines may be used for a wide variety of special optical effects. Most optical printers are step printers, but there are also *continuous optical printers* in which a lens system focuses a moving image onto raw stock moving at exactly the same speed. This combines the benefit of high-speed production with the ability to change size.

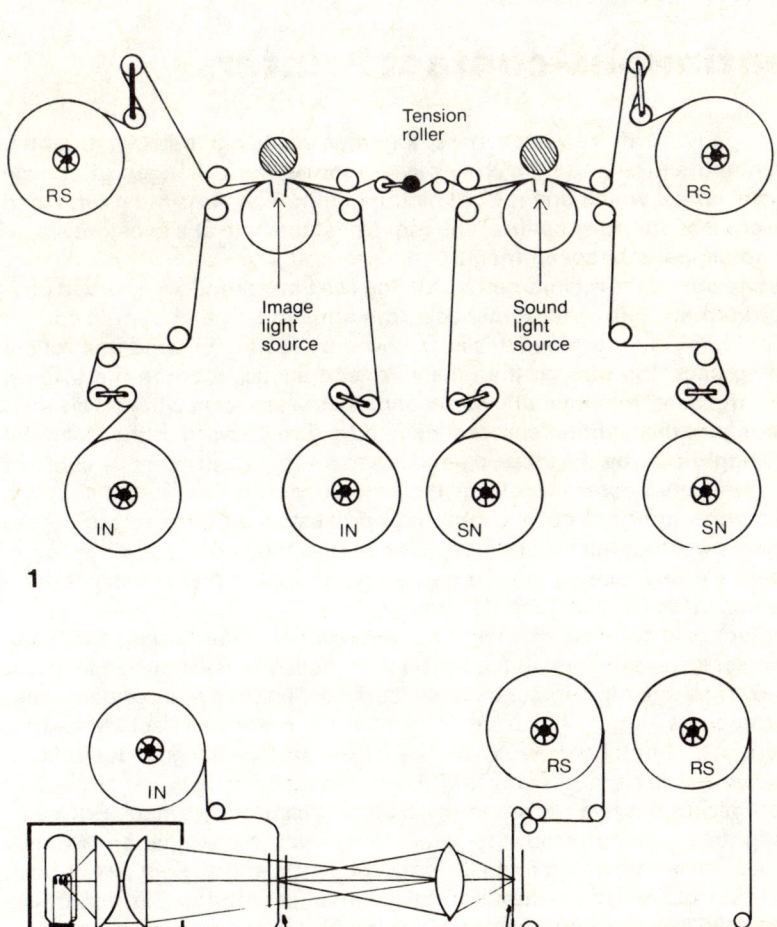

## Types of printer
(1) A continuous contact 'panel' printer used for high-speed release printing. (2) An optical step printer, used for duplication, format changes and optical effects (IN = image negative; SN = sound negative; RS = rawstock).

*The 'workhorse', from rushes to release.*

# Continuous-contact Printers

The negative and rawstock pass together across a narrow, brightly-illuminated slit or gate, which is placed between the flanges of a large sprocket wheel which drives both pieces of film. The films must remain in close contact during exposure, and move past the gate at a constant speed with no slippage between them.

Steady contact is maintained by forcing the films to follow a curved path around the printing sprocket wheel. Both films must be under the correct tension. In many machines this is achieved by sprung or weighted rollers 'holding back' the film on the feed side, and a slack loop on the take-up side of the gate, maintained by a second driving sprocket wheel. This loop ensures that the printing sprocket drives the film forward, rather than the film being pulled by the take-up spool. Modern 'panel' printers by contrast often use servo-controlled feed and take-up motors to ensure that the tension on either side of the printing sprocket is uniform throughout a printing run, thus eliminating the need for a loop. On a bi-directional, double-headed machine this simplifies operation, but places considerable demands upon the machine design.

Contact is further maintained by a hard rubber roller behind the films. This is set so as to barely touch the back of the rawstock. Poor adjustment will produce uneven contact between surfaces, leading to poor definition, and Newton's rings. These are an optical interference effect caused by reflection of light between two very close surfaces, and appear as a 'shimmering' pattern of wavy lines on the image.

Well-perforated film fits smoothly around the sprocket wheel. However, the slightest variation from the ideal pitch in either negative or rawstock will result in an imperfect fit on the sprocket teeth, and a slight jerk as each perforation strips off the tooth and the film slips into the position of the next tooth. This causes a loss of definition and in extreme cases, such as across a badly-adjusted splice between two pieces of film, there is a visible movement in the printed image as the incoming piece of film settles onto the sprocket wheel.

Irregular movement through the printer also results in rapid exposure variations, or 'flutter bars', since the exposure is determined by the time taken for any point on the film to pass across the gate. The effect of such flutter can be reduced by using a wider aperture (averaging the film speed over a longer time), but this in turn can increase the effect of slippage between the two film surfaces.

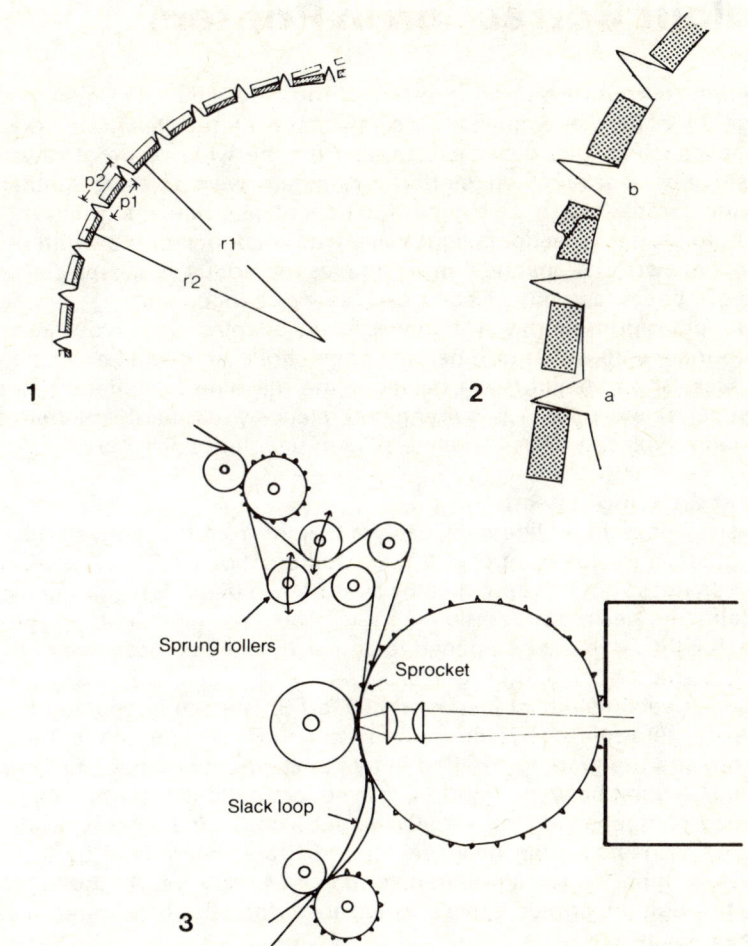

## Pitch and steadiness

(1) The rawstock path around a printer sprocket has a greater radius (r2) than that of the negative (r1) and so its perforation pitch (p2) is greater than that of the negative (p1).

(2) Film is normally driven on the leading face of each perforation (a). If a splice is made inaccurately, the film behind the splice may sit further forward. When the splice passes away from the sprocket wheel, the film will jump back into its natural position with a resultant jump in the printed image.

(3) Model-C film transport: tension behind the sprocket wheel and a slack loop in front of it ensure a steady drive past the gate.

**101**

*Scene-to-scene corrections are made automatically.*

# Colour Correction in Printers

The light output of a printing machine must be adjustable over a wide range of colour and intensity values in order to allow not only for negatives of various densities but also for the wide range of rawstock sensitivities. Black-and-white printers originally were adjustable either by varying lamp voltage or by the addition of neutral-density filters. For scene-to-scene correction a light valve was used to vary the width of the beam, or a strip of opaque film with holes of various sizes was placed in the light beam, and advanced at each scene change.

For colour printing this system was easily adapted, and colour filters of appropriate values were clipped over each hole. An overall correction or 'prepack' of additional filters balanced the machine for different stocks. However, this is a time-consuming and relatively inaccurate method, and has been replaced by the additive system of colour correction.

### The additive light head
A system of dichroic filters divides white light from the lamp so that the red, green, and blue components follow different paths. Each is controlled by a separate light valve, so that the recombined beam at the printing gate contains the desired proportions of red, green and blue light.

Each light valve can be opened to any of 75 settings: each one of these being a step of 0.025 log E greater than the previous one, giving a total range for each colour of just over 1.80 log E. The actual opening of any valve is determined by the sum of the manually-controlled trimmer setting, and the grading data fed in by punched-paper tape. The trimmer setting, ranging between 1 and 24, is used for day-to-day control of printer balance, compensating for overall changes in stock and process, while the grading values, ranging between 1 and 51, are determined by the film grader or timer to suit the particular piece of negative. As the negative runs through the printer, valve settings are automatically changed at each scene change.

Light valves are quite accurately controlled, so that in general, results on any printer should closely match those on any other printer. However, at very low settings, a change of one printer point (0.025 log E) may represent a vane adjustment of less than 0.1 m, so it is helpful to avoid this end of the range by adding neutral-density filters and increasing the trim setting.

**102**

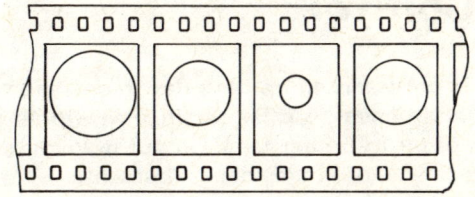

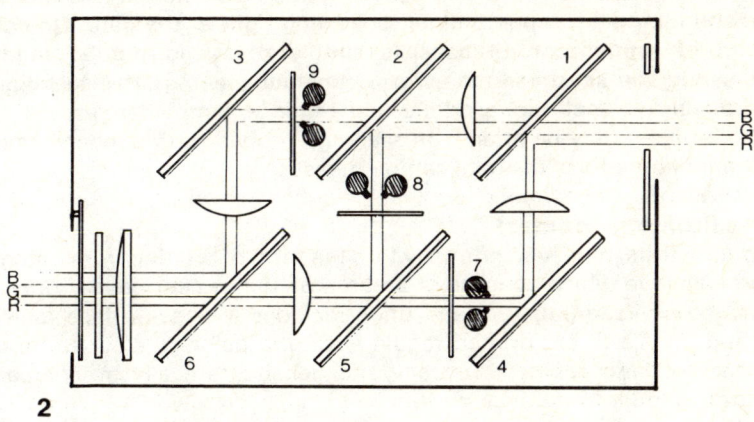

| Dichroic | Reflects | Transmits |
|----------|----------|-----------|
| 1 | Red | Green and Blue |
| 2 | Green | Blue, some Red |
| 3 | Blue | Some Red and Green |
| 4 | Red | Some Green and Blue |
| 5 | Green | Red, some Blue |
| 6 | Blue | Red and Green |

## Colour correction

(1) In subtractive printers a separate filter pack is fitted over an aperture for each scene. (2) The additive-light head uses a system of dichroics so that red, green and blue light may be controlled individually by light vanes, (7, 8 and 9).

# Printer Control

Printer control is necessary to iron out day-to-day variations so that the desired colour and density can be obtained in a print or intermediate. Variations may occur in printer lamp output, transmission of lenses or filters, stock sensitivity, or in the chemical process.

## Photometric control

It is important that printer, stock, and process remain individually within close tolerances so that errors in one part of the system are not masked by changes in another part. The light output of a printer can be measured independently by a photometer, collecting light at the gate. One useful form of printer control consists simply of taking regular readings, adjusting the set-up to maintain a constant reading. This technique is particularly useful during printer maintenance, lamp changes, etc. Many photometers may be fitted with scanning probes so that the evenness of illumination across the gate can be measured.

## Sensitometric control

Routine tests, however, normally take the form of printing from a standard test negative which consists of an area of 18 per cent neutral grey, or a LAD patch, (*see* page 94) and often includes a close-up face for visual reference. Tests are printed regularly on the batch of stock to be used, processed and assessed visually and densitometrically by comparison with a standard reference print.

To correct the density or colour, a change must be made to the exposure set-up. Several controls are available on an additive printer, including

Light – for grading corrections rather than for basic set-ups,
Trims – for small, day-to-day control corrections,
Lamp voltage – to compensate for overall loss of light output,
Filters – for major set-up changes, and to bring trim controls into range.

Sound-track densities are normally corrected by adjustment of the printer lamp voltage.

Sensitometric control has the advantage that it takes the entire photographic process into consideration. Changes in printer speed, process activity, etc., should of course be monitored independently, but overall testing can compensate for the combinations of small errors which may otherwise add up to a significant drift.

Many laboratories cut a few frames of their chinagirl or LAD test into all negatives. So long as the printed densities remain within the tolerances set by the laboratory, the colour of the prints should be within an acceptable standard. This serves as a convenient form of quality control on the product as well as a regular check on the printing and processing systems.

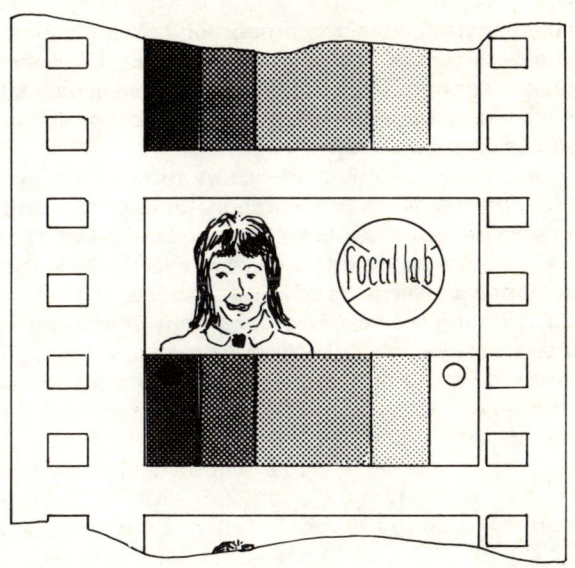

**The chinagirl**
A typical test negative includes a well-lit head and shoulders portrait, and a scale of grey densities. The middle grey square is the laboratory aim density (LAD) patch. The black-and-white steps have small spots of super-black and super-white on them. Poor exposure control in duplication will crush extreme tones and make either black or white spots indistinguishable from their background.

**105**

# Colour Grading

While an experienced technician can assess the exposure required to print a black-and-white negative simply by inspecting the negative over a light box, colour negative presents a considerably more complex problem. Tests, printing two frames from each scene in a cut negative, have now almost universally given way to the electronic colour analyzer. This is basically a telecine machine, in which the negative is scanned and converted to a positive image on a TV monitor. The analyzer is calibrated regularly by the film grader, using a sample of the negative used for printer tests, and the TV image is matched to a projected 'on standard' film image.

When grading any negative, the proportions of red, green and blue in the image can be adjusted in steps that correspond exactly to the light valve controls on a printer. Each scene in a negative is thus adjusted until the result on the monitor is satisfactory, and the settings are then recorded and punched out onto paper tape.

A colour grader has a number of factors to take into account in his assessment: he has to overcome variations in exposure and lighting to balance each shot with others in the same sequence; he has to reproduce exact colours in some material (e.g. commercials, where the advertised product must appear correctly); and he has to interpret the mood required by the director, printing scenes darker for stormy effects, yellow-warm for sunny or romantic sequences, and so on. Control of colour in film printing is limited however, and only the overall balance can be changed; flesh tones for example cannot be corrected without affecting the background tones in the same way.

Laboratories are normally set up so that a well-exposed negative will print in the middle of the range – about 25R 25G 25B – and the trims on each printer are adjusted to suit this. Different laboratories, however, may have chosen slightly different negatives as their standard, and so will arrive at different lights for the same negative.

If a negative is over-exposed by one stop (0.30 log E), the density of mid-tones in the negative will increase by (log E × γ) 0.30 × 0.55 = about 0.17. A corresponding increase in printer exposure of 0.17 log E, or about seven lights, will produce a corrected print. Negatives varying from two stops under-exposed to two stops over-exposed will thus print at lights in the range 10R 10G 10B to 40R 40G 40B.

## FOCAL FILM LABS.  Date _____

Title _Waiting for you_

Client _Miracle Movies_

Roll ___3___  Scenes_____  Fades_____

| No | A | B | | A | | | | B | | | |
|----|------|-----|--------------|----|----|----|---|---|---|---|---|
|    | FCC | FCC | | R | G | B | F | R | G | B | F |
| 1  | 000000 | | Leader | 25 | 25 | 25 | | | | | |
| 2  | 000096 | | Ext Street | 33 | 31 | 27 | | | | | |
| 3  | 000213 | | Ext House | 34 | 32 | 29 | | | | | |
| 4  | 000309 | | Title    CR1 | 36 | 35 | 33 | | | | | |
| 5  | 000531 | | Title    CR1 | 32 | 31 | 28 | | | | | |
| 6  | 000661 | | c/u Door | 25 | 23 | 18 | | | | | |
| 7  | 000982 | | c/u Man | 25 | 23 | 20 | | | | | |
| 8  | 001041 | | c/u Bald man | 28 | 27 | 23 | | | | | |
| 9  | 001221 | | c/u Man | 29 | 29 | 26 | | | | | |
| 10 | 001231 | | w/s 2 men | 34 | 34 | 30 | | | | | |
|    | | | | | | | | | | | |
|    | | | | | | | | | | | |
|    | | | | | | | | | | | |
|    | | | | | | | | | | | |
|    | | | | | | | | | | | |
|    | | | | | | | | | | | |
|    | | | | | | | | | | | |

**Colour grading**

The colour grading lights for each scene are entered on the grading sheet. Often, optical or duplicate negative shots are noted specially, as this material may require a special colour correction due to slight colour differences in the negative dyes.

# Light-change Cues

Although light changes on a printer take place in only a few milliseconds, this represents a measurable distance on the printed film, over which the exposure is rapidly changing. This can appear as a flash on the first frame of a new scene. It is usually necessary to restrict the printing speed of original negatives in which there could be 10- or 15-point changes between scenes.

So far as the positioning of light changes is concerned, the traditional method is to cut shallow notches, or stick metal foil cues, on one edge of the negative a fixed distance away from each scene change. The printer is fitted with a notch probe or 'RF' (radio frequency) cue detector in the negative path a few inches from the printer gate. As each notch or cue is detected, the light valves are activated, and change exactly as the scene change passes through the printing gate.

### Frame-count cueing

Negative handling is reduced by this more modern method, in which an additional punched-paper tape is prepared, encoding the exact length of each scene. This data is fed into the printer at the same time as the grading tape, and a small microprocessor compares each scene length with a frame counter on the printer, firing a cue every time a scene frame count is complete. Frame-count cue data may be recorded either in frames, or in feet and frames: the former leads to quite large numbers, but is transferable between 35-mm and 16-mm systems. Data can be recorded either as a cumulative series, with every scene change measured from a sync mark at the head of the roll, or simply as the length of each individual scene, resetting the count to zero at each cut.

This method is ideally suited to computer assistance. Typically, original negative A- and B-rolls are scanned by a probe that detects black spacing, so that frame counts for each scene are recorded automatically: negative overlaps are interpreted as dissolves, and so on. This data may be stored on disk or in a central data bank, and if interfaced with a colour analyzer, grading information can also be entered directly into memory. When the negative is ready for printing, tapes may be punched out from this data bank, or the computer may be used to control the printer directly. Such approaches reduce negative handling to a minimum, thus reducing the risk of damage. Data handling is also simplified, improving accuracy and speeding up operations such as regrading.

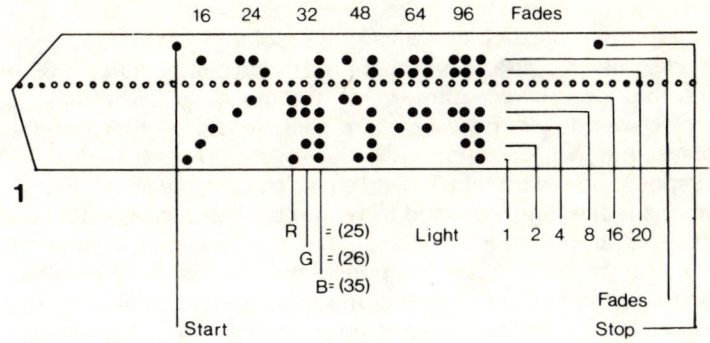

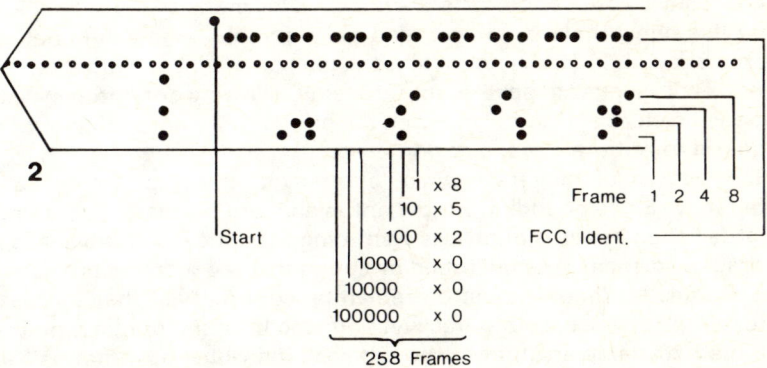

## Punch-paper tape

(1) Colour grading: data for each scene is entered as a series of three coded numbers for red, green and blue.

(2) Frame-count cueing (FCC): each frame count is entered as a six-digit (binary coded decimal) number, representing a count between 000001 and 999999 frames. In the foot-and-frame system, four digits represent feet, and the last two are frames (e.g. 1234 ft 12 frames = 123412).

# Picture and Sound Synchronization

During sound editing, a short 'pip' is placed in the soundtrack leader, to be heard a specified number of frames before the picture starts. One convention is that this pip should sound at the frame marked '2' on a standard 'clock' leader – that is, exactly two seconds before the picture starts.

When a print is projected, any given frame of film passes through the sound head some time after it has appeared in the picture gate: in 35-mm projectors this gap is 20 frames, in 16-mm it is 26 frames. The photographic soundtrack must therefore be advanced by this amount so that it plays in synchronization with the image. The sync pip should therefore appear on the print level with a particular frame ahead of the '2'. In 35-mm this is the fourth '3', and in 16 mm the last but one '4'.

In order that the printer may be laced up correctly, a *sync mark* consisting of a cross with a hole punched in the centre is placed in corresponding positions in the thread-up leaders of the picture and sound negatives. When the printer is laced up with these sync marks in their respective gates, image and sound will be printed in the correct synchronization. Practice on Model-C-type printers is to punch a hole in the raw stock corresponding to the picture sync mark, advance the printer until this punch hole is in the sound gate, and align the sound negative sync mark with it. This is not practicable on panel printers, and a separate sync mark is placed on the sound leader allowing for the separation between picture and sound gates on the printer. Different positions will be required for different types of printer.

The degree of tolerance to an 'out-of-sync' track is hard to assess accurately. Since sounds from distant events are normally heard late, a retarded sound track is often less disturbing than one that is advanced. An average audience is not disturbed by sound that is one frame too early, or two frames too late. It must be remembered, however, that successive errors in post-synchronized track editing, and in sound printing, may add up to a detectable error, even though each individual operation is frame accurate.

### Sound overlays
Since soundtracks are printed some frames ahead of the image, the last few frames of any reel would normally have no sound printed alongside them. If two reels are to be spliced together for projection, the first second or so of the following reel's track must be recorded at the end of the previous reel so that picture and sound are both uninterrupted.

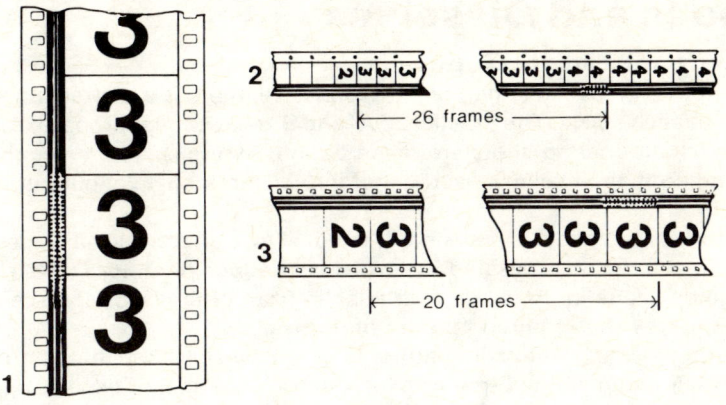

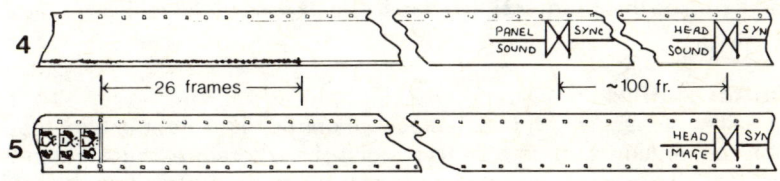

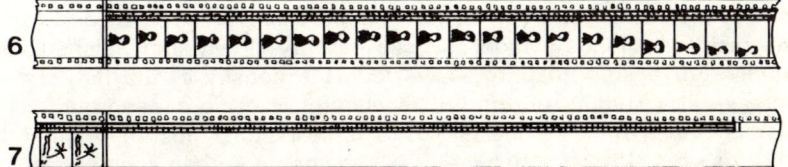

## Picture and sound synchronization

(1) The sync pip may be easily recognized in a photographic soundtrack. (2 and 3) The pip appears a set number of frames ahead of the '2' where it is heard. (4) Sync marks are placed in the sound negative leader so that it may be laced up on the printer correctly with the image negative, (5). The image negative sync mark also serves as a starting point for frame-count cueing (FCC). (6) Sound from the start of reel 2 is printed alongside the end of reel 1 so that nothing is lost when the head leader of reel 2, (7), is cut off in positive assembly.

**111**

*Scene transitions must be as smooth as possible.*

# Fades and Dissolves

### A- and B-roll negative cutting

If 16-mm negative is joined picture-to-picture, there is a distracting white flash at each splice. The practice of A- and B-roll (or chequerboard) cutting in which alternating shots are made up into two rolls, eliminates this by arranging that all splices overlap not into picture negative, but into black spacing.

A further benefit of this system is that it allows effects such as fades and dissolves to be incorporated in normal continuous printing. The tail of an outgoing scene in the A-roll overlaps the head of the incoming scene on the B-roll by the required number of frames.

During printing, the fader shutter is gradually closed as this part of the A-roll is printed. In the B-roll run, the shutter, previously closed, is opened at the corresponding section. Fades to black may be printed from negative by effecting a dissolve from a shot on one roll to clear negative on the other. In reversal printing, it is sufficient simply to close the fader on a single run, as this progressive reduction in exposure will result in a fade to black.

### Shutter profiles

For a steady dissolve, the total exposure on the film from the two images must remain constant. In a 24-frame dissolve, therefore, the exposure as the fader closes is reduced by 1/24 th of the maximum each frame, so that, for example, the 5 th frame represents 19/24 th of the outgoing scene and 5/24 th of the incoming one.

If a simple fade (in reversal printing) were attempted using this shutter, the exposure would fall by 0.30 log E (one stop) in the first 12 frames, another stop in the next six, one more in the next three, and so on. The result would be a fade that started very slowly and finished very rapidly. For a smooth progressive fade the density of the film should increase at a steady rate until it reaches black. This depends upon the characteristics of the stock being used. If the useful exposure range of the stock is, say, 2.40 log E between toe and shoulder, then each frame of a 24-frame fade must result in a reduction of the exposure by 0.10 log E. This means that the exposure would be halved (0.30 log E down) after three frames, and at the mid-point of the effect it would be reduced by a total of four stops.

Clearly, if a dissolve were attempted using this type of fader, the total exposure would dip very noticeably in the middle. Continuous-contact printers are normally fitted with a fader suitable for dissolves, although in some cases a fade profile may be selected.

Mechanical lag and other imperfections may cause a slight departure from the ideal fade or dissolve. This is normally quite unnoticeable, unless two similar – or identical – scenes are being dissolved, in which case a slight fluctuation in density may be noticed during the effect.

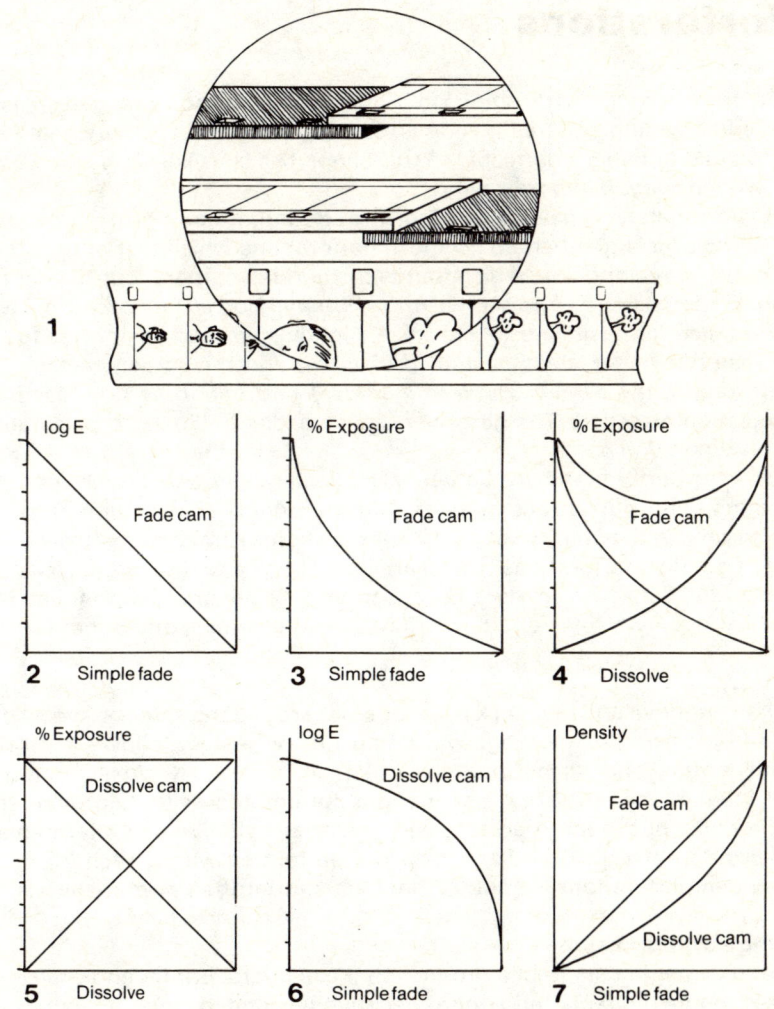

1

| log E | % Exposure | % Exposure |
|-------|-----------|-----------|
| Fade cam | Fade cam | Fade cam |
| **2** Simple fade | **3** Simple fade | **4** Dissolve |

| % Exposure | log E | Density |
|-----------|-------|---------|
| Dissolve cam | Dissolve cam | Fade cam / Dissolve cam |
| **5** Dissolve | **6** Simple fade | **7** Simple fade |

## Scene changes

(1) In A-roll and B-roll negative cutting, alternate scenes are on different rolls, with the splices made on the black spacing side of the join.

Faders: (2) A fade to black uses a logarithmic reduction in exposure so that the shutter closes quickly at first, (3), and then progressively more slowly. (4) Total exposure in a dissolve equals the sum of each scene's exposure. Using a fade shutter this would dip in the middle to less than 100 per cent. (5) Dissolve shutters follow an arithmetic pattern so that the total exposure is always 100 per cent. (6) A fade using this would start slowly and finish rapidly. (7) Density resulting from a fade and a dissolve shutter (on reversal stock) compared.

**113**

# Perforations

The original round perforations in 35 mm film were soon changed so as to have flat leading and trailing edges, and register pins in camera gates are machined to make a perfect fit to this shape, which is known as the *Bell & Howell*, or *negative perforation*.

Unfortunately, repeated running through intermittent projector movements places a great strain on these perforations which tear at the sharp corners. A rectangular perforation with rounded corners, but having the same dimensions, known as the *Dubray Howell perforation*, was introduced for positive-print stocks. A slightly increased height was found to result in better steadiness in projectors, and this larger, rectangular perforation, the *Kodak standard (positive) perforation*, is now used for projection materials. The narrower Cinemascope or 'Foxhole' perforation is now rarely used.

16-mm perforations are universally a rectangular shape with rounded corners. For bulk production of 16-mm prints, 35-mm film may be perforated with two rows of 16-mm perforations, sometimes with an extra set of guiding perforations. These are later slit off and discarded, when the processed film is cut into two 16-mm strands. 8-mm prints can similarly be prepared as two rows on 16-mm film, or as four rows on 35-mm film.

## Pitch
When negative and rawstock pass together around the sprocket wheel of a continuous printer the negative, being on the inside, follows a shorter path length, and its perforations must be fractionally closer together. Nitrate film used to shrink just enought during processing to provide this difference, but modern acetate and polyester negative and intermediate stocks do not shrink, and are therefore perforated with a pitch (distance between perforations) about 0.2 per cent shorter than print materials.

## Image steadiness
If every imaging stage in a production (i.e. camera, printer and projector) were to use pin registration onto negative perforated stock, an extremely steady image would result. This technique is used in process photography (optical effects printing, back- or front-projection, etc.), but normal production equipment, such as continuous-contact printers and theatrical projectors, guide the film by the edge rather than by perforations. Manufacturers' perforating and slitting tolerances are very fine (as little as 0.0004 in or 0.010 mm) and results are steady enough for normal purposes.

Some telecine equipment also uses edge-guidance of the film, and the steadiness required for titling or image combination on video cannot be expected from this equipment, however steady the film image might be.

**114**

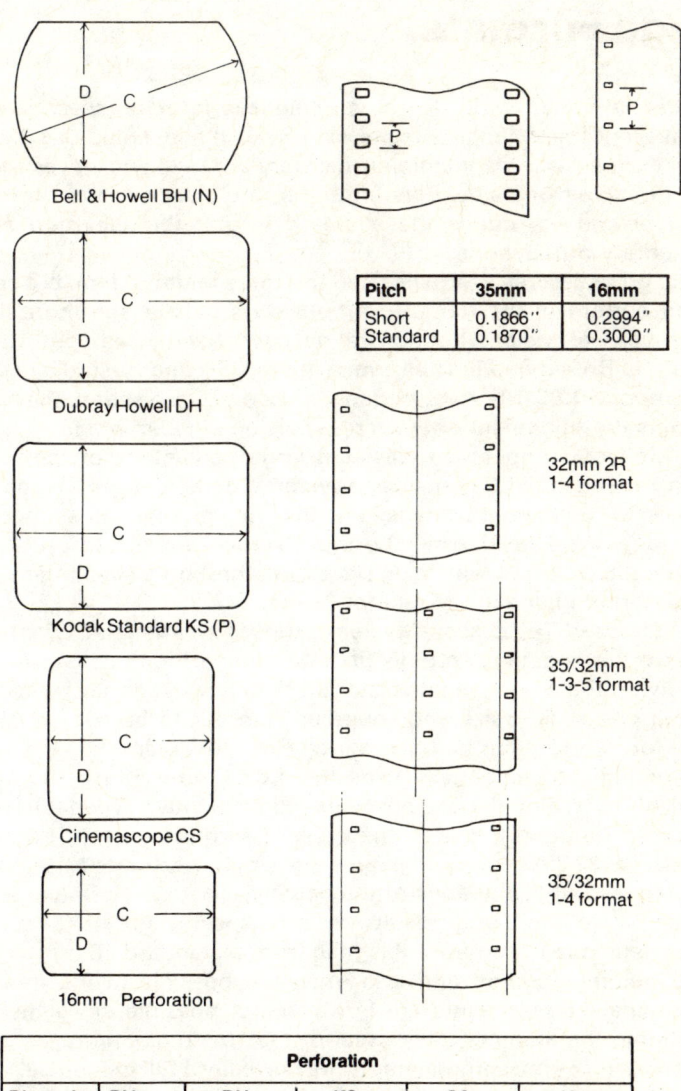

Bell & Howell BH (N)

Dubray Howell DH

Kodak Standard KS (P)

Cinemascope CS

16mm  Perforation

| Pitch | 35mm | 16mm |
|----------|---------|---------|
| Short | 0.1866" | 0.2994" |
| Standard | 0.1870" | 0.3000" |

32mm 2R
1-4 format

35/32mm
1-3-5 format

35/32mm
1-4 format

| | Perforation | | | | |
|-----------|---------|---------|---------|---------|---------|
| Dimension | BH | DH | KS | CS | 16mm |
| C | 0.110" | 0.110" | 0.110" | 0.073" | 0.078" |
| D | 0.073" | 0.073" | 0.078" | 0.078" | 0.050" |
| R | – | 0.020" | 0.020" | 0.020" | 0.010" |

## Perforations

Perforations vary in size and shape, their distance apart and even their position on the film. Measurements are given here in inches.

*Pictures come in a range of shapes and sizes.*

# Image Formats

### Aspect ratio

The ratio of screen width to screen height is termed *aspect ratio*. The original silent frame (approximately 1 in × ¾ in) had a ratio of 1.33:1. The smaller Academy frame maintains this standard ratio and leaves room for a soundtrack on one side. This format is rarely used in the commercial cinema nowadays, but is the standard format for television and for documentary productions.

So-called widescreen formats used the same width of film, but crop the top and bottom of the frame to produce a screen shape more like the normal field of vision. Various ratios have been used, but 1.66:1 is common in Britain and Europe, while in the USA and Australia, a slightly more cropped 1.85:1 is most frequently used. On projection, the cropped frame fills the full height of the screen, giving a wider image.

The widescreen approach wastes a large percentage of the negative area. In Panavision or Cinemascope systems, an anamorphic camera lens produces a 'squeezed' image on the negative so that horizontal dimensions are reduced to half the size of vertical dimensions. A full frame is in the ratio of 1.18:1 which, on projection through a similar lens, yields an undistorted image in the ratio of 2.35:1.

The little-used Techniscope system exposes an image of 2.35:1 aspect ratio onto the negative, and this fits into two-perforations-worth of film, thus halving the use of negative stock. Prints however must be blown up to a four-perforation size and squeezed in order to be compatible with normal four-perforation pull-down projector movements.

16-mm film conventionally uses the 1.33:1 ratio which fits into the normal 16-mm film dimensions very conveniently. When blow-up to widescreen 35-mm is intended, the super-16 format is a useful alternative. This uses a 22 per cent wider area on single perforated 16-mm film, extending almost to the edge of the negative (an area normally used for support on rollers), and results in an aspect ratio of 1.66:1. Less enlargement is required from this than from a standard 16-mm negative, and so better definition and less grain are possible in the final print. Conventional 16-mm prints are however not possible since the image extends into the area normally used for the 16-mm soundtrack.

35-mm and 16-mm camera masks are normally a full height 1.33:1 ratio, slightly larger all round than a projector mask. Although black frame lines are sometimes burnt in to widescreen productions during printing, this practice is unnecessary as projector-gate masks and screen tabs adequately define the edge of the image.

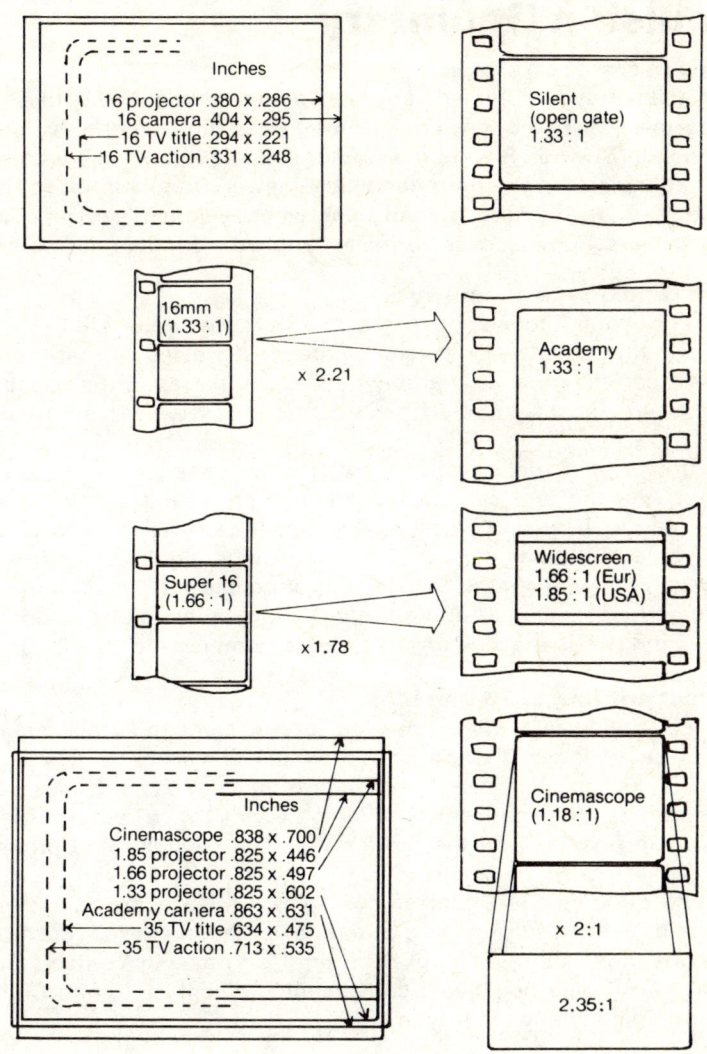

Inches

16 projector .380 x .286
16 camera .404 x .295
16 TV title .294 x .221
16 TV action .331 x .248

Silent
(open gate)
1.33 : 1

16mm
(1.33 : 1)

x 2.21

Academy
1.33 : 1

Super 16
(1.66 : 1)

x 1.78

Widescreen
1.66 : 1 (Eur)
1.85 : 1 (USA)

Inches

Cinemascope .838 x .700
1.85 projector .825 x .446
1.66 projector .825 x .497
1.33 projector .825 x .602
Academy camera .863 x .631
35 TV title .634 x .475
35 TV action .713 x .535

Cinemascope
(1.18 : 1)

x 2:1

2.35:1

**Frame size**

Most productions are shot using either a full-height or an Academy mask, but may be cropped to various sizes by the projector mask. Measurements are given here in inches.

*Take care that the image is the right way round.*

# Emulsion Geometry

### Single-perforation stock

16-mm film may be supplied perforated down either one or both edges. In the former case, the position of the perforations (perfs) is denoted 'A-wind' or 'B-wind'. B-wind rawstock is suitable for use in a camera: the perforations are on the right-hand side (viewed from behind) as the film runs through the camera. B-wind stock, when rewound, becomes A-wind, and *vice versa*. Rawstock is normally supplied wound emulsion-in.

### A-type and B-type geometry

Camera original film has, of course, been exposed emulsion towards the lens, whether negative or reversal material. If viewed so that the image appears correctly (i.e. so that any writing can be read from left to right, etc.), the emulsion is therefore away from the observer. This is referred to as B-type film.

A contact print made from this original is made with its emulsion in contact with the emulsion of the original, producing a 'mirror image'. When this is viewed correctly, therefore, the emulsion is towards the observer, and the base away. This is an A-type film. These terms apply irrespective of whether the film is single or double perforated: however, in single-perf stock, the perforations always run on the left-hand side of the image, and this is the side on which edge numbers are usually printed.

### Contact printing of 16-mm film

Contact printing is always emulsion to emulsion: thus the negative is always cell-to-lamp. A-wind or double-perf rawstock is used. B-type originals are printed head first and produce A-type copies. A-type originals (e.g. CRI negatives), in order to provide the correct emulsion and perforation positions on the printer, must be rewound and printed tail first, producing B-type copies.

B-type geometry is preferred for 16-mm release prints. (These are projected with emulsion facing the lens, the preferred position for optimum sound reproduction.) Such prints, if made by contact, must be made from A-type negatives: conveniently, a contact 16-mm CRI made from original negative is A-type.

### Optical (projection) printing

Projection printer cameras, like other cameras, require B-wind or double-perf rawstock. If the negative (or intermediate) is run from the head, then a B-type print will be obtained. For the image to be correct, it must appear correct when viewed from the camera: thus an A-type original is run cell-to-lamp (away from the camera or observer) while B-type originals are run emulsion-to-lamp.

To obtain an A-type print the original material must be run from the tail and turned the other way around to preserve the correct emulsion position. Thus, if the original is emulsion-to-lamp, the geometry stays the same; if cell-to-lamp, the geometry is reversed.

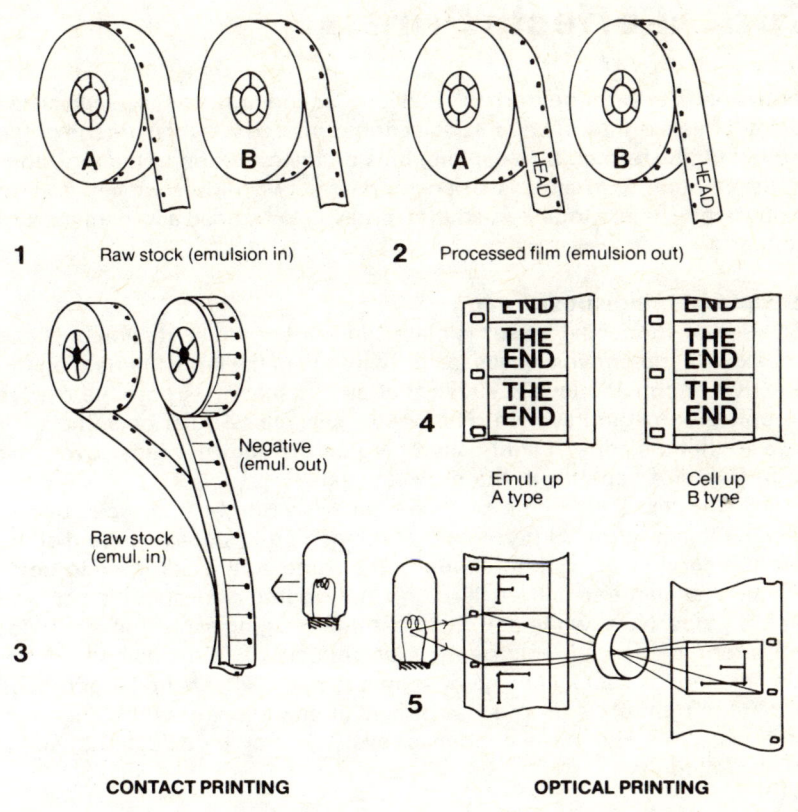

**1** Raw stock (emulsion in)

**2** Processed film (emulsion out)

Negative
(emul. out)

Raw stock
(emul. in)

**3**

**4**

Emul. up
A type

Cell up
B type

**5**

**CONTACT PRINTING**

| To make From | A type | B type |
|---|---|---|
| A type | | Tail first cell to lamp |
| B type | Head first emul. to lamp | |

**OPTICAL PRINTING**

| To make From | A type | B type |
|---|---|---|
| A type | Tail first emul. to lamp | Head first cell to lamp |
| B type | Tail first cell to lamp | Head first emul to lamp |

## Emulsion geometry

(1) Rawstock can be either A-wind or B-wind. (2) Processed camera negative is B-type: a contact print from it is A-type (3). (4) Geometry can be verified by examining writing, etc., on the image. (5) Optical printing inverts the image: negative is normally run upwards through the projector gate.

# Optical-effects Printer

At the opposite extreme from the bulk production printer is the specialized optical-effects printer. This is a projection printer in which an image of the original film is formed by a copying lens on the emulsion of the raw stock in the camera. Provision is often made for two pieces of film to run through the camera together, so that it may also be used as a contact step printer.

### Lenses and image positioning
A system of condenser lenses is placed in front of the light source. These convex or plano-convex lenses focus an image of the lamp filament on the objective or copying lens itself, so that as much light as possible passes through the imaging system. The condenser lenses must be sufficiently large so that the cone of light converging on the objective lens covers the entire frame of negative in the projector gate.

The subject matter in the projector gate is brought into focus by the objective lens, at the camera gate. This imaging system is quite distinct from the condenser system (although the same light is common to both) so that the filament pattern is completely defocused at projector and camera gates. Now, when any change in the imaging system is made (for a different degree of enlargement or reduction), the position of the objective lens is usually changed, so that the condensers no longer focus light in the right place. Some loss of field illumination, or vignetting, may result from this, but some condenser systems may be adjusted to suit a range of settings.

### Aerial image
An additional feature of some optical printers, and rostrum stands, is the aerial image head, in which the light source is moved further back, and the first gate and lens system are used to focus an image onto a second gate, or in the case of the rostrum stand, onto the copying table. The image from the film in the first gate is thus superimposed upon the film or artwork in the second gate, and both images are focused together by the camera lens onto the rawstock in the camera.

Unfortunately, most light from the first (aerial image) gate, while it comes to focus in the second gate, is not travelling directly towards the camera lens, and this would result in a very dim image with a bright spot in the middle. This is overcome by the use of a field lens placed just before the second gate. This converging lens redirects the projected light towards the camera so that a uniform bright field is obtained.

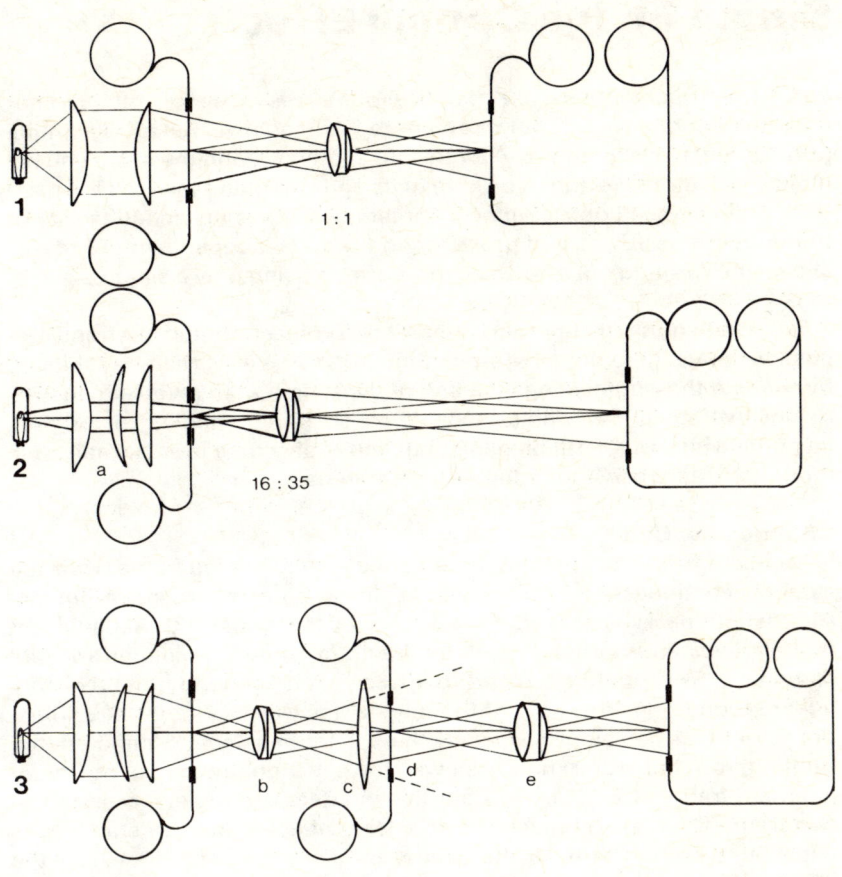

## Optical printing

(1) For 1:1 copying, the lens is placed midway between camera gate and projector gate. (2) For different magnifications, lens distances are changed. An adjustable condenser (a) may be required to focus light onto the repositioned copying lens. (3) Aerial image printer: the aerial image lens (b) forms an image at (d), but light must be redirected by the field lens (c) towards the copying lens (e) so that an evenly-illuminated image is formed in the camera.

**121**

# Single-image Optical Effects

The most straightforward use of optical printers is for simple reduction or enlargement of a single shot or an entire final negative. Relatively simple printers are available to carry out this function only, and these are usually fitted with automatic additive light heads and wet-gate systems (*see* page 132). A single-head optical-effects printer usually has the added facility of frame-by-frame advance of projector and camera independently, and this allows the carrying out of many simple effects using only a single piece of film.

Effects are normally photographed from a contact-printed intermediate-positive image onto negative stock, although some effects can be achieved by running the original negative and duplicating it onto reversal negative or positive stock. Since this involves considerable handling of original negative which may well be damaged, and is of course irreplaceable, it is more usual to work from intermediate materials.

### Change of action

For a freeze frame, the projector is stopped at the required frame while the camera continues to run, resulting in a completely static image. Alternating backwards and forwards between two or three adjacent frames gives an improved result as the grain pattern no longer appears stationary. Skip printing is used to speed up an action, by printing only every second or third frame of the original (so that 24 frames of original occupy only 12 or eight frames of the optical negative). Simple stretch printing, on the other hand, slows down action by repeating every alternate frame (1,2,2,3,4,4,. . .) but this in effect is a rapid succession of two-frame freezes, and gives rise to a jerky effect. If the camera stock is exposed a second time to the sequence of frames 1,1,2,3,3,4,. . . ., the result is that every frame is frozen by the same amount, and the action appears somewhat smoother. The exposure for each run is reduced to 50 per cent (one stop less) so that the total remains the same. This technique is useful in reproducing old silent material shot at 16 fps.

### Change of size

Apart from simple blow-up or reduction, a zoom technique is possible, changing the degree of enlargement frame by frame. Since prime lenses (not zooms) are used, this is achieved by moving both lens and camera between exposure of each frame. An adjustment must also be made to the aperture for each step, as the degree of enlargement has an effect on image brightness, and thus exposure. Many printers are fitted with mechanical or electronic cams to govern these changes automatically.

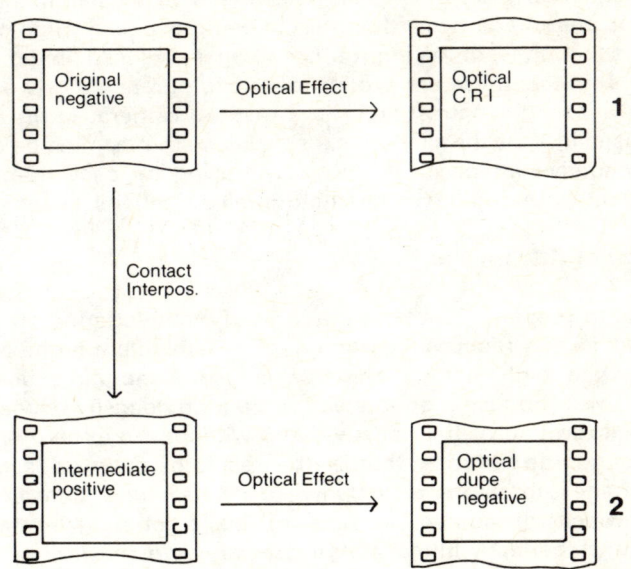

Original negative → Optical Effect → Optical C R I    **1**

Original negative ↓ Contact Interpos.

Intermediate positive → Optical Effect → Optical dupe negative    **2**

**Optical dupe negatives**
These may be printed either directly from an original negative onto CRI, (1) or from an interpositive onto dupe negative stock (2). Some complex opticals require some of the effects to be incorporated into the interpositive stage, in which case this also is carried out on the optical printer.

# Combined Images and Mattes

Most optical effects combine images from more than one piece of film. Such effects include superimposed titles, split screens, wipes, and composite images. In some cases superimposed exposures are required: for example the 'strobe' effect, in which rapid movements leave a trail of images. Here, a series of runs is made on the printer from the same original negative, changing the starting point by a few frames each time. To ensure the correct total exposure is received by the rawstock, each individual run must be at a reduced exposure: four runs at ¼ exposure (two stops down) each, for example.

Other effects require quite separate and distinct images to be combined. To achieve this, it is necessary to mask off, or reserve, the part of the frame required for one image while the other is being exposed. High-contrast mattes, or silhouettes, of the appropriate images are used. In the case of title or wipe mattes these are produced by photographing artwork onto black-and-white high-contrast stock in a rostrum camera: in the case of superimposed images the silhouette, or travelling matte, must be derived from the negative image itself, either by tracing off each frame on a rostrum stand (rotoscoping) or by photographic methods.

### Production of title mattes

It is normal to prepare artwork in the form of white lettering on a black background, as this reduces the amount of possible flare in the camera. Black-and-white high-contrast negative is used, and an exposure is chosen that will produce a good black without any density appearing in the clear background or the negative, and without the excessive image spread around the lettering that is the result of over-exposure. The resultant image is termed a *title negative*, or a *male hi-con matte*. From the negative, which of course consists of black lettering on a clear background, a perfectly-fitting *complementary title master*, or *female matte*, is produced, by contact printing in a registering step printer. This will consist of clear lettering on a black background.

Wipe mattes, used for effects such as iris wipes, left-to-right, diagonal or clock wipes, are usually stored as library footage, and a contact negative and master may be printed from the library master whenever required.

In the case of static titles it is usually sufficient to shoot a couple of feet of each title, as one single frame can be frozen in the optical printer. Roll-up titles must be shot to exactly the required length on the rostrum camera. Titles and mattes should not travel too fast across the frame otherwise they will produce a jerky stroboscopic effect.

**124**

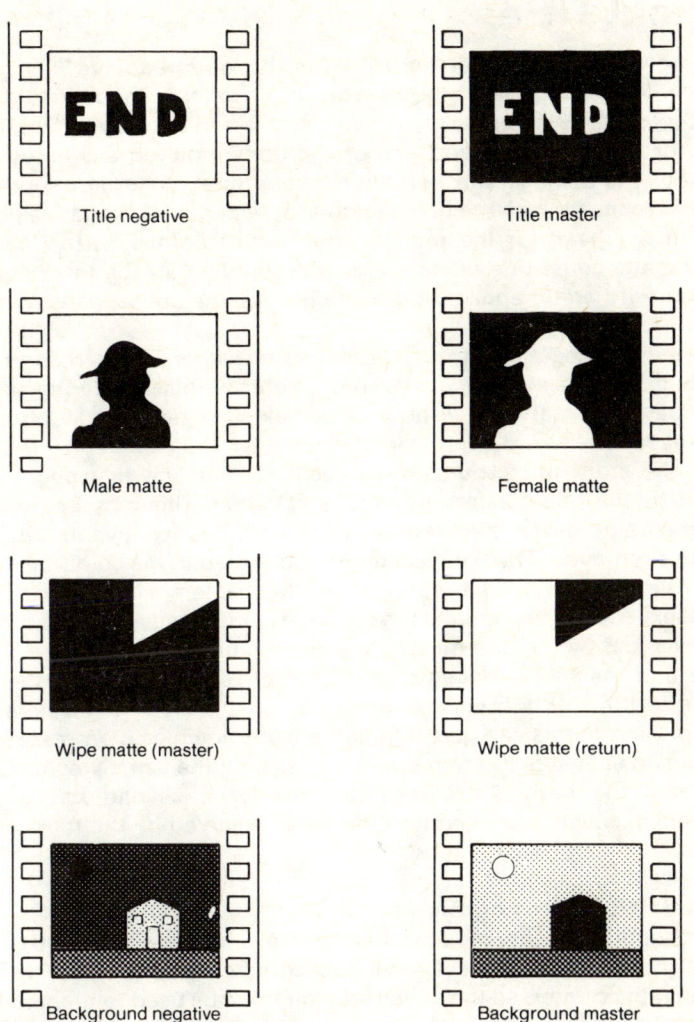

Title negative

Title master

Male matte

Female matte

Wipe matte (master)

Wipe matte (return)

Background negative

Background master

**Optical components**
The various elements required for optical printing, sometimes known as optical 'facilities'.

# Optical Titles

### Coloured titles using intermediate positive and negative

A balanced interpositive of the background shot(s) is made, usually by contact printing. This interpositive is measured, and the appropriate frame counts for the beginning and end of the titles required are noted. The interpositive is then run through the optical printer, either in bi-pack (i.e. laced up in contact) with the title negative, or with the title negative placed in one image head for the required number of frames. In this case, a dummy matte consisting of clear film is substituted for the title negative where no titles are to appear, to maintain the same optical density in the light path.

Intermediate negative stock is run in the camera, and records the background image everywhere except where the black lettering on the title negative has masked it. A print from the optical negative at this stage would reveal a black title.

Next, the stock is rewound in the camera, and the title negative is replaced by the title master, in exact registration. This may be done by aligning a frame of the master in one gate with the negative in the other before it is removed. The light is filtered or trimmed to the colour required for the title, and the stock is run through the camera for a second time. This will expose the title area to the required colour, while the background image, masked by the title master, will remain unaffected.

If the title master is moved slightly out of registration with the title negative, a black fringe will be revealed on one side of the lettering. careful placing of this can give a 'relief' effect, known as a *drop shadow*.

Wipes and split screen are produced in exactly the same way as titles, except that the second printing run includes a second background interpositive, which is printed into the areas reserved by the male matte negative.

### Coloured titles from negative

When the optical is being made from negative or interpositive, or to colour reversal intermediate, titles appear the complementary colour to that exposed in the printer, so that a yellow filter must be used to prepare blue titles, etc. The drop shadow effect would similarly turn out to give a white fringe, and so a third printing pass must be made, using both title mattes together, to expose the shadow outline only.

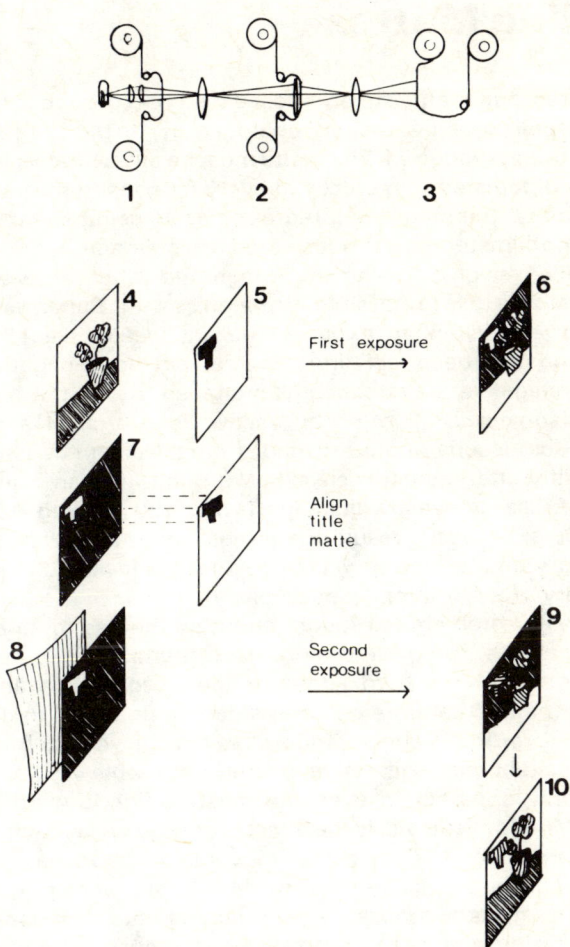

**Printing a coloured title**

(1) Aerial image projector. (2) Projector. (3) Camera. In the first exposure, the background interpositive is placed in the aerial image projector, (4), and copied onto the dupe negative rawstock in the camera, (6), with the title negative in the second projector (5) reserving a blank area in the frame. The background interpositive is then removed and replaced by the title master, (7), which must be perfectly aligned to the title negative. The title negative is then removed, the required colour filtration, (8), for the title is inserted, and a second exposure is made, (9), printing colour into the reserved title space. A contact print, (10), taken from the optical negative reveals the final effect.

**127**

*. . . . to monsters and magic.*

# Travelling Mattes

Where the foreground to be superimposed on a background is not simply a title or graphic, but live action photography, a more sophisticated matting technique is required. The matte must be an accurate silhouette of the foreground, registering perfectly in every frame, and this can only be obtained by photography of the foreground itself, using suitable lighting techniques and filmstocks to produce the correct image.

Most methods involve filming the foreground (often an actor who is later to appear in an impossible situation, as in Superman's flying sequences, or simply in an exotic or distant location) againt a plain background. In the beam-splitting camera, a colour negative and a high-contrast negative are produced simultaneously. In the blue-screen method, the subject is lit, often by yellow light, against a pure blue background. Colour separations are made from the colour negative, which produce a silhouette against a clear background, and an artificial blue record (to neutralize the yellow-lit image) is made by juggling with a series of colour separations. This result in a foreground image that is more or less satisfactory unless blue or yellow colours are included: these tones tend to go very green or pink respectively.

A much greater problem is brought about by the use of high-contrast mattes to separate foreground and background. High-contrast film invariably produces very hard edges to the image. Male and female high-contrast mattes therefore demand a perfect fit, which in the face of lens and film distortion is almost impossible to achieve. The fringing that results from a slight mis-registration is rarely noticeable in titles or wipes, but is invariably apparent in even the most straightforward travelling matte shots. More difficult still is the effect produced when the foreground image has soft edges – due to fast movement, or unsharp focus, or naturally-soft subject matter such as wind-blow hair, or semi-transparent features such as glass or smoke. When rendered onto high-contrast film, these edges produce a very uncertain result, much as cutting out a photograph for paste-up would do, and the final composite image usually suffers from severe fringing, coarse grain, or even 'holes' in the foreground.

Many of these problems can be overcome with care and ingenuity, and techniques have been derived which minimize the need for high-contrast mattes, by using low-contrast colour separations with backgrounds just sufficiently dense to act as a 'self-matte'. These techniques require most accurate sensitometric and optical control at every stage, and the careful selection and use of the appropriate duplicating materials for the various elements of the effect.

**128**

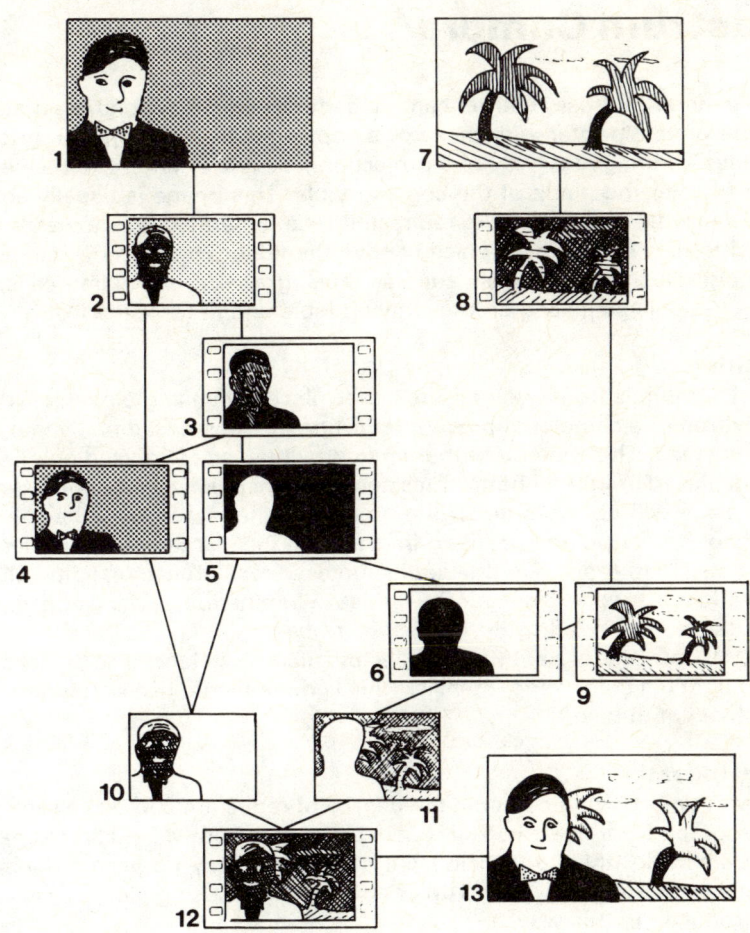

**Blue screen travelling matte (simplified)**

(1) The yellow-lit foreground subject is shot against a blue background, resulting in a yellow background area in the negative, (2). A blue separation positive, (3), from this has a clear background and is dark in most subject areas. An interpositive, (4), printed from the original negative, is given a second exposure from a derivative colour separation to compensate for the yellow cast of the subject lighting. Meanwhile, a female, (5), and a male, (6), hi-con matte are made from the separation.

A normally-photographed background, (7), provides a negative, (8), and interpos, (9). Foreground and female matte are combined in one printing pass, (10), and background and male matte in another, (11), to produce a dupe negative, (12), from which a print of the composite image, (13), may be made.

# Rostrum Camera

The general-purpose rostrum camera combines the functions of an aerial image optical printer with those of a copying stand. A projector system focuses an image (by way of a projection lens and a large, front-silvered mirror) onto the plane of the copying table. This image is usually some 40 cm across, and its light is redirected by a large field lens towards the copying lens of a camera placed above the table. This camera may also photograph opaque artwork such as titles, graphics, animation cells, or even flat objects placed on the copying table and lit from the front.

## Lighting

Front lighting is from two or more lamps placed at an angle of at least 45° away from the camera, to prevent reflection of 'hot spots' directly into the camera lens. This may be further limited by the use of crossed polarizing filters placed in front of both lamps and the camera lens. Light polarized in one plane will not pass through a polarizing filter set in the other plane, and so if the polarizing filter in front of the camera lens is set at right-angles to those over the light sources, directly reflected light will be filtered out, while the more diffuse illumination, which becomes depolarized upon reflection, is allowed to pass.

Light from the aerial image projector must be balanced to match the front lights in colour and intensity: this is done by the use of filters or an additive lighthouse.

## Copying ratio

As with any copying camera, any degree of reduction can be selected to photograph front-lit artwork. It is conventional to copy a field aproximately 30 cm wide (the '12-in field') but other sizes may be accommodated simply by moving the camera up or down and refocusing. Zooms can also be produced in this way.

In the case of the aerial image, the field lens is set to direct image-forming light towards the camera lens at a particular point. If the camera lens is moved up or down, it will collect light only from the centre of the image, resulting in severe vignetting, or edge-masking of the image. Different reduction or blow-up ratios can however be produced by selecting a different focal length camera lens.

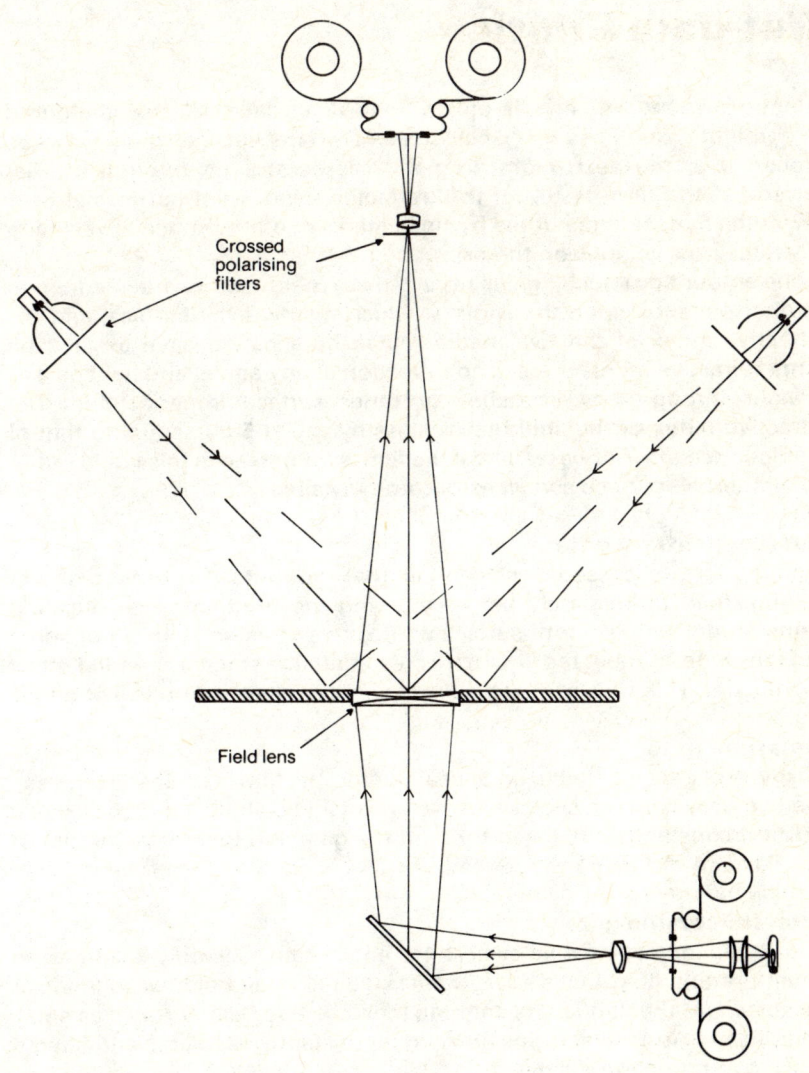

Crossed
polarising
filters

Field lens

**Rostrum camera (animation stand)**
Front-lit and rear-lit images may be combined, or large-scale artwork
photographed.

**131**

# Wet-gate Printing

If loosely-wound negative is pulled tight, its surface will become pitted with minute scratches or 'cinch marks', where each turn of film has slipped over the next. Light normally passes straight through the flat surface of the film base, but it is refracted away from its normal path where the surface is disturbed by cinch marks or other scratches, resulting in white spots or lines on the print.

The amount by which light is refracted as it passes from one medium to another depends upon the angle at which it strikes the surface, and the refractive index of the two media. When both media have exactly the same refractive index, there is no refraction at any angle, and light passes straight through any scratches or other surface imperfections. The refractive index of the liquid tetrachlorethylene (1.50) is equal to that of cellulose acetate (filmbase), and if the film is immersed in this liquid rather than in air, all surface scratches become invisible.

## Wet (application) gate

The negative is passed over a roller that dips into a reservoir of wet printing fluid immediately before entering the printing gate. The fluid forms an optically-smooth surface and covers most scratches, but some surfaces tend to repel the liquid, this resulting in a smeary, mottled effect on the print. This system may be used in both contact and optical printing.

## Aquarium gate

This type of gate is fitted to an optical printer: the film is enclosed between two flat glasses which enclose an evelope of liquid about 1 mm thick. Fluid must be constantly circulated through the gate and there is some risk of bubbles and dirt being introduced.

## Total-immersion gate

In this wet contact-printing system the entire gate assembly is immersed in wet-printing fluid. Once again there is the risk of air bubbles adhering to the surface of the film as it is entering the fluid, and being printed as small white flecks. As in all systems the fluid is constantly circulated and filtered to remove particles of dirt.

Tetrachlorethylene dissolves small amounts of plasticiser from film base, and it must be changed regularly before it becomes dark and oily. Wet-printed negatives must be thoroughly dried after printing: the surface of a film left wet will be damaged within a few hours.

Wet printing was introduced as a salvage system for badly-damaged negatives. It is now routinely used for all printing of 16-mm original cut negative (which has received considerable handling during negative matching, etc.) by many laboratories. Duplicate negatives, however, are less subject to handling damage, and bulk release printing may be carried out by faster and simpler dry-printing methods.

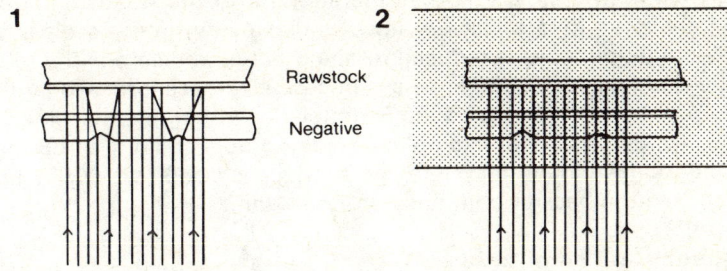

**1**

Rawstock

Negative

**2**

| Liquid | R.I. | Notes |
|---|---|---|
| Perchlorethylene | 1.504 } | Both suitable for wet printing |
| Trichlorethylene | 1.478 } | but dissolve plasticiser slowly |
| Trichloroethane | 1.438 | Used in film cleaning |
| Trichloro-trifluoroethane | 1.358 | Used in hand film cleaning |
| Cellulose Acetate | 1.490 | Film base |

**Wet-gate printing**
(1) Light is scattered as it passes from air into a scratched film. (2) Perchlorethylene (tetrachlorethylene) has a refractive index similar to that of film base, and optically fills in any surface defects.

# Sound Waves

Sound waves are created by vibrations. These vibrations can easily be seen if the strings of a guitar are plucked, or felt by placing a hand on the throat when speaking. Sounds are heard when vibrations are transmitted from the object to the ear, through a suitable medium such as air. With each vibration, or beat, of the sounding object, a series of waves or ripples travels outwards in all directions. When these reach the ear, they set up vibrations in the eardrum, which are in turn transmitted through a series of small bones to the cochlea or inner ear. Here, the various vibrations are converted to nerve pulses and set to the brain.

As sound travels away from its source, the energy is spread over a rapidly-increasing area, and thus the strength of the waves is reduced. This follows an inverse square law, so that every time the distance is doubled, the loudness is reduced to one quarter, and so on. The relative loudness of two sounds is expressed in decibels: these form a logarithmic scale, so that every time a sound is doubled in strength, it becomes 3 dB louder. On this scale, for example, a signal-to-noise ratio of 50 dB means that the loudest sound a system can produce is 50 dB (or 100 000 times) louder than the background noise of the system.

### Frequency and amplitude

As each wave passes any fixed point, the air pressure at that point rises and falls. The variation between highest and lowest pressures represents the strength or loudness of the sound, and is termed the *amplitude* of the soundwave. Now a more rapid vibration will result in more waves arriving per second. This factor is termed the *frequency* of the sound, and is heard as a variation in pitch. A flute, for example, produces higher frequencies than a tuba. Frequency is measured in cycles (complete waves) per second, or Hertz (Hz).

Very few sounds have a single-frequency wave-form. Sounds of speech, traffic noise, or machinery, for example, are a complex mixture of waves of different frequencies and varying amplitudes. Even a single note on a musical instrument consists of a fundamental frequency together with upper harmonics; waves of frequencies exactly two, three or four multiples of the fundamental. It is the presence of these harmonics which gives each instrument its characteristic timbre, and enables us to distinguish, for example, a trumpet from a violin.

Normally, a young person can hear frequencies between 20 Hz and 20 000 Hz. However, in older people, the eardrum tends to thicken and become stiffer, so that the frequencies above 12 000 Hz become increasingly difficult to hear.

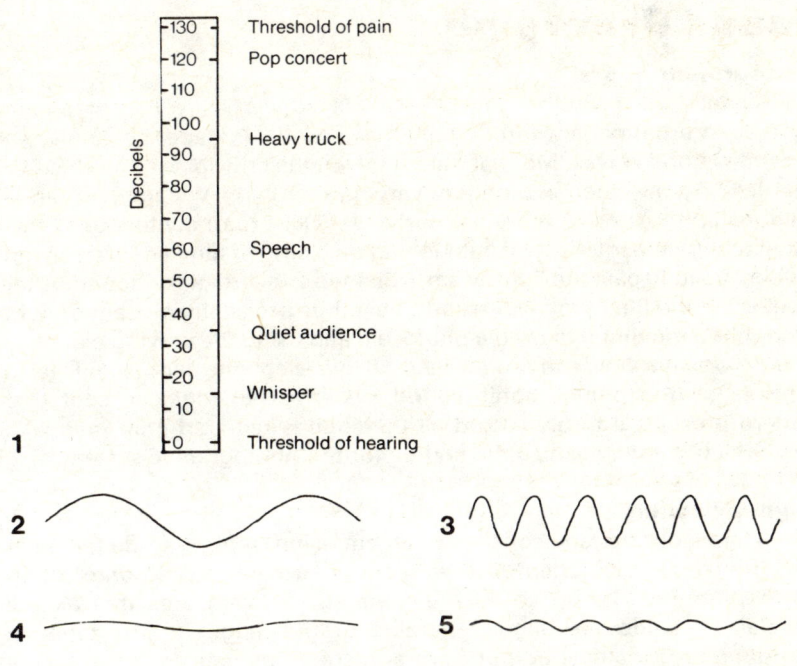

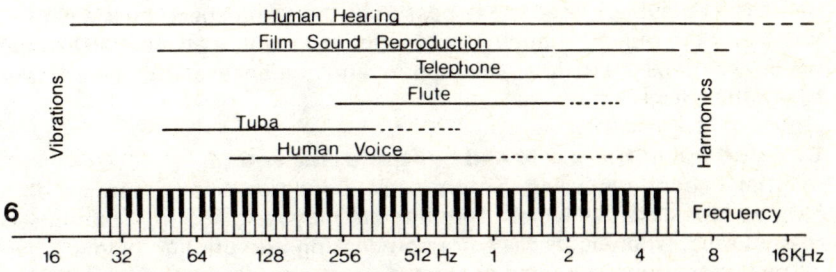

## Hearing sounds

(1) The ear can receive sounds up to about 130 dB above the threshold (quietest audible sound) without pain. Sound levels fall of with distance: these examples are heard at an average distance of 6 ft.

(2) Low-frequency and (3) high-frequency tones; (4 and 5) the same frequencies at a lesser amplitude. (6) Harmonics extend well above the fundamental frequencies of many sounds.

**135**

# Sound Recording

### Photographic sound

Any system of recording sound involves converting transient sound waves into a permanent form which may, at a later stage, be converted back into sound waves. Microphones use various principles to produce an electrical signal — that is, a rapidly varying current or voltage — in direct relationship to a sound wave. As early as 1900, experimenters used this signal to vary the intensity of light falling on a strip of film, and by moving the film steadily past the light beam, obtained a record of the sound. After developing the film, playback was achieved by projecting a beam of light through the moving film onto a photocell, and using the varying electrical output from this device to produce sound in a telephone ear-piece. This, in principle, is the photographic sound system used today, except that modern practice is to pre-record all the sounds required onto magnetic tape, which is then used as the source for the photographic system.

### Magnetic sound

Magnetic recording tape consists of an emulsion of ferric oxide (recently other materials have been used with some success) coated onto a thin flexible support. During coating, a magnetic field ensures that all the particles of oxide are aligned parallel to the length of the tape. In recording, the electrical output from a microphone is used to produce a small, varying magnetic field in the recording head. As tape is passed over the head, each oxide particle becomes a miniature bar magnet, and the signal is recorded as a variation in the degree of magnetization of each particle. In playback, the tape is passed at the same speed over a similar head, and the rapidly-changing magnetic field induces an electrical signal which may be used to drive an amplifier and loudspeaker system, or input to another recorder.

### Comparison of magnetic and photographic sound

Magnetic sound recording is more convenient than direct recording onto film, as tapes are available for immediate playback, and may be re-used many times, whereas film requires processing and printing before it can be played, and may be used only once. Furthermore, magnetic recording produces a much better signal-to-noise ratio than film, so that a wider range of amplitudes can be recorded without background noise becoming obtrusive.

Magnetic tape can also record higher frequencies than can film. For these reasons, magnetic recording is used in most stages of film production, and frequently as the final track of prints for television. However, for bulk release printing, it is far cheaper and more convenient to incorporate a photographic track, printed and processed at the same time as the image, and this basic format of sound on film has remained essentially unchanged over the last half-century.

**136**

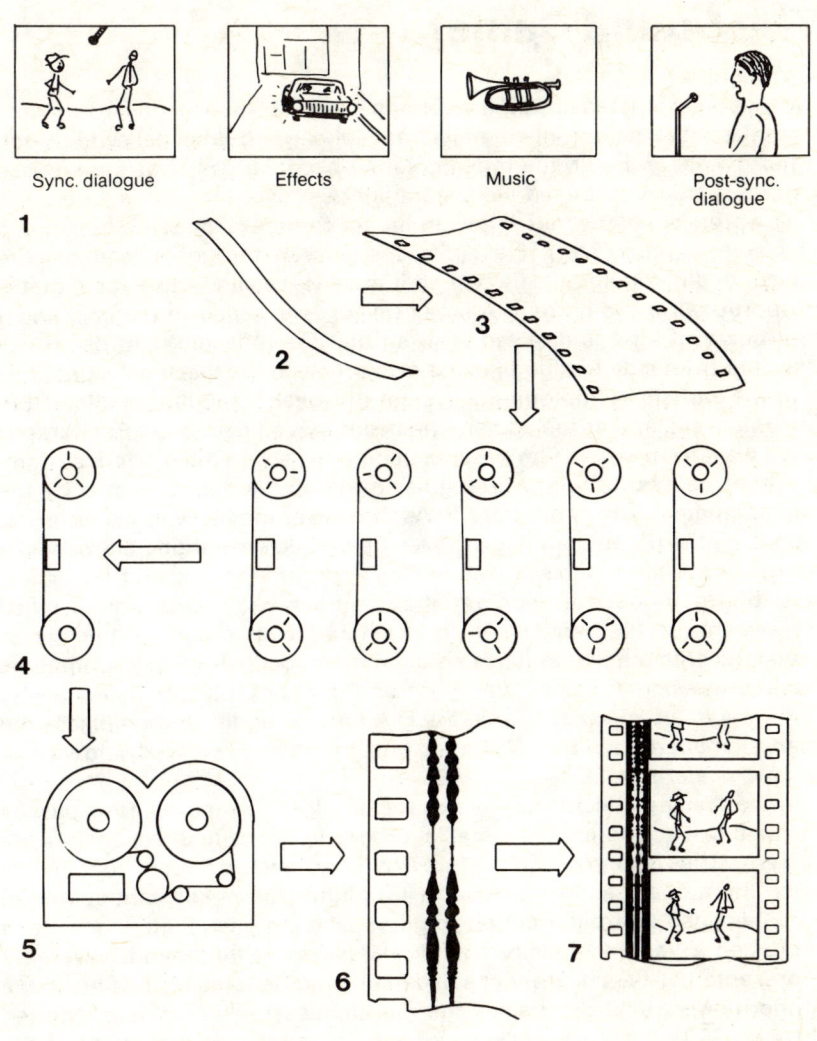

Sync. dialogue Effects Music Post-sync. dialogue

### Film sound production

(1) Sound is recorded from various sources onto ¼-in tape, (2), and then transferred onto magnetic film, (3), for editing. After editing, the sound is mixed from many tracks onto one master 'final mix' (4), from which a signal is fed into the sound camera (5), to expose the sound negative, (6). This is printed alongside the image to produce a composite print, (7).

**137**

*An image of the sound wave.*

# The Sound Camera

Early sound cameras used the incoming electrical sound signal to vary the brightness of a helium-filled glow-lamp, whose light then passed through a narrow slit and onto the moving sound negative. This was superseded by two systems that used a constant light source.

The principle of the mirror galvanometer camera is the same as that of a voltmeter or ammeter; if a current is passed through a coil of wire suspended in a magnetic field, then it experiences a twisting force that is proportional to the current. A small mirror is attached to the coil, and a fine beam of light is directed at it, so that the reflected light beam will oscillate from side to side in exact proportion to the electrical signal.

In the early RCA Photophone system this beam of light was allowed to fall onto a slit, and as the edge of the beam moved back and forth it traced out a waveform on the film passing behind the slit. In the modern system, the light passes through a triangular mask and is then reflected by the galvanometer mirror onto the slit. As the mirror moves with the electrical signal, so the triangular image moves up and down, lighting a broader or narrower portion of the slit. By using an appropriately-angled triangle it is possible to produce a wide variation in track width with only a small movement of the mirror. An optically-reduced image of the slit is projected onto the film as it passes at uniform speed, leaving a continuous trace of the signal. Since it varies on both sides of the light beam, this is termed a *bilateral variable area track*. A further modification replaces the triangular aperture with a W-shaped one, producing two lines, known as a *double bilateral track*.

In the Western Electric light-valve system, the electrical signal is passed through two spring-loaded metallic ribbons in opposite directions. As the current varies, electromagnetic forces either draw the ribbons together or force them apart, allowing more or less light from a constant source to pass between them and fall on the film. Like the glow-lamp system this produced a variable-density soundtrack in which the sound waves are represented by bars or striations of darker or lighter area on the film. In the modern Westrex light valve, the ribbon assembly has been turned through 90 degrees so that the ribbons are parallel to the length of the film, and the beam of light is brought into sharp focus on a slit so that it is lit over a varying width, as in the galvanometer system.

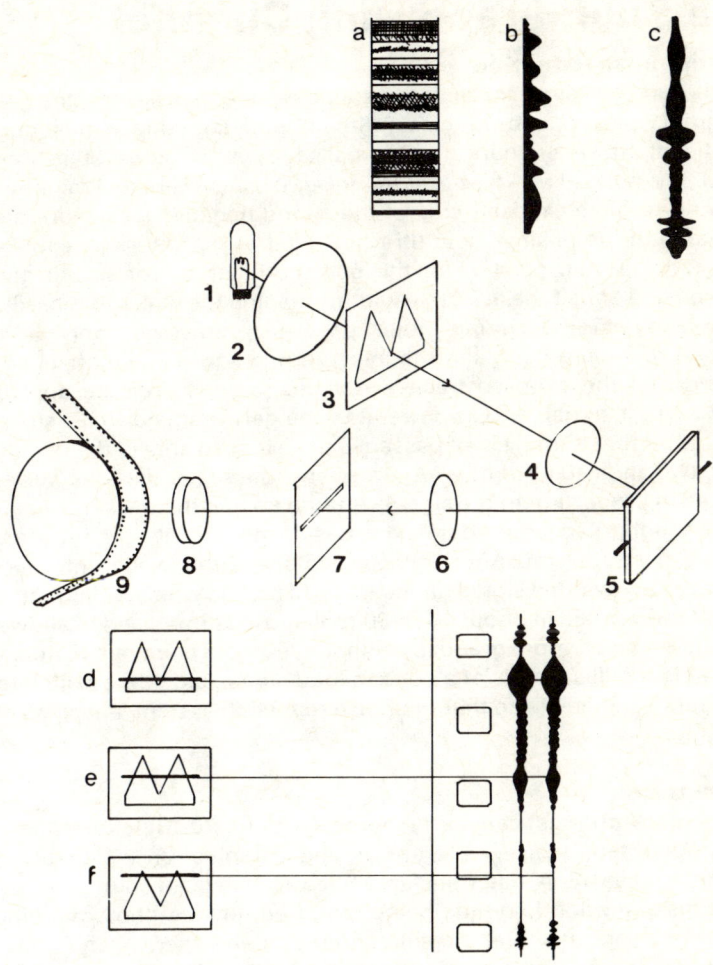

## The photographic soundtrack

(a) Variable-density track; (b) early (unilateral) variable area track; (c) modern bilateral variable-area soundtrack.

The galvanometer sound camera. (1) Light from the lamp is collected, (2), and passes through a W-shaped mask, (3). Lenses (4) and (6) image the mask onto slit aperture (7), but the mirror galvanometer at (5) oscillates with the sound signal, this moving the image up and down and resulting in a varying-width slit beam which is focused by lens (8) onto the moving sound-recording stock (9). Varying positions of the image on the slit result in a wide, medium or narrow (d, e and f) beam of light on the film.

# The Sound-recording Channel

### Ground-noise reduction

When clear film is run through the sound head of a projector, the grain in the emulsion produces a hiss. With a loud soundtrack this may go unnoticed; however, during quiet passages it becomes objectionable. Hiss of this sort is known as *ground noise*; it can be kept to a minimum by ensuring that the exposed area of the sound negative (and therefore the clear area of the positive soundtrack) is kept as narrow as possible.

The normal rest position of the galvanometer mirror would give an exposed line of half the available width, allowing the maximum oscillation in both directions. During quiet passages, however, only a small movement is necessary, and the average position may be offset so that the width of the exposed track is reduced. This is done by applying a direct-current signal, or bias current, to the galvanometer. This current is adjusted so that during silent passages the exposed area of the negative is about two thou (0.05 mm) wide. In louder passages the bias current is reduced in proportion to the signal strength so that the track is always just wide enough to accommodate extremes of movement of the mirror.

The bias current must not vary too rapidly as this would introduce an audible but unwanted signal on the track. In practice the bias line can open up for loud signals in about 15 to 30 milliseconds (ms), and is allowed to close down much more gradually – about 250 ms. To prevent distortion in the first few milliseconds of a sudden loud signal, a delay is built into the main audio signal line so that the noise reduction system 'anticipates' the signal.

### Compression

Magnetic recordings can carry signals up to 70 dB louder than the background tape noise, whereas a photographic track can accept a maximum of 55 dB. A 'flat' transfer would result in quiet sounds being lost in the hiss, and loud sounds being distorted, just as photographing an excessively contrasty scene results in blocked-in shadows and burnt-out highlights. Photographic sound channels therefore include a compression stage in which low-level signals are boosted, and high levels reduced. This raises the average level of a soundtrack but at the expense of losing the impact of very quiet or very loud passages.

### Film loss equalizer

Photographic soundtracks invariably lose signal level at high frequencies. In part this is because accurate reproduction of a 9 kHz signal on 35-mm film requires photographic resolution of the order of 80 lines per mm, and image-spread during exposure and development, slippage during printing, and chemical fog all serve to reduce the resolving power of the system. Some compensation can be made for this by electronically boosting the high frequencies of a recording during transfer.

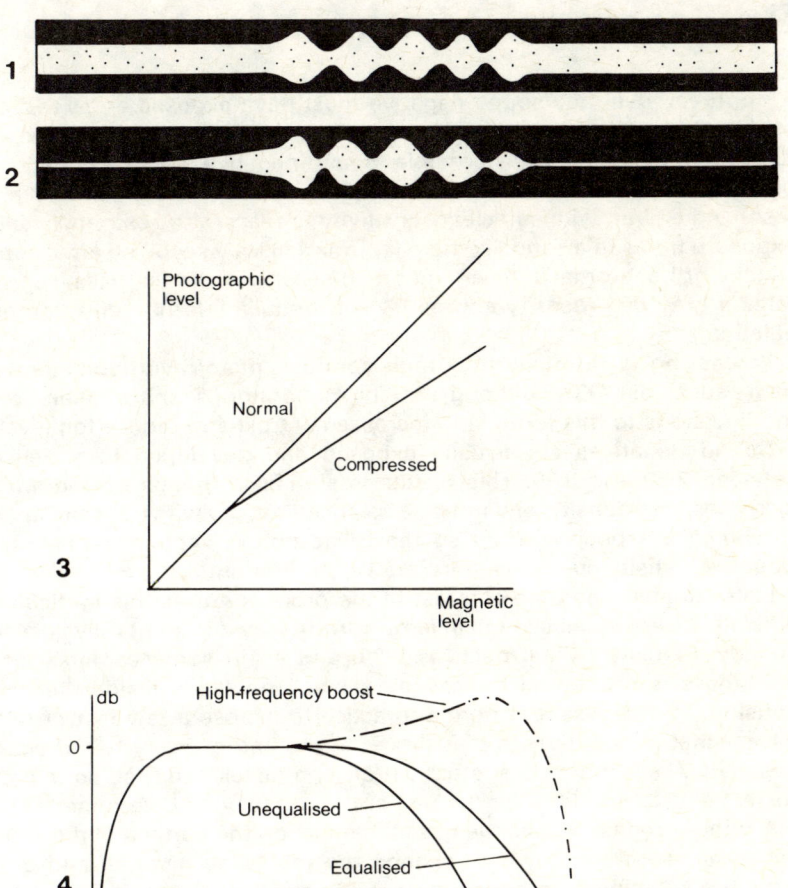

**Improving sound reproduction**
(1) Without ground-noise reduction: (2) with ground-noise reduction: the track adjusts in width to accommodate the signal, remaining as narrow as possible at all times to minimize grain noise in the print. (3) Compression reduces the level of loud signals compared with quiet ones, to accommodate a wider range. (4) Equalization boosts the otherwise deficient high frequencies to obtain an extended overall response.

# Processing the Sound Negative

A good variable area sound negative must have exposed areas that are effectively opaque, unexposed areas free from fog, and the border between them as sharp as possible. Sound negative stocks are therefore black-and-white emulsions of a very high contrast, fine grain, and high resolving power, with sufficient sensitivity to react to the extremely short exposure times in a sound camera (approx 1/80 000 sec). The emulsion is usually orthochromatic (blue- and green-sensitive) and the base incorporates a grey dye (density approx 0.25) to reduce internal reflection and halation.

Processing is normally in a high contrast, metol/hydroquinone-type bath such as D97, although many laboratories make their own modifications to this formula to increase contrast and reduce fog level.

Sound negatives are usually exposed and developed to a density between 2.50 and 3.30. This results in significant image spread which increases with density, and must be balanced exactly with opposite image spread in the positive print so that distortion is kept to a minimum. Negative density control is therefore very important.

Unfortunately the high contrast of the process makes this particularly difficult. A very small change in lamp current (say, 0.1 amp) may alter the negative density by as much as 0.20, and so in some cameras lamp brightness is monitored directly by a small photocell inside the lamp housing. in any case it is normal practice to expose a few feet of *flood track* – that is, a full-width bias line – on the end of every roll of sound negative. A section of this is broken off and developed first, so that the correct developing time for the rest of the roll may be determined.

A minor processing change has little effect on the gamma of the stock: but larger corrections would change the fog level, gamma, and grain structure sufficiently to have considerable effect on the quality of sound reproduction. It is therefore important that the process chemistry be maintained accurately. Normal control procedures are carried out using sensitometric strips exposed on the type of stock used in the sound camera. Note that while sensitometer exposures are usually at least 1/100 sec, soundtrack exposures are approximately 1/80 000 sec, and there is a considerable degree of reciprocity failure between these two times. Sensitometric strips cannot therefore be relied upon for accurate stock comparisons, and exposure tests must be carried out in the sound camera. For routine control purposes, however, sensitometric strips are quite adequate.

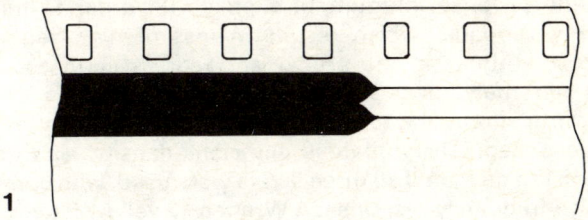

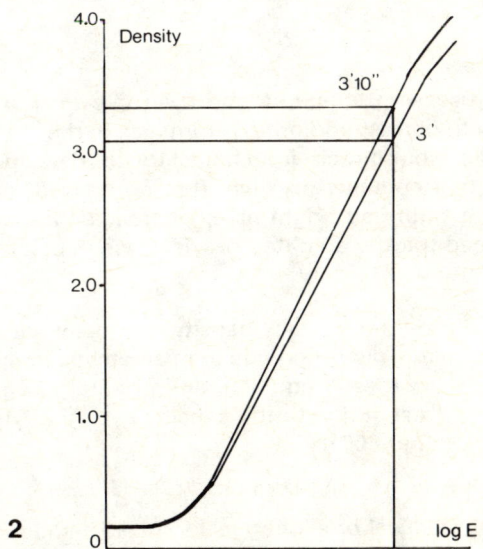

**Process control**
(1) Sound negative density is read on a full-width flood track. (2) High-contrast sound negative is very sensitive to slight processing changes.

**143**

# The Photographic Sound Print

By their very nature, sound prints must be made in a continuous (rotary) contact printer. As with picture negative, sound negative stock is manufactured with a short pitch in order to fit perfectly inside the curved path around the printing sprocket wheel. The back-up roller in the printing gate must be adjusted accurately: if set too tight, it is liable to 'massage' the stock and produce intermittent slippage. In order to minimize the effect of any slippage (which results in loss of high-frequency-signal level), exposure times in the printer are kept as short as possible by making an extremely narrow printing aperture.

In colour prints, only the top two layers of the emulsion (magenta and cyan) are exposed. This provides sufficient density, and results in a sharper track image than if all three layers were used, with correspondingly better high-frequency response. A Wratten 12 yellow filter is inserted in front of the light source to remove blue light, together with a 2B filter to eliminate ultra-violet radiation. This filter pack must be removed for black-and-white printing, in order to expose the blue-sensitive positive stock.

## Processing

In colour positive processing, magenta and cyan dye track images are produced together with corresponding silver images in these two layers. The silver gives the soundtrack its characteristic dark purple-blue appearance; a track that contains no silver (having missed redeveloper application) appears a saturated bright blue, whereas an under-exposed but correctly developed track is a lighter, greyish blue in colour.

## Track density

Any deviation from the optimum track density, normally set at around 1.40, will result in noticeable distortion due to mismatched image spread. Positive track densities are measured using an infra-red-passing filter in the densitometer, to correspond with the sensitivity of the S1 projector photocell, peaking at around 800 nm.

## Direct recording

On occasions it is not practical or economical to make a sound negative, and the soundtrack is exposed directly onto the print stock in the sound camera. The normal W-shaped mask in the galvanometer system is replaced by an opposite form, so that normally-exposed areas are left clear, and *vice versa*. In the conventional negative-positive system the effects of image spread in each stage tend to cancel each other out; with only a single stage this is not possible, and exposures and densities are kept very low in order to retain sufficient sharpness. The resultant soundtrack is lacking in level, particularly at high frequencies, and has a noticeable background hiss. Such prints are mainly used for mechanical tests, or where only a working copy of a soundtrack is required.

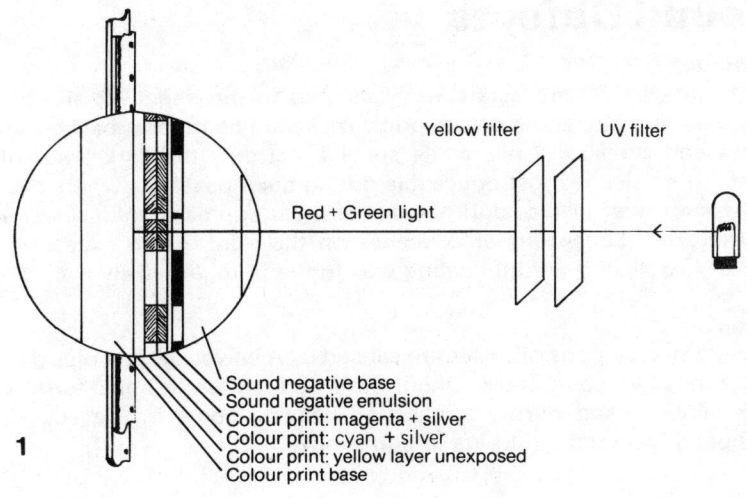

Yellow filter    UV filter

Red + Green light

Sound negative base
Sound negative emulsion
Colour print: magenta + silver
Colour print: cyan + silver
Colour print: yellow layer unexposed
Colour print base

**1**

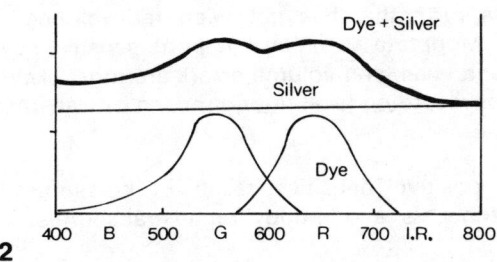

Dye + Silver

Silver

Dye

400    B    500    G    600    R    700    I.R.    800

**2**

**Sound printing**
(1) Printing through a yellow filter exposes the two top layers of colour-positive
stock. (2) Only silver provides density in the near infra-red region just above
700 mm, where the projector photocell is sensitive.

# Sound Defects

### Crackles
Fine particles of dirt, scratches or cinches in the negative, all result in showers of white spots on the print. These are heard as a background of clicks and crackles. Since white spots affect only the dark areas of the track, this noise is most noticeable during quiet passages where the bias line is narrowest. Noise during loud passages originates in the clear areas of the print. Loose dirt or scratches on the print, or an excessive and smeary application of lubricating wax to the print, are likely causes.

### Pops
Low-frequency pops or thuds are caused by relatively large holes or spots in the positive soundtrack. Often these occur when bubbles form in the redeveloper bead during application, leaving spots in the soundtrack without silver, and light blue in appearance.

### Hiss
Hiss results from a random, unwanted signal being reproduced. In an optical soundtrack this may come from a grainy or slightly fogged track area, or from scanning beyond the edge of the soundtrack.

### Low volume
This may arise from a print that has not been redeveloped, or an excessively light print. Moderate variations in print density, however, have little effect on sound level, and volume errors are most likely to be the result of an incorrect recording level during mixing or transfer.

### Sibilance
Incorrect negative or positive densities result in cross-modulation distortion, heard as spitting 's's, and 'muddy' orchestral sounds.

### Clipping
A 'ragged' edge to loud sounds, but acceptable quality at low levels. This may be caused by an incorrectly-positioned scanner slit in the projector, or overloading during sound transfer.

### Wow and flutter
A gradual (wow) or rapid (flutter) variation in pitch is caused by an uneven playing speed at some stage of sound reproduction. This cannot be caused during printing, however, since negative and rawstock must inevitably run through the printer at the same speed.

### High-frequency loss
Some high-frequency loss is inevitable in a photographic system, but is normally corrected by film loss equalization. A frequent cause of excessive high-frequency loss (producing a woolly, muffled sound) is poor printer contact or slippage resulting in a visibly-blurred track.

**146**

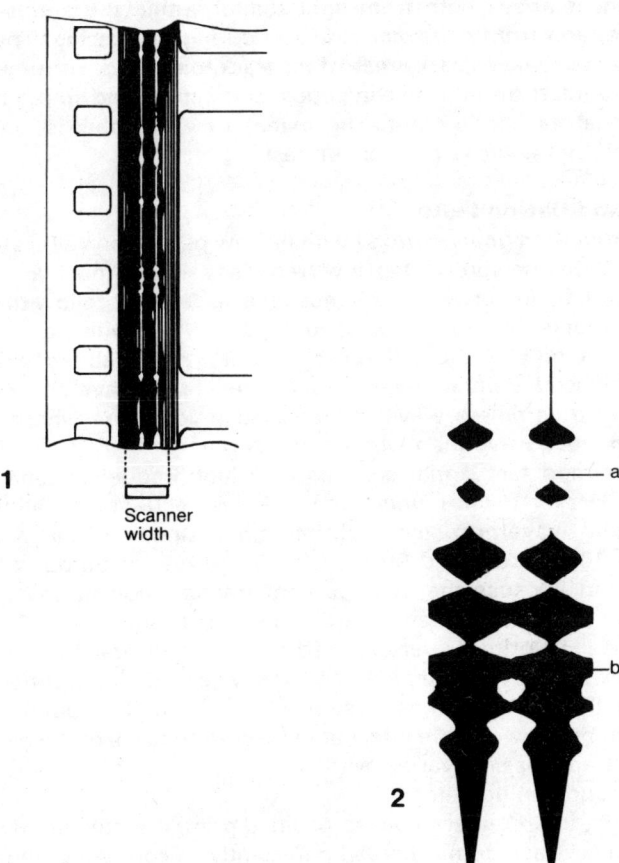

**1**

Scanner
width

a

b

**2**

## Sound distortion

(1) In a poorly-applicated track, the edge of the redeveloped stripe is scanned in the sound reproducer, causing a variable rumble or hiss. (2) Over-modulation because of poorly set ground-noise reduction (a) or an excessively strong signal (b) results in squared-off, rough-sounding waveforms.

# Cross-modulation Tests

## Image spread

The image formed in a sound negative is inevitably slightly more diffused than the light beam generating it. There is a further slight loss of sharpness when a positive print is made from the negative. This unsharpness arises both from light scatter within the emulsion during exposure, and from chemical diffusion during processing. The resultant image spread causes dark areas of the track to expand. Fortunately, in the positive print, the shift is in the opposite direction, and so the two effects may cancel each other out. The extent to which this is successful is measured by the cross-modulation test.

## Cross-modulation tests

High-frequency signals – waves with narrow peaks and valleys – are more affected by image spread than low-frequency waves, much as a thick coat of paint will fill in very fine scratches on a surface but follow the contours of wider marks. In an over-exposed negative track with excessive image spread, not only is the difference between high-frequency peaks and valleys reduced (painting over the scratches) but the average width of the track over a complete wave is increased much more where there *is* a high-frequency wave than where there *is not*.

A cross-mod test signal consists of a high-frequency tone (6 kHz for 35 mm, 4 kHz for 16 mm) modulated by a low-frequency variation (400 Hz). In an ideal waveform, the high-frequency signal varies in amplitude between 10 per cent and 90 per cent of maximum output 400 times a second, but because the average light transmission at any part of the waveform remains constant, there is no audible signal at 400 Hz.

If the positive print is over-exposed, then the dark areas surrounding the clear track spread into the peaks and valleys of the high-frequency signal, lowering the average transmission where the high-frequency signal is strongest, but having little effect at the weaker phases of the signal. Thus, average transmission varies with the modulation of the signal, and a 400 Hz sound can be detected.

Similarly, in an under-exposed positive print, the dark areas surrounding the clear track do not spread sufficiently to counteract the spread of the negative image, and the track area is spread wider in areas of strong high frequency, once again producing a signal at the modulation frequency of 400 Hz.

The cross-modulation signal is purely a test device designed to produce a measurable effect when image spread is not cancelled effectively. In a normal soundtrack the effect is most noticeable when any high-frequency signal changes rapidly, and a spurious wave is introduced. In speech, sibilant sound such as 's' sound 'spitty', while musical instruments such as cymbals lose their clarity and sound muddy.

**148**

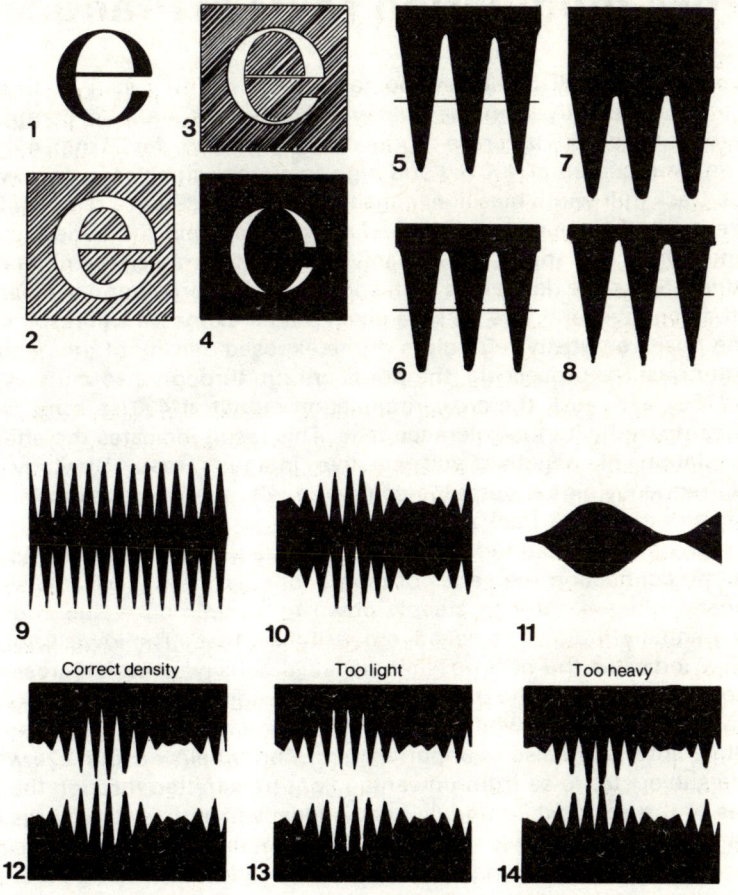

## Image spread

(1) Original pattern; (2) under-exposed negative; (3) correctly-exposed negative; (4) over-exposed negative in which fine detail is lost. (5 and 6) Ideal wave form; (7) over-exposed waveform with filled-in valleys; (8) under-exposed waveforms with feathered peaks.

Cross-mod tests: (9) High-frequency tone; (10) cross-mod signal (a modulated high-frequency tone); (11) low-frequency reference tone. (12) Well-exposed print; constant average width of track, and no low-frequency signal. (13) Underexposed print with feathering of peaks and variation in average width causing a spurious low-frequency signal. (14) Over-exposed print with filled-in valleys, and again, a spurious low-frequency variation.

# Cross-modulation Tests in Practice

A complete family of cross-mod tests must be produced to find the negative and positive densities that will give best results. A set comprising reference tone (400 Hz), cross-modulation signal (6 kHz for 35 mm, 4 kHz for 16 mm, modulated at 400 Hz) and high-frequency signal, together with a flood track (full-width bias line) density test, is exposed at a range of lamp currents in the sound camera, and developed. This full series is then printed onto the appropriate positive stock at a range of printer-lamp settings. Since the dark areas of the positive print correspond to clear film on the negative, and *vice versa*, a given printer exposure will result in the same positive density regardless of the exposed density of the negative.

After positive processing, the prints are run through a sound playback head. For each test, the cross-modulation output at 400 Hz is measured and compared with the reference tone. This result indicates the effective cancellation of negative and positive image spread. Similarly, the high-frequency signal output is compared with the reference tone as an indication of overall track sharpness.

Graphs are now plotted of cancellation against negative density, with one line connecting the series of points for each print. Each line should appear V-shaped, curving steeply down to a minimum value and then rising equally rapidly, as negative density is varied. The lowest point of each V indicates the best possible negative density, at which cross-mod distortion is least, for the print density in question. A light print works best from a light negative, while a heavy print favours a heavy negative.

Other criteria are also of importance: a density below about 1.20 will be more subject to noise from unwanted light transmitted through the dark areas of the print, while unduly heavy negatives and prints will result in greater high-frequency loss. Once a final combination has been decided upon for any combination of stock and printer it is normal for a laboratory to set the print density as a standard so that negatives, once made, can be printed at any time in the future at a standard setting. Sound negatives on different batches of negative stock, or from different sound cameras, should be made to a density that will suit this established print density.

Although this somewhat lengthy test procedure should be carried out regularly, and certainly after any stock or equipment changes, routine control on individual negatives and prints may be carried out using standard sensitometric methods, aiming for the densities indicated by cross-mod testing.

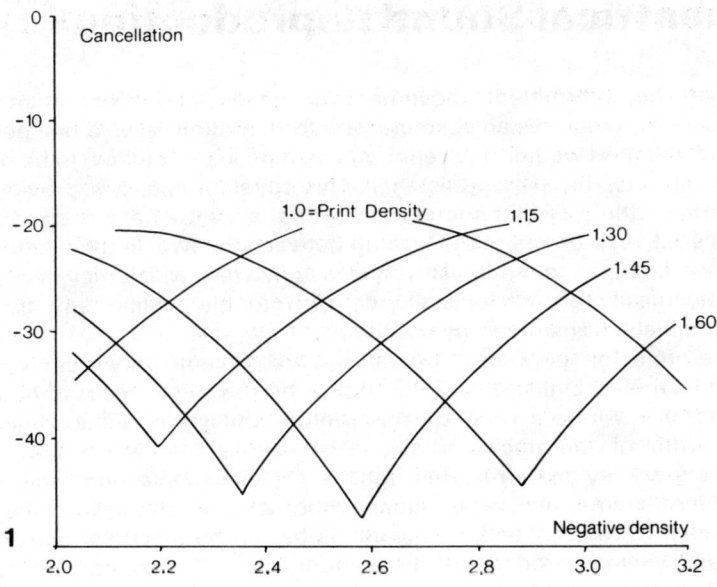

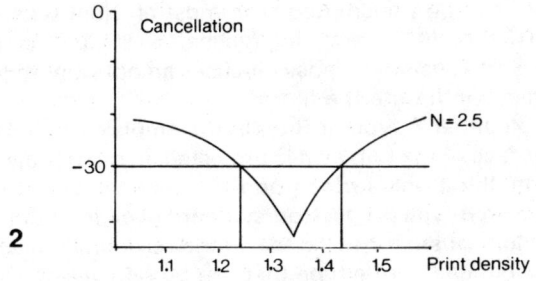

## The cross-mod family

(1) Each curve represents results from a set of negatives at a single print density (P). The value at the V of each curve indicates the ideal negative density for that print.
(2) Control tolerances may be estimated by plotting a series of print results from a single negative. The V width at 30 dB (the normally accepted minimum cancellation result) indicates the upper and lower limits for print density. A minimum of 35 dB is suggested for stereo soundtracks.

# Theatrical Sound Reproduction

Unlike the intermittent movement of image projection, soundtrack reproduction requires an absolutely uniform motion: even a one per cent speed variation would cause enough variation in pitch (wow) to be readily noticeable to the average listener. This constant speed is provided by separating the projector sound head from the picture head and providing for a slack loop of film in the lace-up between the two. In the sound head the film is driven round a relatively heavy flywheel which may in addition be electrically or mechanically damped to elimination any trace of vibration still transmitted by the film.

The projector sound head operates in a complementary manner to the sound camera. Light passing through a narrow slit is focused onto the soundtrack, where a varying proportion is transmitted depending upon the width of the track (variable area) or its density (in the earlier variable-density system). This light is collected by a photocell which produces a small electrical signal proportional in strength to the light received. Once amplified, this signal is fed to the theatre's loudspeaker system where it produces audible sound. As in the sound camera, the width of the slit is of great significance. Too wide a slit results in high-frequency loss: if it is too narrow there is an overall loss of output since not enough light can be transmitted. The most efficient width has been found to be 0.0013 thou (0.033 mm). In practice, the slit itself is many times wider than this, and a system of lenses focuses an optically-reduced slit image of the correct width onto the film.

16-mm prints may be either A-type or B-type: the emulsion may be on either front or back surface of the film as it is projected. In most projectors the slit is focused on the front surface and so best high frequency response is obtained from B-type prints. Non-standard (A-type) prints may be played but a slight loss of sharpness in the sound reproduction will be noticed unless the soundhead is of a type that can be refocused.

Photocells in 35-mm and 16-mm projectors are sensitive predominantly to infra-red radiation, peaking at around 800 nm. This standard was established when black-and-white prints were the norm. Unfortunately, the dyes used in colour prints have a very low density to infra-red, so it is necessary during processing to restore the original silver image in the soundtrack area by means of redevelopment. Super-8 projectors use a newer type of photocell which is responsive to visible light, and a simple dye track is adequate in this format.

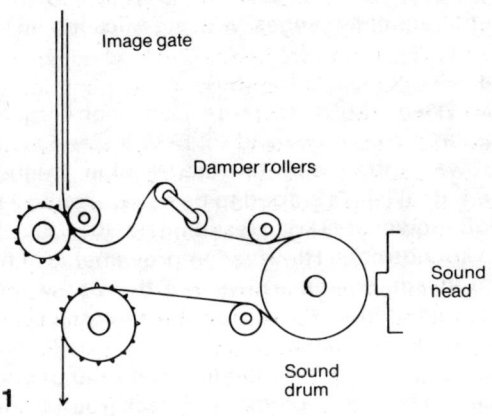

Image gate

Damper rollers

Sound
head

Sound
drum

**1**

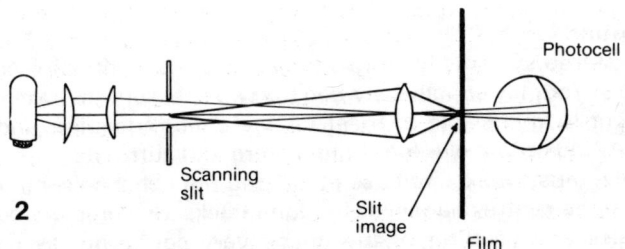

Photocell

Scanning
slit

**2**

Slit
image

Film

### The projector sound head
(1) The intermittent movement of the film through the image gate is smoothed out
to a perfectly steady movement around the heavily-damped sound drum. (2) A
reduced image of the scanning slit is formed on the film soundtrack.

# Dolby Stereo Soundtracks

### Noise reduction

Noise-reduction systems work by boosting low-level signals at the time of recording, and then cutting them back on playback. The proper relationship between loud and quiet signals in the soundtrack is maintained; but the hiss from the recording system is reduced in the quiet passages. In the Dolby system, separate channels of noise reduction operate at different frequency ranges, with significantly improved results.

### Academy curve

Early film-sound systems suffered more from high-frequency loss and distortion than today's tracks do, and in 1938 a standard known as the *Academy Curve* was introduced to restrict high frequencies in the film-sound chain. Signal levels started to be cut at around 2 kHz, and were as much as 10 dB down at 9 kHz, resulting in the dull, flat sound of conventional film soundtracks. However, improvements in film stocks and photographic sound equipment, as well as the Dolby noise reduction system, mean that soundtracks can now be reproduced faithfully with frequencies of up to about 14 kHz.

Dolby noise-reduction yields a signal-to-noise ratio of about 55 dB (the difference between maximum volume and background noise), enabling tracks to range louder, but without the distraction of noise in quiet passages. Stock and equipment improvements lead further to an extended frequency response giving a brighter, more realistic sound, particularly in music.

### Stereo sound

Domestic stereo systems have two tracks (left and right) and require the listener to sit roughly equally between the two speakers. In the cinema this requirement is impossible to meet for the entire audience, and so film stereo uses four channels: left, right, centre and surround.

Normally, music makes full use of left and right channels, but dialogue is placed in the centre channel as in mono tracks. (A stereo dialogue track would make cross-cutting of the image very confusing, as characters would appear to change position with every camera angle.) The surround channel feeds speakers along both sides of the auditorium, and is used for atmospheric tracks and occasionally to bring sounds 'right out of the screen' such as spaceships flying overhead.

A stereo sound camera produces a double bilateral track from two galvanometers, each reflecting a single beam and producing one of the two bias lines. An encoding device mixes the four separate channels of sound into two signals in such a manner that they can be analyzed into the original four signals during replay. Left and right channels correspond to the left and right bias lines, and the combined signal in both lines produces the centre channel. Surround sound is recorded in both lines, but with a phase shift to distinguish it from the centre channel.

## 154

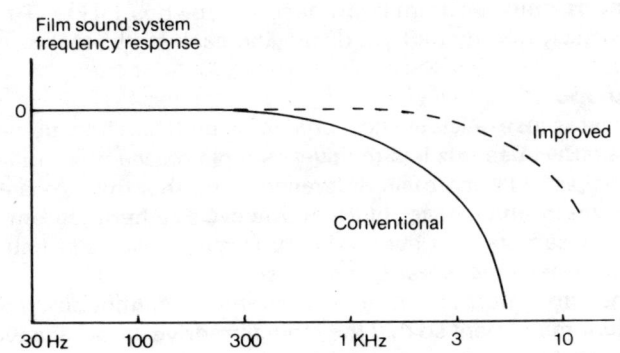

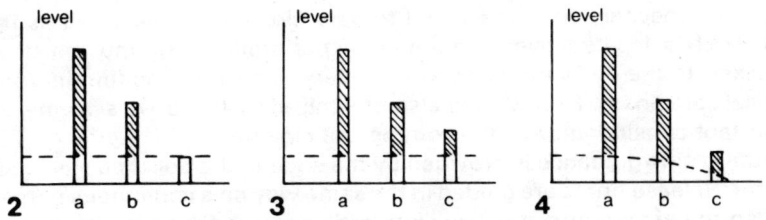

## Improvements in sound reproduction

(1) Extended high-frequency response, resulting in crisper soundtracks. (2) Noise reduction: high-level (a) and mid-level (b) sounds only can be heard above the noise level of a conventional soundtrack. (3) Noise reduction applied during recording boosts low-level signals, (c). (4) On playback, the correct relationship is restored, thereby cutting noise level in the quiet passages.

**155**

*Every frame is shown twice.*

# The Film Projector

## Persistence of vision

The basis of the cinematic process is a rapid sequence of still images, photographed and later projected at the same rate, which merge into a moving picture. This effect works because of a psychological effect known as *persistence of vision.* The brain holds an image for a fraction of a second after it has been removed from sight: long enough, in the cinema, for the next frame of film to replace it. The effect of motion is apparent at speeds as slow as 12 frames per second (fps): but below about 48 fps the dark periods between frames produce an obvious flicker. To avoid this flicker, projectors run at 48 fps, displaying each frame twice.

## Film transport

Film cameras use a claw mechanism to pull the film down between exposures. Because this is a relatively simple device it is usually fitted to 16-mm projectors – the main difference being that the film is completely pulled down in one quarter of the frame cycle rather than one half, as is the case in a camera. However, in 35-mm projectors an alternative system, called the *Geneva movement,* or *Maltese cross,* is used. This is essentially a pin-and-cam mechanism that converts a continuous drive to an intermittent movement so that the main film-drive sprocket advances four perforations during one quarter of the cycle and is at rest for the next three quarters.

## Image steadiness

The cross-mechanism is machined to very close tolerances, and as the film itself is located over a number of perforations around the drive sprocket, frame-by-frame placement is very accurate, resulting in good vertical steadiness. Film wear is also minimized by this drive system – an important consideration in the commercial cinema.

Side-to-side guidance is provided by the edge of the polished steel gate runner. Release prints are guided in the same way on a continuous printer, and so the screen image is usually steady enough for normal theatrical requirements. Normal projectors, however, cannot provide the precise steadiness required for process photography (rear-projection etc.); a pin registering movement is required for this application.

## The lens

The projection lens is normally of fixed focal length and has an aperture of *f*/2 or larger. The required focal length may be calculated using the magnification formula: $o/i = u/v$. In this case the object distance is almost exactly equal to the focal length, and so the formula becomes

$$\frac{\text{film gate width}}{\text{screen width}} = \frac{\text{focal length}}{\text{throw (projector-to-screen distance)}}$$

**156**

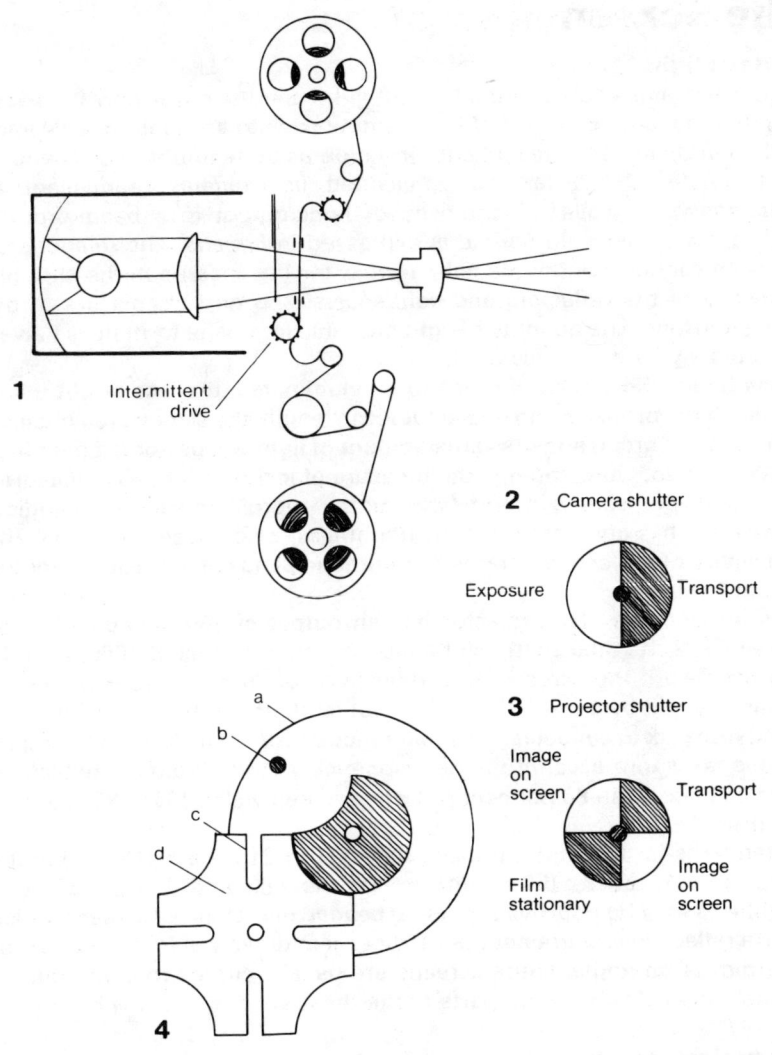

1

Intermittent drive

2   Camera shutter

Exposure      Transport

3   Projector shutter

Image on screen      Transport

Film stationary      Image on screen

a
b
c
d

4

## The 35 mm projector

(1) Basic layout. (2) In a camera, exposure is 1/48 th of a second, followed by a dark period of 1/48 th of a second. (3) In a projector, two exposures of 1/96 th of a second are made of each frame. Fast movements can appear jerky because of this difference. (4) The Geneva movement, or Maltese cross: as the wheel (a) rotates, pin (b) engages in slot (c), advancing wheel (d) a quarter-turn each time. The precision of this movement determines the steadiness of the screen image.

# The Screen

### Units of light

A lamp radiates energy in the form of light, and its power may therefore be rated in watts. However, this does not take into account the efficiency of the lamp, and so gives little information as to its brightness. The total light emitted by a lamp is measured in *candelas* (equivalent to 'candlepower'), while the intensity of light output in a beam from a projector or other light source is expressed in *lumens*. The relationship between candelas and lumens in a projector depends upon the size and efficiency of the reflectors and condensers, and on the aperture of the projection lens. The quantity of light available for image forming is halved immediately by the projector shutter.

The larger the screen that has to be illuminated, the less bright it will appear. If the projector throw is doubled in length, the screen area must be four times as great, and the same amount of light will be spread over four times the area. Illumination – the measure of incident light – is measured in lumens per square metre (*lux*) or the more familiar foot candles. However, the apparent screen brightness also depends upon the reflectivity of the screen, and is measured in candelas per square metre, or foot lamberts.

As an example, if a projector has an output of 1000 lumens, then a screen 6 ft × 10 ft (60 sq ft) will be illuminated at a level of 1000/60 = 17 foot candles. If the screen has a reflectivity of 80 per cent, then screen brightness will be 17 × 80% = 13.6 foot lamberts. In the metric system, going from lux to candelas per square metre ($Cd/m^2$) includes dividing by pi; this takes into account the hemispherical nature of diffuse reflection. Thus 180 lux on an 80 per cent reflective screen yields 180 × 80%/3.14 = 46 $Cd/m^2$.

Standards for screen brightness specify $16 \pm 2$ ftL ($55 \pm 7$ $Cd/m^2$) in the USA, and $14 \pm 2$ ftL ($50 \pm 7$ $Cd/m^2$) in the UK and Europe. Screen brightness may be improved by using beaded or metallized screens which have a reflectivity far greater than 100 per cent directly in front, but appear very dim at an angle. Large screens are usually curved to give uniform brightness to viewers in all parts of the theatre.

### The projector lamp

The once universal carbon arc has now been largely displaced by the xenon arc which provides light at an approximate colour temperature of 5400 K. Some portable 16-mm projectors are fitted with tungsten lamps of about 3200 K, but xenon lamps are becoming more widely used for 16 mm (exclusively so in telecine machines), and 16-mm prints are now normally balanced for xenon projection.

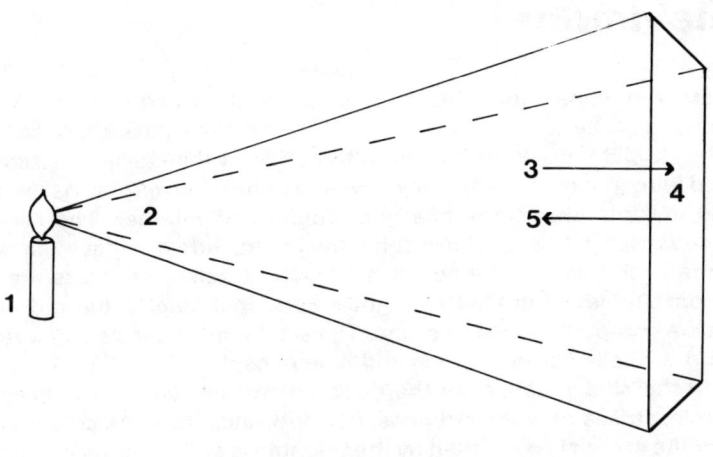

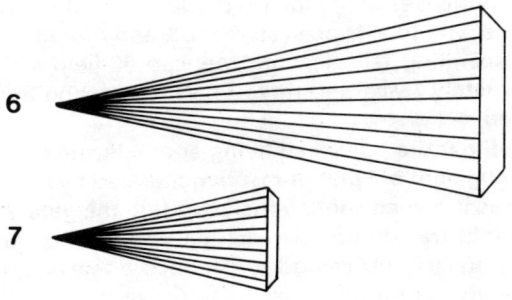

## Units of illumination
(1) Candela = total light emitted by one standard candle. (2) Lumen = intensity of a light source; equal to total luminous flux received over 1 m² at a distance of one metre from a source of one candela. (3) Illumination = brightness of light falling on subject: 1 lux = 1 lumen/m²; 1 footcandle = 10.76 lux. (4) Reflectivity = percentage of light reflected in a given direction. (5) Luminance = brightness of reflected light: 1 footlambert = 3.4 candela/m² (or nits).

Inverse square law: intensity of light varies inversely as the square of the distance. Light at twice the distance, (6), is spread over four times the area, as (7), and so is only one quarter as intense.

**159**

# Television

In black-and-white television, an electron beam formed at the back of the cathode-ray tube scans the front of the tube or screen, painting a complete picture of 625 lines from top to bottom (525 in the USA). The screen is coated with a phosphor that glows when struck by electrons. As the beam varies in strength, so the line gets brighter or dimmer. The screen is scanned twice in 1/25 th of a second, tracing the odd numbered lines first, and the even lines on the next scan. In colour television there are three electron beams, controlled by signals corresponding to the red, green, and blue components of the scene. The screen itself consists of a regular pattern or mosaic or red, green and blue phosphor dots. A shadow mask behind the screen separates the three beams so that the red beam, for example, strikes only the red phosphor dots, etc. Thus, the colour on any part of the screen is controlled by the brightness of the red, green and blue dots in the area.

## Telecine machines

The simplest telecines – camera-tube telecines – consist of a film projector which focuses an image on the screen of a television camera. In 50 fields per second television systems (UK and Australia) film is run at 25 fps to fit the scanning rate. In the American 60-field system frames are scanned alternately twice and three times, corresponding to the basic 24 fps film speed.

In the more advanced flying-spot telecine typified by the Rank Cintel, a moving spot of light, or *raster*, generated by a cathode-ray tube, scans the film as it moves continuously through the gate. A photomultiplier collects the light transmitted by each part of the film, and the resultant signal is electronically processed to produce a television image. Frame rates are the same as for camera-tube telecines.

## Colour-correction in telecines

The individual red, green and blue images may be adjusted for level (overall brightness), gain (contrast), and purity (colour saturation). In this way, for example, shadows can be corrected without affecting the highlights, or flesh tones made warmer without affecting the neutral balance – both corrections that are not possible on film. Thus even the most carefully graded film print may require further corrections on telecine. With the greater number of controls available, care must be taken that the telecine is set up to a correct neutral balance, and test films are available for this purpose.

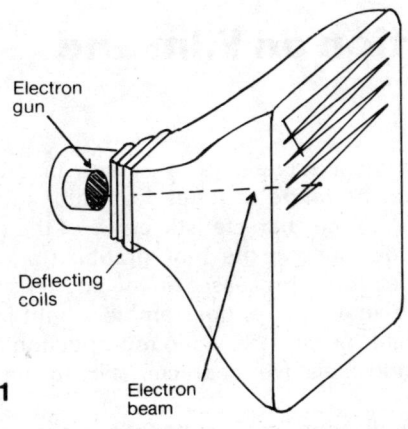

1

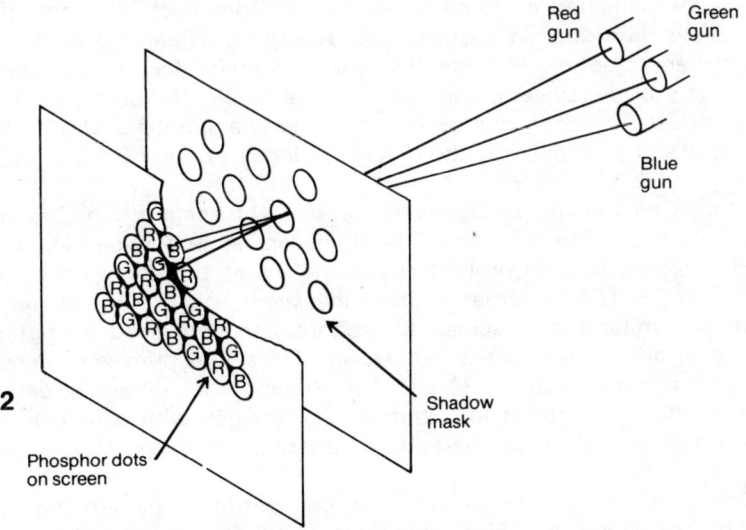

2

Electron gun

Deflecting coils

Electron beam

Red gun

Green gun

Blue gun

Shadow mask

Phosphor dots on screen

**Television**
(1) Cathode-ray tube: an electron beam scans the screen from left to right as it moves from top to bottom, then returns to the starting point top left for the next scan (or raster). (2) The shadow mask in a colour tube ensures that the electron beam from each gun will strike only the appropriately-coloured phosphor dots. Electron-beam strength controls screen brightness at any point.

# Image Reproduction on Film and Television

Copying an image from the original scene onto a screen involves a number of stages. In each stage the range of tones from highlights to shadows is reproduced according to the characteristic curve of the stock. A full account of the system includes not only the photographic stages but also the various optical and electronic processes involved: lens flare contributes to the tonal values in an image, as does ambient light falling on a cinema screen. Similarly a telecine camera, video reproduction chain and TV receiver or monitor all add their own characteristics to the final image.

As with each stage of film duplication, a characteristic curve can be drawn relating the range of exposures or luminance values input, to the range of densities or luminances output from each element of the complete reproduction system. The average gradients of each curve, multiplied together, indicate the overall transfer factor – or gamma product – of the system, and should come to slightly more than 1.0 for best results. Theatrical prints have a final gamma product of about 1.6, but when this is multiplied by the projection factor of around 0.8 a result of just over 1.2 is obtained.

In telecine transfer an additional problem of image brightness range presents itself. Theatrical print densities can range between about 0.10 and 2.80, which upon projection yields a screen brightness of between 50:1 and 100:1. A TV screen, on the other hand, because of ambient light and the limitations of screen phosphors, cannot exceed a brightness range of about 20:1, which corresponds to a film print with densities ranging between about 0.30 and 2.10. Attempts to reproduce densities greater than this result in extremely flat images with a high level of electronic 'noise' – comparable to printing from an under-exposed negative.

The film density range can best be controlled by limiting scene brightness ranges in original photography, although this is not so easy in the harsh sunlit exteriors of Australia and California as it is in the studio or under European skies. Contrasty subjects can be dealt with by the use of a low-contrast print stock with a gamma of around 2.6 (compared with 3.2 for projection stock). This doubles the scene brightness range that can be reproduced on the screen, at the expense of slightly reducing the overall contrast throughout the tonal range. Alternatively the original negative may be run on the telecine machine: this ensures that the full range of tones can be transferred to the television signal, but of course does not alter the inherent low-contrast capability of the screen.

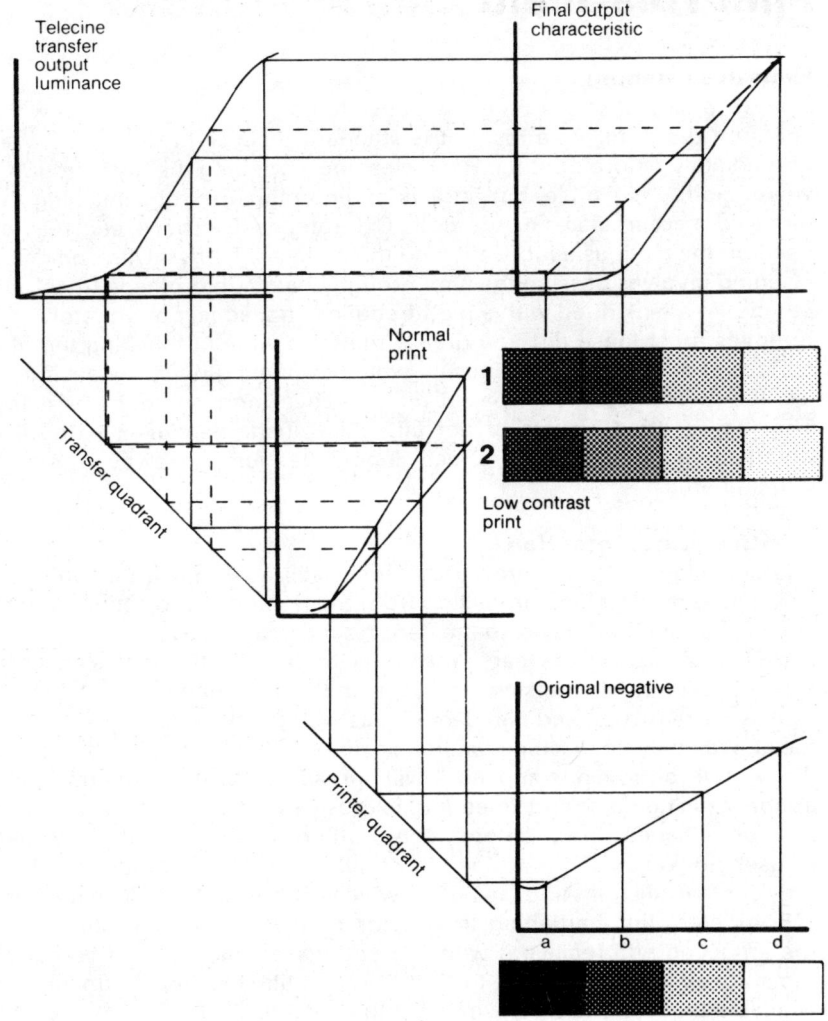

Telecine
transfer
luminance

characteristic

Transfer quadrant

Normal
print

**1**

**2**

Low contrast
print

Printer quadrant

Original negative

a     b     c     d

## Telecine reproduction characteristics
A contrasty original scene, printed normally, will yield a very wide range of
brightnesses to be input to the telecine, resulting in severe black crushing on the
screen. (1). A low-contrast print reduces the luminance range to within the
capabilities of a television screen, (2).

# Film Treatment

### Negative cleaning

Any trace of dust or dirt on the negative to be printed will result in white spots on the print. As a result it is standard practice to clean negatives immediately before printing. Hand-cleaning — winding the film through a velvet cloth — is simple, but attracts an enormous risk of scratching the film as dirt accumulates on the cloth. Chlorothene (Genklene, etc.) may be used on the cloth as a lubricant, and this reduces the risk. Ultrasonic film cleaning involves passing the film through heated Chlorothene (trichloroethane) in a tank fitted with a high-frequency transducer or vibrator. This removes most loose dirt and greasy materals without touching the film surface at all. Buffing machines, in which a spinning buffer wheel lightly 'scrubs' the Chlorothene-soaked film, remove more-stubborn particles. The film is dried by jets of hot air. Chlorothene vapour is harmful if breathed in quantity, and fumes should be pumped away from the working area.

### Positive-print protection

The emulsion of freshly-processed film is still quite moist ('green') and soft, and requires some protection from the rigours of projection. A light application of paraffin wax to the perforation area acts as a lubricant, and prevents excessive film wear in the projector gate. Friction in this area can cause a build-up of emulsion scrapings on the gate runners which in turn causes more friction and film damage, as well as throwing the film out of focus. Wax may be machine-applied or simply wiped onto the sides of the film roll. If too much is applied it will spread across the soundtrack and image, causing noise and smearing. Excessively dirty, oily, or waxy prints can be cleaned in a chlorothene buffing machine and re-waxed. Household waxes and machine oils should be avoided completely since they contain silicones and fatty acids which can cause dye fade in the film.

Proprietary film-hardening treatments remove surplus moisture from the emulsion and replace it with oils and waxes that act as a barrier to moisture as well as lubricate the film. Various film coating treatments are available that are extremely resistant to damage.

Provided that the emulsion has not been scratched sufficiently to remove image dyes, even quite badly-worn prints can be given a new lease of life by a treatment which softens base and emulsion in turn and then allows them to re-dry and harden, healing over scratches as they do so.

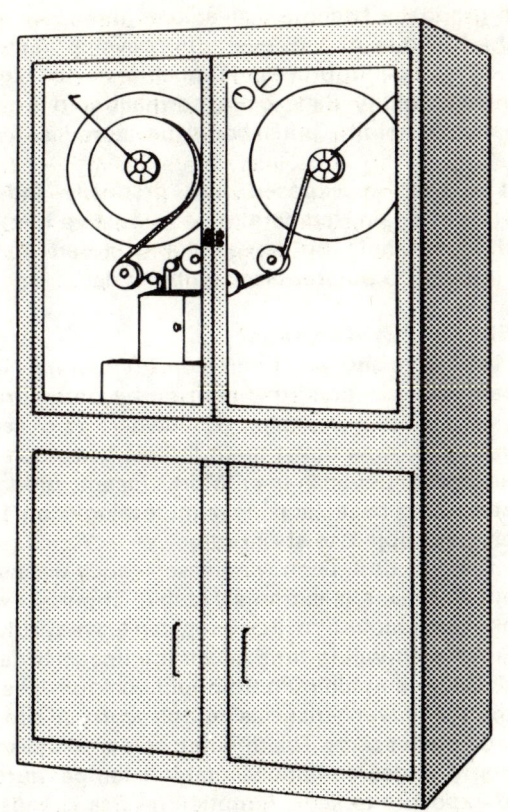

**Ultrasonic cleaning**
All negatives should be cleaned prior to printing: in the ultrasonic cleaner, a high-frequency vibration loosens dirt, grease, etc. from the film. Some machines are fitted with buffing rollers as either an addition or an alternative.

# Film Storage

## Unprocessed film

From the time it is manufactured, film is subject to change. Emulsions can be fogged by radiation or by exposure to many gases and vapors (e.g. ammonia or formaldehyde), but even without these agents the film's sensitometric properties change over time. The silver-bromide crystals in the emulsion gradually become activated of their own accord, and this results in a high D-min or fog level after development, and a flat and grainy image. This ageing process is much faster at high temperatures and high relative humidity. Rawstock is normally sold in cans sealed at the optimum relative humidity, and should be stored as cold as possible before use.

The latent image on exposed film gradually fades if it is left unprocessed. Once again, temperature and relative humidity affect this, and exposed film should be resealed and stored under deep-freeze conditions if it is not to be processed within a day.

## Processed film: archival storage

Films before 1950 were shot and printed on stock with a highly-flammable cellulose nitrate base. In time, this shrinks, becomes brittle, and finally decomposes into a sticky, explosive powder. Low temperature and relative humidity can slow down this process, but much nitrate film has already deteriorated beyond use. More recent productions are on cellulose acetate film base (and now increasingly on polyester stock) which is much less subject to shrinkage.

Assuming that it has been processed and washed correctly, a black-and-white emulsion is extremely stable. Imperfect washing of both black-and-white and colour film, however, can leave residual thiosulphate in the emulsion which will in time cause the image to fade, and stain it with brownish silver sulphide. Photographic colour dyes are rather less permanent than a silver image although current emulsions are an improvement on earlier ones. The different coloured dyes fade at different rates, particularly under conditions of high temperature, high relative humidity, and exposure to light. A motion picture spends very little time exposed to light, leaving temperature and humidity once again as the principal factors. Tests have been carried out to study dye fade at a range of extremely high temperatures and humidities, and from the results, quite precise predictions can be made of dye changes over tens and even hundreds of years at reduced temperatures.

**166**

| | Short term (up to 6 months) | | Long term | |
|---|---|---|---|---|
| | °C | %R H | °C | %R H |
| **Raw stock** | 13 | 70% | –18 | in sealed cans |
| **Exposed stock** | –18 | 70% | not recommended | |
| **Processed film (acetate)** | | | 10 | 15 – 30% |
| **Processed film (nitrate)** | | | 10 | 40 – 50% |

**1**

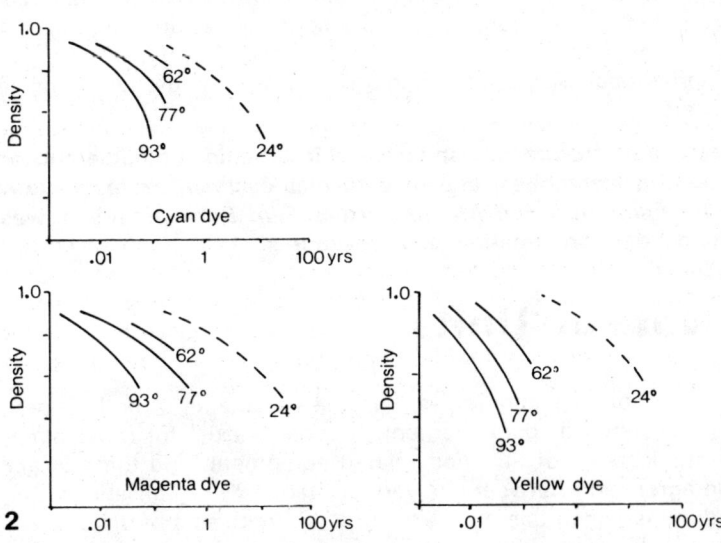

**2**

## Film preservation
(1) Unprocessed stock must be protected from heat damage and latent-image fade. Processed film is subject to dye fade: accelerated tests at high temperatures enable predictions to be made of long-term dye stability at normal or reduced temperatures, (2).

# Further Reading

Bernard Happé's *Your Film and the Lab* (Focal Press, London, 2nd ed, 1983, also in the Media Manual series), deals with the practical aspects of film laboratory procedures from the point of view of laboratory technicians, camera operators and editors alike.

A theoretical approach is provided by *Photographic Theory for the Motion Picture Cameraman* (Russell Campbell, Tantivy, London, 1970), although many technological advances have been made since this book was published.

Books such as *Principles of Cinematography* (Leslie Wheeler, Fountain Press, Watford, 4th ed, 1969), *Basic Photo Science* (Walls and Attridge, Focal Press, London, 2nd ed, 1977) and *Basic Motion Picture Technology* (Bernard Happé, Focal Press, London, 2nd ed, 1975) are all standard works, and give thorough and detailed accounts of their topics.

*Basic Motion Picture Laboratory Techniques* (BKSTS, London, 1981) is a more recent publication, based on a series of lectures organized by the British Kinematograph, Sound and Television Society. Other volumes in the series deal with photographic sound technology, television technology, etc.

Stock manufacturers publish technical information on film emulsions and processing techniques, and in particular *Eastman Professional Motion Picture Films* and *Fuji Motion Picture Film Book* provide a wealth of technical data on materials and procedures.

# A Note on Units

Like many other technologies, film uses elements of both Imperial and metric systems of measurement. Standards exist for most dimensions and applications of film and related equipment, and there is generally good agreement between the various standards organisations. Engineering dimensions in this book are quoted in both sets of units.

Nominally, film width is quoted as a metric value (35 mm etc). However, while some European manufacturers supply raw stock in metric measurements, film length falls more naturally into the Imperial system, as 16 frames of 35 mm film (40 frames of 16 mm) equal almost exactly one foot. In this sense, a measurement such as 13 ft represents not a length, but a frame count. Film for television, however, is increasingly being measured using the time-code system established by the Society of Motion Picture and Television Engineers, in which scene lengths are denoted by a seven-digit count of hours, minutes, seconds and frames.

## Conversion tables

### LENGTH

| Microns (10⁻⁶m) | Millimetres | Thou | Inches |
|---|---|---|---|
| 1 | 0.001 | 0.04 | 0.00004 |
| 25.4 | 0.025 | 1 | 0.001 |
| 1000 | 1 | 40.0 | 0.04 |
| 25 400 | 25.4 | 1000 | 1 |

| | | | | |
|---|---|---|---|---|
| 30.4 cm | = 12 in | = | 1 ft | |
| 1 m | = 39.4 in | = | 3.29 ft | |
| 304 m | = | | 1000 ft | |

### FILM LENGTH AND RUNNING TIME
**16 mm**

| Frames | Feet | Time (24) | Timecode (25) |
|---|---|---|---|
| 24 | 0.6 | 1.00" | .24 |
| 25 | 0.625 | 1.04" | 1.00 |
| 40 | 1 | 1.67" | 1.15 |
| 1000 | 25 | 41.67" | 40.00 |
| 1440 | 36 | 1'00" | |
| 1500 | 37.5 | 1'02.5" | 1.00.00 |
| 4000 | 100 | 2'46.7" | 2.40.00 |
| 40000 | 1000 | 27'26.7" | 26.40.00 |
| 86400 | 2160 | 1h. | |
| 90000 | 2250 | | 1.00.00.00 |

**35 mm**

| Frames | Feet | Time (24) |
|---|---|---|
| 16 | 1 | .67" |
| 24 | 1.5 | 1.00" |
| 25 | 1.56 | 1.04" |
| 1000 | 62.5 | 41.67" |
| 1440 | 90 | 1'00" |
| 1500 | 93.75 | 1'02.5" |
| 1600 | 100 | 1'06.7" |
| 16000 | 1000 | 11'06.7" |
| 86400 | 5400 | 1h. |
| 90000 | 5625 | |

### TEMPERATURE

| F | C | | F | C | | F | C | | F | C |
|---|---|---|---|---|---|---|---|---|---|---|
| 0 | −18 | | 50 | 10 | | 70 | 21.1 | | 86 | 30.0 |
| 14 | −10 | | 59 | 15 | | 77 | 25.0 | | 100 | 37.8 |
| 32 | 0 | | 68 | 20 | | 80 | 26.7 | | 104 | 40.0 |

### LOGARITHMS

| No | Log | | No | Log | | No | Log |
|---|---|---|---|---|---|---|---|
| 1 | 0.00 | | 1.12 | 0.05 | | 3.55 | 0.55 |
| 2 | 0.30 | | 1.26 | 0.10 | | 3.98 | 0.60 |
| 3 | 0.48 | | 1.41 | 0.15 | | 4.47 | 0.65 |
| 4 | 0.60 | | 1.58 | 0.20 | | 5.01 | 0.70 |
| 5 | 0.70 | | 1.78 | 0.25 | | 5.62 | 0.75 |
| 6 | 0.77 | | 2.00 | 0.30 | | 6.31 | 0.80 |
| 7 | 0.84 | | 2.24 | 0.35 | | 7.08 | 0.85 |
| 8 | 0.90 | | 2.51 | 0.40 | | 7.94 | 0.90 |
| 9 | 0.96 | | 2.82 | 0.45 | | 8.91 | 0.95 |
| 10 | 1.00 | | 3.16 | 0.50 | | 10.00 | 1.00 |

# Glossary/Index

**A- and B-rolls** (112) Assembly of alternate shots of original film in two rolls.

**A- and B-type** (118, 152) A way of denoting emulsion position in 16-mm film.

**A- and B-wind** (118) A way of denoting perforation position in single-perf rawstock.

**academy curve** (154) Frequency-response curve used to limit distortion in film sound systems.

**academy frame** (116) Standard 1.33:1 ratio frame not extending into 35-mm soundtrack area.

**acetate** (30, 132) Cellulose acetate: safety film base used since 1951.

**acutance** (36) Measure of sharpness at image edges.

**additive colour mixing** (18, 102) Colour production by the mixing of light of the three primaries, red, green and blue. See SUBTRACTIVE COLOUR MIXING.

**adjacency** (36) Development effect producing enhanced edges of outlines.

**aerial image** (120, 130) Image formed in an optical printer by a projection lens which is then recopied by a camera lens.

**amplitude** (134) Sound-wave signal level, corresponding to the subjective measure of loudness.

**ambient light** (162) General non-image-forming room lighting in cinema or TV viewing area.

**analyser** (106) Video system for assessing colour corrections required prior to printing a negative.

**analytical density** (68) Colour density due to each individual dye.

**animation stand** See ROSTRUM STAND.

**anamorphic lens** (116) Lens that squeezes a wide view into half its width on film, or re-expands the image upon projection.

**antihalation layer** (30, 48) Light-absorbing layer in rawstock that prevents reflection of light back into the light-sensitive emulsion.

**aperture** (12, 70) Lens opening, controlling amount of image-forming light.

**applicator** (50) System for applying viscous redeveloper to soundtrack area of print.

**ASA rating** (78) See EXPOSURE INDEX.

**aspect ratio** (116) Ratio of frame width to height.

**base** (30) Transparent support on which the light-sensitive emulsion is coated.

**batch** (30, 86) Consignment of rawstock coated at one time having uniform sensitometric properties.

**B & H perforations** (114) (Bell & Howell) 35-mm negative perforations.

**bias line** (140, 146, 154) Exposed line of soundtrack resulting from unmodulated signal.

**bi-pack** (126) Running two films through a gate.

**blow-up** (98, 116, 120, 122) Image enlargement: e.g. from 16 mm to 35 mm.

**brightness range** (76, 158, 160, 162) Ratio between brightest and darkest significant image areas in a scene.

**cancellation** (148, 150) Effect of limiting cross-mod distortion by matching negative and positive soundtrack densities.

**candela** (158) Basic unit of quantity of light.

**cell-side** (52, 56, 118) Non-emulsion surface of a film: the base.

**characteristic curve** See SENSITOMETRIC CURVE.

**chequerboard cutting** (112) See A- AND B-ROLLS.

**chinagirl** (104) Standard laboratory test film usually incorporating a face and a greyscale; used for printer line-up.

**Chlorothene** (164) Brand name of organic solvent used for film cleaning.

**chroma** (22) Television measure of hue or colour.

**cinch marks** (132) Minute scratches on film surface caused by slippage between turns of a loose roll.

**cinemascope** (116) System using anamorphic lens to project an image of aspect ratio 2.35:1.

**circle of confusion** (12) Size of 'spot' of light in image produced by a lens from a 'point' on the object.

**colour grading** (106) Balancing the red, green and blue components of a colour image in film printing or in video transfer, to produce a pleasing colour balance.

**colour temperature** (16) Proportion of yellowish to bluish light in a light source: a bluer balance corresponds to a higher colour temperature.

**compression** (140) Boosting of low level sound and reduction of high levels to reduce dynamic range.

**condenser** (12, 120) Lens which collects and directs light through both gate and lens.

**cones** (18) Colour-sensitive light detectors in the eye. See RODS.

**contact printer** (98, 100, 118) Printer in which the rawstock is exposed while in contact with the original.

**contrast** (34, 52, 64, 76, 80, 82, 160, 162) Density difference between tones in an image.

**coupler** (40, 42, 96) Chemical in the film emulsion which reacts during development to form a coloured dye image.

**CRI** (92) Colour reversal intermediate: duplicated negative prepared in one stage from an original negative.

**cross-modulation test** (148, 150) Testing system for determining best negative and positive densities in the soundtrack.

**cyan** (18, 20, 96) Secondary colour: a mixture of green and blue light.

**decibel (dB)** (134, 140, 154) Logarithmic comparison of sound levels. Doubling the level is equivalent to an increase of three dB.

**definition** (36, 98, 100) Clarity of detail in an image.

**density** (62, 64, 74, 142, 144, 150, 162) Darkness, or light-absorbing power of a film or filter.

**depth of field** (12) Range of object distances for which the image remains acceptably sharp at a given setting and aperture.

**developer** (32, 42) Solution used to make a latent image visible.

**dichroic filter** (102) Glass with thin coating that transmits certain wavelengths of light and reflects others.

**diffuse density** (64) Measurement of density that includes all scattered light, corresponding to contact printing. See SPECULAR DENSITY.

**dissolve** (112) Gradual transition whereby one image merges into another over a number of frames.

**D-min** (74, 166) Density of unexposed processed film, due to film base plus chemical fog.

**Dolby stereo sound** (154) Film soundtrack system that encodes four channels of sound (left, centre, right and surround) into a photographic sound track, incorporating noise reduction and extended frequency response.

**dupe** (76, 88–94, 98, 128, 132) Duplicate negative; laboratory printed negative that is an exact copy of an original negative.

**dynamic range** (140) Difference between loudest and quietest levels in a soundtrack.

**dye** (20, 40, 42, 68, 96, 166) Yellow-, magenta- or cyan-coloured chemicals that form images in developed colour film.

**edge (key) numbers** (118) Sequence of numbers printed, usually every foot, in the perforation area of the negative, to identify specific frames for editing purposes.

**emulsion** (28, 56, 98, 118) Light-sensitive layer on one side of film base, in which the image is formed.

**equalization** (140, 146) Adjustment of frequency response during sound transfer stages.

**exposure** (32, 62, 70, 76, 78, 86, 106, 162) Total amount of light allowed to fall on film emulsion. Product of intensity and time.

**exposure index (EI)** (78) Indication of film stock sensitivity, used in determining correct exposure. Formerly ASA rating.

**fade** (112) Gradual disappearance of an image, usually to a uniform black.

**FCC** (108, 126, 168) Frame-count cueing. System for cueing light changes during printing.

**field lens** (120, 130) Large lens used to redirect light in an aerial image towards the camera lens.

**fine grain** (90) Low-speed, high-resolution film: specifically a black-and-white intermediate positive used in duplication.

**fixer** (32, 42, 48) Solution of sodium or ammonium thiosulphate that dissolves silver bromide from an emulsion, rendering the exposed image permanent.

**flare** (82, 88, 124, 162) Scatter of light by a lens system resulting in loss of definition and thin shadow tones.

**flashing** (82) Reduction of image contrast by adding a slight uniform exposure.

**flood track** (142, 150) Full width exposure of track area of sound negative.

**flutter** (100) *Image:* density variation caused by irregular frame exposures or uneven printer speed. (146) *Sound:* rapid fluctuation in frequency caused by vibration in film or tape transport.

**focal length** (10, 156) Distance behind a lens at which an image is formed of an infinitely distant object.

**fog** (44, 82, 166) Accidental or unwanted density in a film caused by exposure to light, heat, radiation or chemicals.

**fog level** (52, 74, 84, 142) Density of unexposed but developed emulsion.

**foot candle** (158) Measure of incident light intensity: the light falling on a surface one foot away from a standard candle, equal to one lumen per square foot.

**foot lambert** (158) Measure of reflected light: the amount of light reflected from a perfectly-reflecting surface illuminated by one-foot candle.

**forced development** (84) Increased development to compensate for under-exposure.

**frame** (8, 108, 116, 168) Single complete image of motion picture film: the area occupied by one such image.

**f/stop** (12, 70) Ratio of diameter to focal length of a lens; an indicator of the light-gathering power of the lens.

**galvanometer** (138) In a sound camera, an electromagnetic device that swings a mirror in response to signal variations.

**gamma** (80, 142) Slope of the straight-line portion of a characteristic curve; a measure of contrast.

**gamma product** (80, 90, 162) Multiplication of gammas of each stage in an image-forming chain; overall gain or loss of contrast.

**gate** (8, 98, 100, 120, 156, 164) Aperture in which each frame of film is held stationary during exposure in a camera or projector.

**Geneva movement** (156) Pin-and-cam system of intermittent motion used in 35-mm projectors.

**grain** (32, 34) Individual particle of silver or cloud of dye, comprising a single element of an image. See FINE GRAIN.

**graininess** (34, 54, 78, 84) Coarse-textured appearance of a film image due to its grain structure.

**granularity** (34) Objective measurement of graininess.

**green film** (56, 164) Newly-processed film whose emulsion is still comparatively soft.

**halation** (30, 48) Flare around an image caused by light reflection within the film.

**harmonics** (134) Whole-number multiples of fundamental frequencies that give a sound its characteristic 'timbre'.

**Hertz (Hz)** (134) Frequency: cycles per second.

**hi-con** (124, 128) High-contrast image or lettering used in optical-effects printing.

**hiss** (140, 144, 146, 154) Unwanted background noise in a sound system.

**hue** (22) Attribute of colour that identifies its position in the spectrum.

**humidity** (56, 166) See RELATIVE HUMIDITY.

**hypo** (48) Sodium thiosulphate, fixer.


**image** (10, 118, 120) Pattern of light from scene, brought into focus by lens on film surface and recorded as silver or dye in the emulsion.

**image spread** (36, 124, 142, 144, 148, 150) Slight enlargement of exposed areas of image due to light scatter, chemical diffusion, etc.

**infra-red** (14, 144, 152) Invisible radiation above 700 nm; used in projector sound optics.

**integral density** (68) Colour density due to all three dye layers.

**integral masking** (96) System of compensating for colour deficiencies of dyes, giving colour negative its orange appearance.

**intermediate** (90, 122) Any film stage between camera original and projection print.

**intermittency effect** (70) Reduced effect of a series of short exposures as compared with a single long one.

**interpositive** (92) Positive printed on intermediate stock from which duplicate negative may be printed.

**ion** (26, 58) Electrically-charged atomic or molecular particle.

**iris** (12, 70) Adjustable diaphragm controlling amount of light transmitted by a lens.


**Kelvin** (16) Scale of temperature related directly to thermal energy. Used in photography to indicate colour temperature.

**KS perfs** (114) (Kodak Standard) 35-mm positive perforations.


**LAD** (94, 104) Laboratory Aim Density exposure control system.

**latensification** (82) Slight preflashing of camera stock to increase shadow sensitivity.

**latent image** (32, 86, 166) Invisible exposed but undeveloped image.

**latitude** (76, 78, 80) Range of acceptable exposures.

**light** (14, 158) Radiant energy visible between wavelengths of 400 to 700 nm.

**light** (grading) (104, 106, 108) Red, green, blue printer settings for correct colour printing of a given negative. See also POINT.

**lighting ratio** (76) Difference between intensity of key light and fill (shadow) light in a scene.

**light valve** (102, 106) *Image:* or light vane: device controlling light output of a printer. (138) *Sound:* device that produces a variable width light beam in response to electrical sound signal in a sound camera.

**logarithm** (62, 134) System of numbers used in measuring exposure, density, sound level, etc.

**log E** (70, 72, 106, 112) Unit of exposure.

**loudness** (62, 134, 144, 146) Sensation of volume, or strength of sound.

**lumen** (158) Unit of light output.

**luminance** (162) Measure of brightness.

**lux** (158) Unit of illumination.


**magenta** (18, 20, 96) Secondary colour: a mixture of red and blue light.

**Maltese Cross** See GENEVA MOVEMENT.

**master** (92, 124) Positive film used for generating duplicate negatives.

**matte** (124) High-contrast silhouette used in optical effects printing.

**modulation transfer** (36) Measure of lens's or film's ability to resolve fine detail.

**monitor** (106, 162) Video display screen.

**173**

**nanometre** (14) One millionth of a millimetre ($10^{-9}$m).
**negative** (42, 76) Image in which tonal and colour values are reversed.
**Newton's rings** (100) Optical interference pattern resulting from close proximity of two surfaces.
**nitrate** (cellulose) (8, 166) Flammable film base used before 1950.
**noise reduction** (140, 154) System for reducing the effect of background noise introduced in recording and transfer systems.

**optical effects** (88, 120–130) Image effects produced on optical printer.
**optical printer** (98, 118, 120) Film printer in which the image is copied onto the rawstock through a lens.
**optical sound** (136–154) Photographic soundtrack.
**orthochromatic** (38, 142) Sensitive to blue and green light.

**Panavision** (116) Camera system using anamorphic lens to photograph a 2.35:1 ratio.
**panchromatic** (38, 92) Sensitive to all colours.
**panel printer** (100, 110) Continuous-contact printer often used for bulk release printing.
**perforation** (perf) (30, 100, 114, 118) Precisely-punched hole at edge of film used for film transport and location.
**pH** (26, 46, 60) Degree of acidity or alkalinity of a chemical solution.
**phosphor** (160, 162) Coating on television screen that emits light when struck by an electron beam.
**photocell** (136, 152) Device that converts light into an electrical signal.
**photomultiplier** (66, 160) Highly-sensitive type of photocell.
**pitch** (perforations) (100, 114, 144) Distance between successive perforations.
**pitch** (sound) See FREQUENCY.
**point** (102) Single increment of red, green or blue printer light, usually a value of 0.025 log E.
**polyester** (30) Very strong type of film base.
**positive** (42, 90) Image in which tonal and colour value reproduce those in the original scene.
**primary colours** (18, 20) Set of three colours (red, blue and green) that can be mixed to produce all other colours.
**processing** (32, 44, 48, 52, 54, 84, 86, 142) Sequence of chemical reactions that render an exposed image visible and permanent.
**process (or projection) plate** (98, 114, 156) Motion-picture print used as a background in front- or rear-projection copying.
**purity** (22, 160) Colour saturation of a video image tone.
**push-processing** See FORCED DEVELOPMENT.

**rawstock** (98, 110, 118) Unexposed film.
**reciprocity** (70, 142) Normal relationship between exposure time and intensity of light.
**redeveloper** (50, 144, 146, 152) Viscous developer solution applied to colour soundtrack.
**refraction** (10, 132) Bending of light passing at an angle from one medium to another.
**register pin** (8, 92, 98, 114) Precisely-fitting pin in gate that accurately locates film perforation.
**relative humidity** (166) Water vapour content of air at a given temperature, expressed as a percentage of the maximum, at which condensation occurs.
**release print** (88, 98) Finished print, intended for distribution and exhibition.
**replenishment** (54, 58) Addition of fresh chemicals to a partially exhausted working solution.
**resolution** (36) Fineness of detail that is clearly reproduced in an image.

**reticulation** (54) Break-up of emulsion caused by extreme changes of temperature during processing.

**reversal** (44, 92) Single-stage film system in which a positive original is reproduced as a positive image, or a negative image as a negative.

**rods** (18) Non-colour-sensitive light receptors in eye, predominant in night vision. See CONES.

**rostrum stand** (120, 124, 130) Equipment for copying artwork onto film.

**rushes** (98) First print of camera negative. See WORK PRINT.

**safelight** (38) Light filtered to reduce fogging wavelengths to a minimum so that unprocessed film can be handled for a limited time without fogging.

**saturation** (22, 160) Degree of richness or purity of a colour.

**scene** (76, 78) Subject matter as photographed.

**scene (shot)** (102, 108, 112) In printing, a single shot in a final cut negative. In a script, a sequence of shots set in the same time and place.

**secondary colours** (20) Set of three colours (cyan, mangenta and yellow) produced from combinations of two primary colours.

**sensitometer** (72, 86) Device for producing accurately-repeatable series of exposures on test strip of film.

**sensitometric curve** (74, 76, 84, 90, 94, 162) Graph relating density to exposure.

**sensitometry** (60–86, 104, 142, 150, 166) Study of relationship between exposure and density.

**separation** (92, 128) Single-colour record on black-and-white film produced from colour original.

**shoreline** (56) Disturbed emulsion surface around film perforations caused by uneven drying.

**sibilance** (146, 148) Sound distortion, heard as a 'spitting' effect on 's' sounds.

**signal-to-noise ratio** (134, 154) Ratio (dB) between loudest (fully-modulated) sound and background noise in a sound-reproduction system.

**silver bromide** (32, 42) Light-sensitive chemical: the basis of photography.

**sound camera** (138, 142, 150) Device that records a sound signal as variations in an exposed stripe on film.

**sound negative** (110, 142) Black-and-white film bearing the photographic sound track.

**sound track** (50, 104, 136, 144, 148) Area of film used for recording audio information. Also, the sound program itself.

**sparkle** (164) White spots on print caused by fine dirt on negative.

**specific gravity** (SG) (60) Mass of volume of liquid compared with equivalent volume of water.

**specular density** (64, 90) Density reading obtained from directly-transmitted light only, ignoring diffused or scattered light.

**speed** (34, 78, 82) Sensitivity of a film. See EXPOSURE INDEX.

**splice** (112) Join between two pieces of film.

**sprocket** (52, 100, 114, 144, 156) Wheel with teeth that engage in film perforations to transport film.

**squeeze** (116) Copy image through anamorphic lens, compressing lateral dimensions.

**status filters** (68) Standardized filters used in colour densitometry.

**step printer** (98) Printer with intermittent movement that exposes film one frame at a time.

**step wedge** (72) Accurately-calibrated filter strip that provides a stepped range of exposures in a sensitometer.

**stereo sound** (154) Sound system with two or more channels, so that sound appears to come from a number of differently placed sources.

**stop** (70, 106) Lens setting (see $f$/stop). Generally, a change in exposure by a factor of 2, or 0.30 log E.

**subtractive colour mixing** (20) Colour synthesis by overlaying coloured filters. See ADDITIVE COLOUR MIXING.

**super-16** (116) 16-mm widescreen negative format: release prints are in 35 mm.
**synchronization** (110) Correct alignment of image and sound tracks.
**sync mark** (108, 110) Frame mark on lace-up leader of image and sound negatives to enable printing to be 'in sync'. Also zero point for FCC counts.
**sync pip** (110) Short 'pip' that sounds at a specified place in the leader.

**telecine** (106, 114, 160) Machine which converts film image to video signal.
**threshold** (74, 82) Least exposure that has a measurable effect on unexposed film.
**throw** (156, 158) Distance between projector and screen.
**time code** (168) Standardized frame identification used in video editing.
**toe** (74, 76, 78) Curved region of characteristic curve below the straight line.
**tonal value** (74, 76, 94, 162) Gradation of light and dark in any part of a scene.
**transfer function** (162) Curve relating input and output luminance in any stage of an imaging system. Cf SENSITOMETRIC CURVE.
**travelling matte** (128) System of combining two separate images on one piece of film.
**trend chart** (86) Graph showing variation of processing results over a period of time.
**tri-separations** (92) Set of three black-and-white film images corresponding to red, green and blue components of an image.
**T-stop** (12) Effective value of *f*/stop, allowing for light loss etc. in lens.
**tungsten light** (16, 158) Illumination of 2500 K to 3200 K used in domestic and some studio lighting.
**turbulation** (54) Agitation of solution to remove exhausted developer from film surface.

**ultrasonic cleaner** (164) Film cleaner using organic solvent and high-frequency vibration.
**ultra-violet** (UV) (14, 38, 144) Radiation of wavelengths below 400 nm.
**unsqueeze** (116) Restoration of compressed image to normal proportions through an anamorphic lens.
**useful exposure range** (76, 78) Range of exposures that fall on the linear portion of the characteristic curve.

**variable area track** (138) Photographic soundtrack in which the signal is represented by a line of varying width.
**variable density track** (138) Photographic soundtrack in which the signal is represented by a line of varying density.
**videotape** (162) Magnetic recording tape used to store motion-picture information in the form of a television signal.
**vignetting** (130) Loss of exposure at edges of frame due to inadequate field illumination.
**viscous developer** (50) Treacle-like developer applied to colour positive soundtrack area.

**wax** (146, 164) Lubricant used on release prints to prolong projection life.
**Weber's law** (62, 70) Law relating strength of a stimulus (light, noise, etc.) to the sensation produced.
**wet gate** (122, 132) System of printing that renders negative scratches invisible.
**widescreen** (116) Film image with aspect ratio 1.66:1 or 1.85:1.
**work print** (98) Print used for checking or editing purposes.

**Xenon arc** (158) Light source used in most modern projectors.
**X-mod** See CROSS-MODULATION TEST.
**X-rays** (38) Penetrating radiation that fogs unprocessed film.

**Yellow** (18, 20, 96) Secondary colour: a mixture of red and green light.